ROCK
ROADIE

ROCK ROADIE

BACKSTAGE AND CONFIDENTIAL
WITH
HENDRIX, ELVIS, THE ANIMALS, TINA TURNER, AND AN ALL-STAR CAST

JAMES 'TAPPY' WRIGHT
AND ROD WEINBERG

JR
BOOKS

This book is dedicated to the memory of
Ivy and Joseph Wright
Hetty and Ben Weinberg

First published in Great Britain in 2009 by
JR Books, 10 Greenland Street, London NW1 0ND

ISBN 978-1-906779-06-1

1 3 5 7 9 10 8 6 4 2

Printed by MPG Books, Bodmin, Cornwall

www.rockroadie.net

Contents

Acknowledgements

Tappy Wright would like to thank all his family, especially Maureen, James, Joanne, Steve, Antony, Kerry, Jacqueline, Alexander, William, Hannah, Andrew and Max for all their help, encouragement, patience and love.

Rod Weinberg would like to thank all his family especially his wife Julie, Julia, Steven, Amanda, Ben, Spencer, Christina, Sebastian, Max, Roman, Clara, Oscar, Matteo and Jasper for all their help, encouragement, patience and love.

Also thanks go to Alison Shaw-Henderson with Laura, Rachel, Rebecca and Dylan, Alison Chaplin, Bob Levine, Bryony Chaplin, Guy Rose, Ray Marshall, Mark Borkowski and all the team at Borkowski PR, Maurice Sutherst, Ray Gillon, Dr Tim Irvine, Avril Macrory and all at Silverapples Media, Nick Pedgrift, Roger Pomphrey, Sally Alexander, Tony Garland, John McDermott and the Hendrix Estate, all the team at JR Books, William Burdett-Coutts and all the team at Riverside and Assembly.

We unreservedly apologise to anyone who should have been mentioned and were not.

Foreword

There's an old cliché: 'If you can remember the Sixties, you weren't there'. There may well be some truth in that, as most drank and many did drugs. Tappy Wright's only vice was women. Hence his clarity of memory. It was certainly a truly exciting period in history. In reality, there were probably only 500 people at the core of this British cultural change. Tappy was at the centre of this short-lived whirlwind that changed the world for ever.

In 1996 when I had finished my documentary, *The Making of Electric Ladyland*, I thought that after all the research I had done and all the interviews I conducted with so many who'd been associated with Jimi Hendrix, that I had heard everything about Jimi that was worth knowing.

Until now.

Tappy Wright's book certainly blows the lid off so many rumours that have abounded for decades. He was there. This book adds the final chapter to Jimi's life and, more importantly, his tragic death.

This book is a real page-turner. Full of humour about Tappy's own sexploits, it also gives an insight into what life was really like on the road during pop music's fledgling days in the UK and USA. He toured with many legends of the rock industry. Then he ran the London office establishing the ground work for an industry that was just born. A true pioneer.

I highly recommend this book that highlights new facts on the death of a true legend, whose music changed rock 'n' roll history for ever.

Enjoy the read.

Roger Pomphrey,
Director of At last the beginning, The Making of Electric Ladyland.

Prologue

Jimi Hendrix was found dead on the morning of 18 September 1970. The coroner's report stated cause of death due to barbiturate intoxication and inhalation of vomit. An open verdict.

1973, and I'm sitting in an old friend's apartment. We're working; doing what we're good at; what we've done for a decade. A collection of glasses and ashtrays are propped up amongst sweeps of paperwork on the table in front of us. The hours tick by, the details are completed and we talk.

More than 30 years on, I can still hear that conversation; see the man I'd known for so much of my life, his face pale, hand clutching at his glass in sudden rage:

'I had to do it, Tappy. You understand, don't you? I had to do it.'

'What are you talking about?'

'You know damn well what I'm talking about.'

And I did, though I didn't want to believe it. I knew what he was telling me and now I'm going to tell you. Because of all the crazy theories there were about Hendrix's death, there is one I know to be true. There are secrets I don't need to keep any more, and I'm going to tell them all.

Introduction

June 2004, Dallas, Texas

'Five minutes to go, Tappy,' a voice says behind me, interrupting those thoughts of murder and lies. 'Are you ready?'

I nod and force a smile. The stage manager grins, laying a hand on my shoulder.

'If anyone should be good at this it's you, Tappy. Not nervous are you?'

'Nah . . .' I try to say more, but the words catch at the back of my throat. I watch the stage manager push through the heavy glass doors to the stage. They close behind him and leave me to face my own hazy reflection in the glass. A man standing alone in an empty corridor. A man who looks, frankly, terrified.

I should be good at this, he's right. I've spent so many years of my life touring the world with the greatest bands that ever played. But it's his job that I know, not this one. Tonight, the stage is going to be mine and mine alone.

'C'mon, Tappy, you can do it,' I whisper to the familiar face in the glass. The encouragement is familiar, too; it is as if this man in the glass was one of my former employers waiting nervously in the wings before a performance. Yes, there is that same fear in my eyes tonight that I've seen a thousand times before in others, but never in myself.

I shake my head and stare critically at my full reflection: it's pretty good. I wipe my sweaty hands against my khakis and adjust my shirt. A little older and a little wider than the man who faced the nervous band members all those years ago, but the hair's still there and I'm thankful for it being plenty. The 'do-it-yourself' ear piercing is empty now. There is no sad old rocker to meet the crowd tonight. But, although these days I'm free from piercing, my waistbands are elastic and my shirts are worn loose to hide the signs of a once-hedonistic lifestyle, the stories are still with me.

'You can do it,' I repeat to myself and step back as the stage manager appears again through the glass doors.

'Right, Tappy, you're on. Good luck mate.' He holds the door open for me; I brace myself and step through.

'Ladies and gentlemen, please welcome, all the way from England, one of the élite roadies of the Sixties . . . Mr Tappy Wright!'

So this is it. This is the spotlight. Not just applause, but the odd wolf-whistle follows me to the microphone where I stand grinning at the rows of eager faces, waiting for the steamy tales of a life on the road with their heroes. I pause as a shriek of feedback echoes around the hall and someone coughs from the gloom of the back rows. Can I really do this?

I clear my throat, slick back my hair with a shaking hand and begin to speak. Suddenly my nerves are gone, absorbed by the gasps and laughter of the crowd. Finally, the stage is my home and the tales of a rock roadie pour out without hesitation. Sex, drugs, rock 'n' roll, and finally the truth: about The Animals, Herman's Hermits, Elvis Presley, Ike and Tina Turner and, most importantly, about the legendary Jimi Hendrix.

CHAPTER 1

Clubs, Coal Dust and Cubs: The Start of The Animals

From the Very Beginning

It all started with a boy. An average miner's son, brought up in the hard, bare, post-war years in the north-east of England. I was born in Whitley Bay, a small town outside Newcastle, the third son of Ivy and Joseph Wright. Struggling to bring up their children with rationing still in operation, and probably to keep me quiet, they indulged me with Taffy, a saltwater candy that passed for toffee. With a mouth gummed up in this substance, I earned my nickname when only a small boy: Tappy. It has never left me.

I was 12 years old when I held my first guitar. A teacher at my school, Mr Glegg, brought one with him to class and played us a tune. He taught me three chords and, as I held it, feeling the strings bite into my fingers, I think I knew then what my life would be: music, music and more music.

Remember your first car? The smell of the seats; the colour of the paintwork; the pride of sitting behind the wheel, after all those years of waiting? Well, I wanted a guitar. But this was the Fifties and money was short, and there was no way that I could afford something like that. So, with a few words from Mr Glegg to my woodwork teacher, and driven by my own new-found passion, I made one myself.

She was a poor thing really, chipboard and paste. She must have sounded terrible. But, like that first old banger you never forget, to me she was beautiful and I loved her.

I took her home and borrowed or stole the books to teach myself

1

how to play. Every evening, to the despair of my poor parents, I practised and practised until I had mastered every chord. I played until she fell apart in my hands. Finally I managed to save the money for a deposit on a Hofner guitar and was able to play in tune at last. Now I was a guitarist; all I needed was a band.

There were plenty of those to be had. The depression that sank over England after the war had left the new generation desperate for something different. Rock 'n' roll was pouring across the Ocean from the States and we were listening. I moved from band to band. The Alley Cats: me on guitar, Ronnie on the washboard and Harry on the T-chest bass (a broom and a string). We just wanted to be making music.

I got better and so did the bands. I was 16 and heading back from a talent competition at the Newcastle Empire when I first met future Animals guitarist Hilton Valentine. Neither of us had been successful and, as we headed to the train station together, we founded a friendship on an agreement that the winners (Hank Marvin and Bruce Welsh, who went on to be part of Cliff Richard's band, The Shadows) would never amount to anything.

Hilton was back then a skinny, wild-haired teenager, with skin even worse than mine. He lived in North Shields, a town close to me in Whitley Bay, and soon after that first meeting we arranged to merge our bands. My old school friends, Ronnie and Harry from The Alley Cats joined us and we formed The Wildcats.

Hilton and I always got on well. I'd lost my mother the year before I met Hilton, when I was 15 years old. Hilton's mother had died when he was 14. Both missing our mothers, we understood one another.

The Wildcats offered me some relief from the now difficult home life. My father was a fantastic man, but my mother's death had been a terrible shock. They'd attended a dance at the Rex Hotel in Whitley Bay and it was on the marble steps, dressed up for an evening out and laughing with my father, that Mum slipped and fell. She struck her head against the marble and the resulting blood clot killed her. My brothers, Alex and George, are seven and 14 years my senior and had already left the family home at the time of my mother's death. So, in just one tragic night, our household shrank to my father and me.

My dad had taken the job that men were expected to take in our area: down the coal mines and, despite his shock and grief, he had to keep working. Ours had been a traditional family; my mother had taken care of all the household chores, the cooking and the cleaning and, with my father hard at work, it fell to me to fulfil those duties in her absence.

Hilton was probably the only person who could truly understand my situation (his home life was even more complicated than mine). I worked early mornings as a milkman, and then I'd cook my dad's dinner and clean the house before heading off to play a gig with The Wildcats. Hilton never questioned me about it: in fact, I even found that he was a little jealous of the close relationship that I had with my father. Dad was always happy to see Hilton at our house. Kind and gentle man that he was, I think that he even began to look on Hilton as a surrogate son. Hilton repaid his affection generously; it was only Hilton who could manage to fill that grieving house with laughter.

But, as well as being a true and good friend to me during that difficult time, he was also an amazing guitarist and that was what mattered to The Wildcats. We were getting gigs and playing hard and, even with the hardships at home, I was having fun.

Early promotional material for The Wildcats – no MySpace in those days!

Too Wild for The Wildcats?

The places to play if you were a small band starting out in the north-east of England were Working Men's Clubs. Most of the great bands known from the Sixties started out in these smoky dens, playing down crackling microphones to local drinkers. The entertainment was always varied but the audience was usually reliable: old boys with their pints of ale and bitter, out with their wives for the evening. Drinks were cheaper in these clubs and so, as working men ourselves, the younger parts of the crowd were still usually friends or family. We got used to recognising our audience and our popularity with them. That was until one night at the Seaton Terrace Working Men's Club in Seaton Delaval, where we were forced to see whether The Wildcats really could 'measure up' to the competition.

We arrived for the gig as usual, unpacked the equipment from the van, and settled down with a drink to wait for our set. As soon as we took our seats we noticed that there was something different about the crowd.

'Lot of women here tonight, aren't there?' Hilton said, lighting a cigarette and eyeing the tables around us.

'You're right there, son,' Ronnie agreed. 'And they're looking mean.'

Now I have as much of an eye for the ladies as the next man, but the boys were right. There were only a handful of men in the audience; the place was packed with women, and this was back in the days when a woman would rarely venture into a pub unaccompanied by their husband or a date. Where were all the working men in this Working Men's Club? We sank down in our seats as the shouts of female laughter got louder and waited to see what would happen next.

The compère took to the stage, tapping the microphone and rolling off a few gags, but these girls were impatient for something and, hidden in our corner table at the back of the club, we doubted it was a set from The Wildcats they were waiting for. Eventually, the compère admitted defeat.

'All right then, ladies, it's time for this old boy to pass the floor over to the young one you've all been waiting for . . . be gentle with him now.'

The crowd went wild and we had to stand up in our seats to catch a glimpse of the act that now strode on to the stage.

I caught Hilton's eye. 'What the hell is he doing?'

You may think that in the regimented atmosphere of post-war England, where a woman would be frowned on for drinking alone, let alone mentioning anything to do with sex, the idea of *male* strippers would be decades away. But long before the Chippendales and *The Full Monty*, it seemed that the women in a small Northern club in 1961 knew exactly what they were expecting.

The Wildcats watched, mouths agape, as the young male stripper strutted his stuff across the stage and dodged the hands that reached out to grab at him. With a lifetime spent amongst groupies, I was to see women behaving far crazier than this, but I think that this was my first taste of just how wild they could get when they got the chance. But, more than the reaction of the female audience, was the dawning realisation that it was The Wildcats that would have to follow this guy!

We finished our drinks in a nervous silence and shuffled around the crowd to find our equipment. We were standing, ready to go on as the stripper fell into the tiny backstage area, looking exhausted.

'You've earned your money there, kid,' Hilton commented as we watched the man stagger to his feet and reach for a spare set of clothes.

'Don't I know it; I'm off home before they tear me apart. Good luck to you, lads.'

We could hear the girls shouting for more as the compère announced us. As soon as we hit the stage we knew that it wasn't music they were after and the shouts of 'Get 'em off!' soon drowned out the crackling acoustics. What all these women wanted was male flesh and Wildcats flesh was as good as any!

Now, this may sound like a treat rather than a chore. You couldn't be blamed for thinking that a venue full of screaming women is every teenage boy's dream. But, to be honest, I was terrified. What if they lost patience and ripped the clothes off our backs? All I could think about was what would happen if I wasn't wearing clean underwear! I had changed them this morning, hadn't I?

Luckily for us, Ronnie wasn't feeling shy. After just a couple of minutes listening to those screaming girls, he lost control. Jumping over his drum-kit and pushing past Harry, Hilton and myself, who were all still standing rooted to our places on the stage, Ronnie threw himself into the crowd.

'Strip me naked!' he bellowed, as he disappeared into the sea of waiting arms.

I hope that his underwear was clean . . .

So, in 1961, the year the Russians beat the Americans into orbit, with Yuri Gagarin floating above our heads, I was safe in my place on rhythm guitar and Hilton on lead. The Berlin Wall was under construction and John F Kennedy was inaugurated as President. But for Tappy Wright and Hilton Valentine, all that mattered was to lose ourselves in hammering our guitars for The Wildcats and keeping the clothes on our backs. Little did we know that we were taking the first steps towards our own mark on history.

Rivals and Just Good Friends

The Wildcats had rivals in the North-East: The Alan Price Combo. They were a popular band with a residency at the now infamous Club A Go Go, at the Haymarket in Newcastle. They were known for whipping their audience into frenzy as they blasted their sets to a close with 'Boom Boom' and the Ray Charles classic, 'Talking About You'.

They watched us and we watched them. We met regularly at gigs. I liked their lead singer immediately. Eric Burdon was a small, cock-sure man with an incredible voice. He knew where he was heading, even back then in the clubs of Newcastle: straight to the top. The namesake of the band, Alan Price, was on keyboards. Long-haired and baby-faced; in fact, spotty kid that I was then, I think I envied his smooth face more than his swift talent on the keys. But towering over them all, even the quiet John Steel on drums, was their bass player, Chas Chandler. At 6ft 4in (1.93m), he dwarfed tiny Eric, particularly when, in the throes of a set, his unruly hair would spring up and add still more inches.

So we were rivals, but in a small community like that we met so often that any animosity was impossible. Anyway, we liked each other. Still, it's strange the moments that cement a friendship. For me, it took a field of cows, two policemen and some very swift talking.

It happened on the night both bands were invited by a well-known sax player, Nigel Stanger, to a party in Gosforth. The Alan Price Combo had no transport of their own, nor the money to arrange any, so we all piled into my van. We were crammed in like sardines, laughing and shouting to be heard over each other and raring to go party.

Halfway to Nigel's house Hilton decided, inconveniently, that he had to piss. There and then, he had to go. I was driving and the only place I could pull over was a spot known locally as the 'Town Moor', a stretch of field used to graze cows. With Hilton already tugging the door open, I stopped.

Now this was the early Sixties and we were young and on our way to a party, so you have to allow us a little stupidity. Hilton staggered off into the field and, welcoming the chance to get out of the hot, overcrowded van and to relieve ourselves, we followed him. There we all stood, cocks out in the breeze, playing silly boy's games and seeing how high we could piss. Then Hilton spotted the cows, which were standing watching us, huge impassive lumps in the dusk.

With a shout, Hilton ran off towards them. If you could call it running. We fell back into the grass laughing as we watched Hilton's white arse bobbing away, trousers still round his ankles with a dark wet patch spreading across the crotch where urine ran down his legs. The cows were obviously not keen to meet the half-naked lunatic who was to become one of the most famous guitarists in the world; they took off across the field, kicking sods of wet earth up behind them.

Not to be outdone, I decided to help Hilton in his pursuit.

'Come here, ladies. Come chew on this,' I shouted across the field at the fleeing cattle, my trousers bunched round my knees and my cock in my hand.

'Go on, Tappy!' the lads shouted from behind me.

Hilton pulled up his trousers and laughed.

'Go, Tap, it's the best offer you'll get tonight.'

Yes, this would be the time that I realised I loved being in the limelight. Centre stage was exactly where I wanted to be. I started to strut my stuff in the middle of the field. Catching up with one of the cows, I turned round and bent over, treating the poor creature to a full close up of my bare arse. Hands aloft, I waited for my applause from the boys. Nothing. Silence. It had got darker; I could barely see my hand in front of my face. Where was everyone? Then suddenly: 'OK, son. Enough is enough.'

I jumped, yanking up my trousers and half-tripping on the dewy grass. A light flashed into my eyes.

'You're under arrest for indecent behaviour, bonny lad.'

Oh, Christ!

Back at the police station in Newcastle, I was led into a brightly-lit room and thoroughly grilled about my intentions towards livestock. That's right. They were convinced that if they had not arrested me when they did, I would have performed a 'sexual act' on one of the cows. And I was going to have to tell my dad this!

I squirmed in the hard plastic seat.

'Seriously, officer, I swear it was nothing like that. Me and my mates were just messing about.'

'What mates would these be?'

Yeah, what mates? As soon as they saw the police the other guys had fled, leaving me to be led, still half-unzipped, into the waiting police car. The cops had seen the abandoned van and had decided to investigate. Then, sitting quietly in the dark, they had watched the whole spectacle. My first touch of the limelight and the audience were now convinced I was some kind of sexual pervert. My dad was going to kill me.

Finally, though, the begging and pleading paid off and they let me go. All charges dropped. Thank you, God.

I called a cab from the grubby public phone outside the holding room, still grateful not to be phoning my dad to explain my disgrace. The police officer at the desk leant towards me with a grin.

'Tell me, son, you know the difference between a four-legged cow and a two-legged one?'

Smutty bastard. I nodded, biting my tongue, and smiling politely.

'Take my advice and stick to the two-legged kind.'

I could still hear them laughing as I stood alone in the car park, waiting for my cab to arrive.

When I finally reached Nigel's house (hours late) the music was blaring and the party was in full swing. The boys were waiting for me. As I walked through the door, Eric spotted me and shouted out across the music, 'He's here ladies and gentlemen. Mr Tappy Wright, the famous cow lover. You'll need bigger udders than that, love, if you want to turn him on. Ain't that right, Tappy?'

The laughter was loud and long. The boys had obviously wasted no time in telling everyone there what had happened in the field.

'You're bastards, you know that? Fucking bastards!' I said, laughing with them as someone passed me a well-earned drink. 'And the Pigs have minds as filthy as yours, Eric.'

'Oh, it's pigs, too, is it, Tappy?'

Strange night. From joker, to sexual deviant, to laughing stock, to . . . well, that was the strangest. Who would have thought that such a stupid prank could have put me on the path to so much? I was the hit of the party. People I knew, and those I didn't, came to slap me on the back and hear the story again. Tappy Wright was walking entertainment. I had shown them, quite literally, that I had bollocks and my credibility soared. I was popular, and with Eric, Chas, Hilton, John and Alan laughing along with me, I'd formed friendships that would take me further than I had ever dreamed.

Animals at Last

Mike Jeffery was the Alan Price Combo's manager; he was also the owner of the Club A Go Go in Newcastle, where the band had their residency. I had first met Mike when The Wildcats played at his other nightclub an all-nighter called The Downbeat. He looked every bit the London spiv: dark pin-stripe suits and always a full-length black leather coat over the top; shoulder-length dark hair, which he combed back to disguise its thinning. But his trademark was the dark lens glasses he always wore, glass tinted, in fact, to disguise just how thick those lenses had to be to fulfil his prescription.

He was a shrewd businessman, even a little frightening. He'd left London to serve with the Special Forces in the Middle East, and it wasn't until the late Fifties that he'd moved up to Newcastle to study Languages and Sociology at Newcastle University and there became involved in the music industry. By the time I met him, he'd moved well beyond his humble beginnings at Student Unions and built up several nightclubs. He was well known in our area and the Alan Price Combo were glad to have him on their side.

It was only a couple of weeks after my arrest that Mike called his band to let them know he'd secured them an audition for the BBC's *Saturday Club*, in Manchester. This was Britain's most popular radio show at the time and a big chance for the Alan Price Combo. In the days before commercial radio – before the pirate stations that would storm the British airwaves later in the Sixties, when the BBC ruled the frequencies and only the rich could afford a television – there were few places to listen to pop music in the UK. This was the time and place for the Alan Price Combo. There was just one thing missing . . . a guitarist.

Hilton was, and is, a great guitarist, but he's also a fabulous show-man. Back in the days of The Wildcats (these are the early Sixties, remember) he would throw himself around the stage, abandoning years of quiet English upbringing to the pursuit of the song, ripping his shirt and falling to the floor. The Alan Price Combo had watched our gigs, as we had watched theirs, and they knew who they wanted playing for them on the day of their big break. Hilton agreed, and they played that night at Club A Go Go.

Eric Burdon, Alan Price, Chas Chandler, Hilton Valentine and John Steel took to the stage for the first time together and I cheered them on. Mike Jeffery met them after the gig to congratulate them on their performance and tell them that the time had come for a new name for the band. They were on the brink of something big, and Mike didn't think that the Alan Price Combo would work commercially. I sat with them in the hours after the gig, drinking and laughing and thinking up names. The Animals fitted perfectly; they agreed that it fitted their characters, and their antics, down to the ground. The only note of dissent came from Alan Price. He'd always made sure that his name was the foundation of every band which he'd been a member of. But, with the radio chance coming, any fuss was short-lived: cubs no longer, The Animals were born.

Now you are probably thinking that I'd have been disappointed in this turn of events: losing Hilton to the newly-founded The Animals, and finding myself absent from the line-up? But Hilton was my best friend and, although by today's standards it would sound like poaching, band changes, mergers and shifts were commonplace in the Sixties, particularly in our small musical community. Anyway, I was excited for them. They were my friends and I had no doubt they were going places. And as it turned out, I wasn't going to be left out after all.

Just before Christmas in 1962, the day of the *Saturday Club* audition arrived. Although they were heading for their big break, The

Animals had as little capital as the Alan Price Combo had before them. Chas approached me to ask if I could drive them to Manchester in The Wildcats van and I was happy to help.

They passed the audition and were booked to appear on the radio the following week. Packed back in the van that had carried us halfway to Nigel Stanger's party just a few short months before, we celebrated on the way back to Newcastle. They were securing a future that would take them across the world, to Number 1 in the charts, and to having their names screamed in hundreds of languages; as I offered to take them back to Manchester the next week, I was securing my place alongside them.

That performance for *Saturday Club* was electrifying. Every band, unsigned or well established, had to play live in front of an audience and the pressure was intense. I'd played with Hilton and watched the other guys for over a year, but I knew I was watching something special.

Apparently, everyone listening knew it, too. The work poured in. Best of all, The Animals were offered the chance to appear live at the Scene Club in Piccadilly Circus, London. Graham Bond, one of London's top jazz performers, heard the broadcast and had seen The Animals play at Club A Go Go. He wanted to book them for a series of gigs in the January of 1963.

Opportunity was waiting for them. On one of the nights they performed at the Scene, Don Arden and Peter Grant (who were to become the band's agents) brought an unknown record producer called Micky Most to watch The Animals play. Sharon Osborne has already documented many events that went towards creating the tough reputation of her father, Don Arden, but at the time he was just one of those men, like our manager Mike Jeffery, that you knew it was best to keep on the right side of. It was said that he rarely used lawyers in business disputes; Don Arden's lawyers were likely to be replaced by two large men who 'sorted out' problems without the paperwork. Peter, so it was told, had started out as one of these henchmen and had worked his way up until he was Don's right-hand man and tour manager for the acts he represented.

Micky Most was a lucky man, destined to be in the right place at the right time, and the fact that he was holding company with Don and Peter proved that he had the right contacts, too. But he was not the only record producer in the audience that night who could recognise new talent.

After the show Micky, delighted with what he'd seen and heard, approached the band and offered to record them. The lads were thrilled and accepted. Don and Peter then left, satisfied that they had managed to get The Animals their record deal.

Soon after the agents had gone, however, another man approached the band. Ian Samuels was a record producer with a great deal more notoriety than Micky Most. He'd worked closely with Cliff Richard and had produced his first hit, 'Move It'. Samuels promptly offered The Animals a similar recording contract to the one Micky had presented moments before.

Micky Most listened, obviously horror struck, as Samuels talked to the band. I saw Micky leave in a hurry, but only when he returned with Don and Peter did I see what he was up to. Don simply walked over, leant down and had a quiet word in Samuels' ear. Then it was Ian Samuels who left in a hurry, not to return. Like Mike Jeffery, Don Arden was not a man you upset. The charmed life of The Animals continued with the right people on their side.

Now don't go thinking that Tappy Wright was forgotten in all these dreams of impending stardom. I have to admit, though, there were a couple of moments there, when the boys were talking excitedly about the new record deal, where I worried that I'd be driving myself back to Newcastle and reconstructing The Wildcats with Ronnie and Harry while they headed off for the glamour of London. Trying not to feel too self-pitying, I approached the band.

'You know, if you want, I could drive you guys. I mean, you'll have loads of gigs in London and that. And with the deal and everything . . .' I finished lamely.

'For Christ's sake, Tappy, we thought you'd be driving us anyway! You should be our road manager, son, not our driver. We need you, Tap.'

So this was The Animals and I was with them all the way to the end.

CHAPTER 2

Tooth and Claw and Chasing Tail: The Animals Fight Their Way to the Top

Goodbye Newcastle . . . Hello London

So, six working-class boys from Newcastle set off for London. The Big Smoke. Like six Dick Whittingtons heading for those streets lined with gold. Only it was gold records we were hoping for and instead of a handkerchief tied to a stick we were, once again, all crammed into my trusty Bedford van. Christ, if we'd thought we were crowded on the way to that party in Newcastle it was nothing compared to the long drive to London with us, the equipment and just enough space for a suitcase apiece.

It was a scary move for us. Despite our excitement, we really knew very little about London. It was 1963 and I was 19 years old; most of the lads were barely older than me. But, from what we had heard about London, it was going to be one long party, beautiful girls, free booze, the full star treatment . . . sure it was!

It seemed to start out all right. When we arrived we met Ronan O'Rahilly at a show biz party, a big Irish entrepreneur, who lent us a flat. Ronan's grandfather was rumoured to be one of the founding members of the IRA, and he had plenty of connections and plenty of money. The money was useful as it was funding our sleeping arrangements, and the connections would prove their use later on.

Ronan owned the first pirate radio station in England, Radio Caroline. A boat would sail in the North Sea outside the three-mile border and broadcast the music that the BBC felt unsuitable for tender young ears, i.e. the music which tender young ears were desperate to hear. O'Rahilly loved The Animals and his broadcasts of our tunes secured their popularity and requests for playtime on commercial stations. He also used his influence to introduce us around town, getting us into nightclubs and letting us meet the right people. Still, I do wonder quite how we managed to surround ourselves with Britain's most terrifying men as our greatest supporters.

When we got to Ronan's flat in South Kensington, it was as huge as he had promised, but completely empty. There was not a stick of furniture in the place. In the three months before we could afford our own apartments, we made do with sleeping bags and camp beds. We slept a couple of hours in the bare rooms and then headed out to cheap cafés and our local Wimpy bar to eat. So much for London glamour! But we were hardly going to complain to O'Rahilly. He was a good friend to us, but I was in no hurry to meet the darker elements in his network of connections.

Don and Peter, meanwhile, had not forgotten us. Far from it. We were kept busy with gigs around town. (So busy that we wore my poor Bedford van into the ground. It limped back home one evening and died there on the street. We all said a few words before we crawled back to our makeshift beds; our own little memorial service for its hard work. I couldn't even bear to have it towed away when I got my replacement Commer, and left it parked there outside Ronan's flat, as a testament to our humble beginnings.)

But, whilst The Animals were with Micky Most recording their first single, 'Baby, Let Me Take You Home', Don and Peter found a great opportunity for the band to become what they wanted more than anything: to raise popularity.

Chuck Berry was about to embark on his first British tour and Don asked if The Animals wanted to go along with him. Don Arden specialised in tours like this: packaged promotions of rock stars of the time. He promoted the *Who's Who* of the pop business, but liked to have a mixture of headliners and unknowns for a tour. A slot in one of his shows was a well-known golden ticket for future success (The Rolling Stones had helped to launch their careers by touring with Bo

14

Diddley and The Everley Brothers). Also, we all loved Chuck Berry's music, he was a legend even then. Not only was it a great chance, it was an honour. Then Don turned to me. 'Do you fancy coming on board as Peter's assistant, Tappy? Give you the chance to find out what being a tour manager's all about.'

I'd just been given the opportunity to assist the man who would go on to be the manager of Led Zeppelin. Peter Grant was one of the best in the business. Fancy it? Give me the chance and I'd get down on bended knee and marry it!

Chuck and Carl

Chuck Berry was a hero of mine. I couldn't wait to watch him perform; to hear 'Johnny B Goode' and 'Roll Over Beethoven' played live. I had to keep reminding myself that now I would be on the same side of the stage as he was. I was staff; I was the assistant tour manager, and I really mustn't embarrass myself by getting star-struck on my first big job. But this was *the* Chuck Berry.

Second on the bill was Carl Perkins; I didn't know him or his music as well as I knew Chuck's. He was a Southern rock star coming out of the Sun record label and had written Elvis Presley's hit, 'Blue Suede Shoes'.

Figuring that I'd get to meet them both and see them perform enough times on tour and still delighted with my new job title, I settled down to watch the lads rehearse. Which didn't go strictly to plan.

Mike Jeffery was back with us, of course, and although the music was still amazing, our businessman manager had more plans to make The Animals a commercial success. The first single, 'Baby, Let Me Take You Home', had gone into the charts at Number 20, but there was plenty more work to be done if they wanted to hit the big time. First, and to much grumbling, the regular stage uniform of T-shirts and jeans was replaced with smart suits, to bring them into line with other young British acts like The Beatles. Then, to the band's horror, Mike brought in a choreographer. He wanted to bring dance routines into the act.

There was one attempt; the boys stumbled over their own feet and each other's, and wore looks of pure fury on their faces. It wasn't long before Eric had had enough. 'We'll wear the fucking Beatles suits, but we are not the sodding Shadows, Mike.'

The description that Eric gave of where Mike could stick his dance routines seemed to convince him. That, along with my laughter, which finally broke free at the sight of Chas Chandler, red-faced with concentration as he tried to learn dance steps.

So, all-singing, but thankfully not all-dancing, The Animals were ready for their first tour.

The show opened on Saturday, 9 May 1964 at the Astoria, in Finsbury Park, London, the venue that would later become famous as the Rainbow Theatre. Larry Burns, the compère, introduced Chuck Berry as the 'living legend of rhythm 'n' blues' and I joined the cheers and applause as he took to the stage.

He was everything I, and the banner-waving crowd, had hoped he would be. And, man! Chuck Berry could play an audience as well as he could play a guitar! With his shiny suits and velvet lapels and all that crazy glamour that had run over from the black acts of the late Fifties, Britain went wild for him! The Astoria managed to get the curtain down between him and the howling crowd at the end of his set. The second concert we played that evening brought out dancers in the aisles, but by the end of his performance the stage was packed with fans dancing alongside Chuck.

At the Hammersmith Odeon the audience invaded the stage again, but this time only 15 minutes into the set. It took me and half the management team to pull down the safety curtains and rescue Chuck from his over-adoring fans. Someone switched on the National Anthem, to try and remind this crowd they were English; stiff upper lips and afternoon tea seemed impossible in that mob. Still, it seemed to quieten them down after a while and Chuck took to the stage once more. But it only took an example of the celebrated Berry 'duck walk' to set them screaming again. Chuck was obviously loving it. He treated them to an improvised Cossack dance, performed while still turning out those glorious tunes, note-perfect on his guitar.

Chuck Berry was a resounding success. He could do no wrong that tour. The crowds screamed and stamped their appreciation for the up-tempo rock of 'Guitar Boogie' right through to the slow moody blues of 'Wee Wee Hours'. You would have thought that the obvious triumph of his British début would have made him happy and voluble backstage, but he was isolated and difficult to talk to.

Now, I flatter myself that I'm a pretty easy guy to get to know, and I have always liked the chat and laughter backstage. The performances are only a small part of the touring experience and the monotony of travel, setting up and rehearsing is saved by the banter and stories that are passed. But, for all that I respected Chuck Berry and my many efforts to get to know the man, he seemed arrogant and, at times, impossible even to pass the time of day with.

Carl Perkins was a different story. He was a real Southern gentleman, ready to tell the enthralled young tour manager all his tales of Elvis Presley, Johnny Cash and Jerry Lee Lewis, all the greats that I'd been worshipping for years. He was happy with his place as my 'adopted grandfather' for the tour as long as I was willing to help him supply his new-found addiction: fish and chips.

'You just can't get them in the States, Tappy.'

We had to stop the bus at every 'chippy' we passed so that Carl could run in and come back laden with greasy newspaper wrappings. I was surprised that he hadn't developed gills by the end of that tour. He was a sweet guy and a real professional.

Despite following Chuck Berry on the billing, a task that would have struck fear into the heart of any lesser man, he was a huge success, even with the Berry fans baying for more. In marked contrast to the flamboyancy of Chuck's performance, Carl Perkins would stroll on to the stage like a lost cowboy. Accompanying himself on guitar, he performed 'What'd I Say', 'Big Wheel', 'Match Box', 'Mean Woman Blues' and then finished off with his own composition, 'Blue Suede Shoes'. The venues shook with the cheers and applause of his audience.

The Swinging Blue Jeans didn't fare so well in their task of following Carl Perkins, however, much to Carl's embarrassment. The crowd wanted an encore from Perkins, and seemed more determined in this than they had been even for Chuck Berry. When The Swinging Blue Jeans came on and started their set, the music was drowned out by calls of 'Off! Off! Off!' Music is a cruel business, but to give them their dues, the band played on through the catcalls, although I hardly think that tour is a memory they look back on fondly.

Much as I liked Carl Perkins, and despite my problems with Chuck Berry, there was one situation that confused me: they barely spoke to one another. Innocent English boy that I was, I couldn't understand how two great artists from the States, travelling and performing together, hadn't developed some kind of relationship over the years. At first I put it down to Berry's arrogance, which I'd experienced first-hand, but one day as Berry took his place at the back of the bus and Carl noted his position and sat down at the front, I asked Perkins what it was all about. Had they had some kind of falling out? Was I going to get another great story about the names that, until a few months ago, had only been known to me through magazines and newspapers?

'He's black, son.'

This was not the reply I had expected, and Carl must have seen it on my face.

'Tappy,' he said quietly, 'I've got nothing against black people or black musicians. Hell, I love black music. But, if the folks back home found out that I'd spoken to a black man, even if that man were Chuck Berry, they'd smash the windows in my house. My family would be totally outcast. I have to think of my family.'

I just couldn't understand it. This was my first experience of racism and it had come from a man I both liked and trusted. But Carl wasn't a racist; he was just a man at the mercy of an American prejudice who was trying to protect his loved ones back home. Could the world of Sixties America have been so different to that of Sixties England? Looking back, it was, and, even at that moment, I was glad to be English.

But let's not forget my boys and The Animals' first taste of touring. They suffered none of The Swinging Blue Jeans' misfortune and went down well with the crowds. The loudest applause, predictably, came for their hit, 'Baby, Let Me Take You Home', but the greatest shock was the response to a cover of a little 18th century American folk song about a brothel, 'The House of the Rising Sun'.

Rising Sun

'Break time, guys,' Micky Most ordered as he left the Kingsway studio. 'I'll only be a couple of minutes.'

We relaxed. Hilton slumped down in front of me, a cigarette

hanging from the corner of his mouth and his guitar still strapped across his chest. The Animals had been working hard on the Chuck Berry tour. We'd get to the studio as quickly as possible after a gig; we had travelled to London by train with our equipment and borrowed a porter's cart and pushed it to the studios. Long hours had been put in, but the band had nearly finished recording the tracks for their first album. It's strange to think of it now, all those famous tracks being turned out in that dark basement studio deep underneath the Midland Bank in Kingsway, in the early hours of the morning. As the Kingsway Studios were only equipped with a 4-track analogue recording machine, whereas today's studios can have over 100-track digital machines, I often took up my old position from The Wildcats days on rhythm guitar, leaving Hilton to concentrate on playing lead. But now they had a break, a few spare minutes to relax, before Micky got back from whatever he was doing. Eric sat quietly, watching Hilton as he idly strummed his guitar and let his fingers find a familiar tune on the strings.

'Oh, fuck it!' Eric said suddenly, jumping to his feet. 'Let's record "The House of the Rising Sun". Come on, all five minutes of it. We'll never get to do it when Micky's here.'

The sound engineer agreed and one of the greatest pop singles ever recorded was laid down in one take. It was completed before Micky Most could get back from the bathroom.

The average single in the 1960s lasted approximately two-and-a-half minutes. The four-and-a-half minutes of 'The House of the Rising Sun' was therefore considered only as an album track. But Eric loved that song. He'd loved it since we'd first heard Bob Dylan's version (the same album that 'Baby, Let Me Take You Home' had been taken from) and Hilton, playing about with the tune in a jamming session, had first plucked out that famous arpeggio. Eric literally pleaded with EMI to release it. Eventually, with great reluctance, in 1964, they agreed and 'The House of the Rising Sun' became The Animals' second single. By 22 August, 'The House of the Rising Sun' was the Number 1 single in the British charts.

But here something strange happened. 'The House of the Rising Sun' was an 18th century folk song, but its lyrics had been written in 1928. This still meant that its composers, Georgia Turner and Bert Martin, had been dead long enough for the song to be free from copyright. This was good news for us, as it meant that any new arrangement could claim the title and the rights to the song: 'The House of the Rising Sun' could now belong to The Animals. However, when the single was released, Mike Jeffery said that it would look ridiculous to have five names crowded under the song title. Whether it was favouritism or the memory of forcing Alan to change the band name all those months ago, I can't say, but it was Alan Price's name, and his name only, that went on the record. The intention was that at some point a contract would be drawn up to give each member of The Animals their own share of the rights, but for now they were Alan Price's. This agreed, we forgot about it, with consequences we could never have guessed at.

But Great Britain was not going to be the limit of the song's success.

Before 'The House of the Rising Sun' had been released, The Animals signed a contract agreeing to appear at the Blackpool Pier with Manfred Mann for six weeks. We kept to our promise for two weeks before the news came, news that we could only have dreamed of back in rainy Newcastle two years before. The Animals had entered the American charts. On 5 September 1964, 'The House of the Rising Sun' was Number 1 in the US, where it would remain for three weeks.

This was big. The only other British band to have had a Number 1 in the US was The Beatles. Our agent booked us a live appearance on the *Ed Sullivan Show* the following Sunday.

We were forced to buy our way out of the contract with the Blackpool Pier and leave immediately for New York. It all happened so fast. The successes in Britain, the recording contract and the first tour were only months and weeks behind us. They had seemed such huge achievements, and yet here were The Animals on their way to America with a Number 1 in both countries. I was their road manager, the sixth Animal, and I was going with them.

Goodbye England . . . Hello USA

The airport was heaving; a crush of bodies; tangles of legs poking from under skirts hitched higher than any mother would approve of, certainly any mother near Newcastle. But we weren't anywhere near Newcastle, we were in New York City surrounded by smeared

20

lipsticked mouths which screamed and screamed . . . for us. We were a collection of ordinary lads from the North-East, who stood in the middle of the scrum, trying not to look terrified.

'This way. Let me through.' A short chubby man forced his way out of the crowd of fans. 'I'm Bob. This place is about to blow. Follow me, I've sorted Customs.'

The Animals were, in fact, the first British group to be routed through a new immigration and Customs procedure in an attempt to protect the band from the fans.

Bob Levine looked up at me and grinned. 'You'll get used to it.'

Bob was a US roadie. He'd worked with all the greats, right back to Glenn Miller, Doris Day and Frank Sinatra. Frank Barcelona from Premier Talent, one of New York's top agents, had sent him to meet us from the airport. He wasn't an inch over 5ft 4in (1.62m) and his suit was as tight as the skin on a sausage. I followed his balding head as he ushered us out through a side exit to the waiting limousine, little knowing that I'd just met the man who would be one of the greatest influences on my life.

You'll get used to it, he'd said. Propped up in the back of that massive limo we were a group of nervous working-class boys from England, used to family rules and embarrassed fumbles in back lanes, being driven like royalty. And it got better. Our agent arranged for each member of the band to transfer from the limo into their own convertible Cadillac, where they could sit on top of the back seat and wave to the New Yorkers as they passed. This was the Sixties and The Animals were better than royalty; they were pop stars, the girls were screaming and we were going to make the most of it.

America, though, proved a culture shock in ways we had never anticipated. It dazzled us. Everything was bigger, brighter and more exciting. Travelling through New York, in the line of our grand entrance, I realised that I couldn't see the sky. I hadn't believed that buildings could get this high. That night at our hotel was the first time I'd seen a colour television. We had all grown up in terraced houses with outdoor toilets; it was novelty enough for us not to have to go outside to piss, and here was colour television! And the girls . . . well, the girls were the best of all.

In that whistle-stop, five-day visit to the USA in the September of 1964, The Animals were to appear live, five times a day, at The

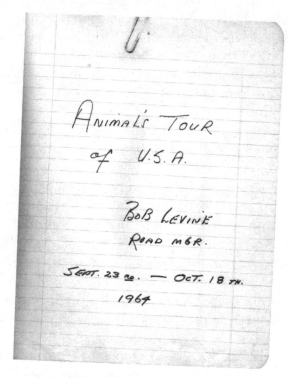

Expenses tour book of the Animals first American tour

Paramount Theater in Times Square. Then we had our live performance on the *Ed Sullivan Show* on Sunday, 13 September. And the fans were coming with us every step of the way.

Groupies, Groupies Everywhere

America had gone crazy. Girls climbed the elevator shafts of our hotel and sat in vigil outside our windows, desperate for just a glimpse of The Animals. They may have been shouting for The Animals, but I had been with those boys from the beginning. That was more than enough for the girls, and there were more than enough girls for me.

You'll get used to it, and we did. We were young men, and there were girls crawling out of elevator shafts to get close to us. If there was one lesson we held on to from Merry Ol' England, it was to be

Accounting for The Animal's first date on the US tour – Norfolk, Virginia

polite. And if they are begging at your door . . . well, it's only polite, isn't it?

Now, I don't want you to misunderstand me. I have slept with a lot of women, and each of them was wonderful in her own unique way. Women in the Sixties were something special; those were beautiful, smooth-limbed, wonderful days, where we could get any woman we chose. And I thank every one of them for the time she gave me.

But there were *so* many! We were young boys and although the attention was fantastic, sometimes we were too scared even to leave our hotel rooms. America on that first visit and the subsequent tour will always live in my memory as a place of static nylon carpets, colour TV, indoor toilets and screaming women.

Arriving for Ed Sullivan, we were mobbed, the girls surging forward and grabbing at our hair and clothes. A security guard pulled us through a back entrance and slammed the door closed behind us. I

23

turned and three fingers fell at my feet. We stood there, horror struck, and stared down at the three painted fingernails on their fleshy stubs, just laying there on the concrete floor. John Steel wretched the door back open and pulled the injured girl into the building. We tried to comfort her while he ran off for an ambulance, but the girl, apparently oblivious to her severed fingers and bleeding hand, just seemed delighted to meet the band.

The *Ed Sullivan Show* was something else (this was the show that broke The Beatles into America, remember) and The Animals did themselves proud. It's hard to explain just how huge that show's influence was in the US and I don't think that we even realised it at the time. Performing on a stage shared with a collection of variety acts, from jugglers to other singers of the day, it was easy just to view *Ed Sullivan* as another television performance. But when Paul Simon approached me at the end of the show, asking if he could meet Eric Burdon, I think that I began to get a taste of what success in America could mean for us.

But we were leaving America, just as suddenly as we had arrived. The Animals were a Number 1 band and they were in demand at home as well as abroad. So with a few more notches in our bedposts and a little less terror in our hearts, The Animals and I jumped straight from the stage of the *Ed Sullivan Show* into the waiting limos. Before we knew it, we were waving goodbye to Bob Levine, the screams at the airport and the glamour of the New World and heading back to the UK.

CHAPTER 3

100% Animal: On the Road with The Animals

Goodbye, Chas Chandler?

We were back in England. In Manchester, to be exact, and straight back on stage. When I said our exit from the US was sudden, I meant it; The Animals went straight from the plane to a gig, still wearing the make-up that they'd been plastered with for the *Ed Sullivan Show*.

Now here I just have to explain another nickname I'd acquired during my time with The Animals: Captain Filth. I know you'll presume that this was something to do with the girls, but in fact it was my face that earned me that little tag-line. I'm a dark man and a hairy one. I'll have a shave in the morning but by mid-afternoon there will already be a dark shadow of new growth. Unfortunately this does not take the form of sexy stubble and even I have to admit that my face can look filthy. The guys were quick to pick up on this particular weakness, hence the nickname.

It did get to me. Tired of their ribbing, I even tried make-up to cover the inevitable afternoon shadow. Pasting my face in pan stick, I got away with it a couple of times, but one day after a rather hurried application I noticed Alan looking at me strangely.

'Tappy,' he said, with a sudden shout of laughter. 'You bloody fag, you're wearing make-up!'

With memories of their laughter at my expense I must admit a moment of satisfaction at the newspaper headlines that greeted The Animals' return to the UK: SHOCK! BRITISH BAND MADE UP LIKE GIRLS FOR GIG!

Thanks to the success of The Animals and 'The House of the Rising Sun', we were saved from returning to the bare boards of Ronan O'Rahilly's flat in London. Eric, Hilton, John and I rented apartments in Earl's Court; Chas and Alan in Kensington. These were the places to be when London started to swing and we were surrounded by the other artists of the day. But, if I'm honest, rent and location were mostly wasted on us; it hardly felt like we lived in London at all. The fever surrounding 'The House of the Rising Sun' showed no signs of abating and The Animals were in greater demand than ever before.

On the whole it was great. We were good friends; we'd known each other nearly all our lives and we were getting the chance to experience a new world together. The tour bus is a funny place though, and touring itself quickly becomes claustrophobic and repetitive. The Animals were a Number 1 act and they knew they had to make the most of it. But, from behind the wheel, in those hectic early days, I began to see the differences that could drive The Animals apart.

Chas Chandler was a problem. From the large, hard man we'd known in Newcastle, he had proved himself to be an intimidating bully. Anyone who knew Chas knew not to cross him. That was fine for a knockabout band in the North-East, but now we were in the big time and having to deal with living in each other's pockets. Chas's domineering behaviour was getting out of control and intolerable.

The only one not affected was Eric. Chas knew as well as the rest of us, that without Eric Burdon's vocals, The Animals would be over, and even in his worst moods I don't think he ever wanted that. It shouldn't have surprised me then that it was Eric who ordered me to pull the van over on a long drive from a gig in Scotland back to London. It was time for Chas to be confronted with the consequences of his behaviour.

It was in the early hours of the morning and all members of The Animals were, or so I thought, sleeping peacefully in the back of the van. When Eric shouted at me to stop, Hilton, John, Chas and Alan stretched and shook themselves awake.

Well, they didn't seem to know what was happening and someone had to ask it: 'What's this about, Eric?' I said.

In truth, I was pissed off. I'd been driving for hours and now Eric was delaying us even longer. It was all right for them, they could just get back to sleep and . . .

'We need a meeting. Chas, we're sorry but we've decided that it would be best for you to leave the band.'

Now that was unexpected!

'What the fuck do you mean "leave the band"?' Chas snapped at Eric, very much awake now and looking murderous.

'Just what I said, Chas.'

Maybe it wasn't so unexpected. I'd turned round in my seat now and could see the rest of the boys keeping their eyes directed anywhere that was away from Chas Chandler. Chas himself started to rave at Eric.

Eventually, even loudmouth Eric Burdon seemed to lose his nerve. 'It's not just me, we've all agreed. Look, let's put it to the vote. Hands up everyone who thinks we'd be better off without Chas.'

Eric, Alan and John all raised their hands. Hilton, who was a little stoned and sat glassy-eyed at the back of the van, waved both his hands wildly in the air. I kept my hand down. I certainly didn't want to get in the middle of this one.

'C'mon, Tappy,' Eric said, looking more confident now that he had the rest of The Animals behind him. 'Get your hand up, son.'

'That's not fair, Eric. It's nothing to do with me. I'm not even a member of the band so leave me out of it.'

'You're the sixth Animal, Tappy, and you know it, so cut the crap and cast your vote.'

Slowly, and avoiding Chas's eye, I raised my hand. I did like Chas, but he had been getting worse and worse lately; he made all our lives miserable. But what followed was awful.

Surrounded by a unanimous show of hands, Chas began to cry. That's right, Chas Chandler was weeping like a baby. He begged us to give him one more chance; told us that he was sorry for all that he'd done; pleaded for forgiveness. It was horrible. There could certainly have been a time and place to confront Chas with his behaviour, but two o'clock in the morning on a slip road in the back of my van was not it. Nice one, Eric!

Alan was the first to speak. 'Look, lads, can't we come up with another solution? We don't have to sack him. This could just be a warning, couldn't it?'

Eric wasn't happy about it, but in the face of Chas's tears the rest of the band agreed. Chas would stay with a warning.

The rest of the trip home passed in a strained silence. Hilton was the only one to get any more sleep that night. I was furious with Eric because he'd made me put up my hand just before Alan stepped in with a change of heart. Chas loved The Animals, he'd never do anything to threaten the band, but I was just the roadie. Despite Eric's comments about me being the sixth Animal, I didn't think that Chas would see me as irreplaceable. Would I be the one to face Chas's revenge for a conversation that had reduced him to tears?

As it turned out, I'd misjudged him. After that incident, Chas really tried to change, the bullying stopped and we seemed to find our friend again. He became a better man, I think, after the shock of seeing us all turn against him. Chas was not a man to cross, but if there was any revenge for that night it never found me. Maybe Chas, as well as Eric, credited me as the sixth member of the group?

Lady Fate

When we did get some time off in our schedule and weren't bouncing around the country or abroad, we were able to spend some time in London. In the August of 1964, I enjoyed my Earl's Court flat. Upstairs, directly above me, lived two young sisters. I knew that they were foreign and that the pretty one was studying to be a doctor. I'd see her on the stairs now and then. I always made sure to stop and wave, to shout a good morning. She would nod and smile at me politely, hiding her face behind a sweep of long blonde hair. This was a change for me; I'd quickly become used to the screaming of fans and dodging the thunder of chasing high heels. But this was nice, sweet even.

Still, as I say, we were busy and I was driving the boys all over the country for bookings and gigs. My apartment was a place I crawled back to, desperate to catch up on lost sleep and to rest my aching limbs. But the sweet smile on the stairs stayed with me, I suppose. Though I thought little about my pretty neighbour in the hectic months that followed, it seemed that Lady Fate was just waiting her time.

So Many Women . . .

Despite our loyalty to the British fans and the wonderful chances that the boys were being offered back home, the success of The Animals' performance on the *Ed Sullivan Show* and their gigs at the Paramount had secured their first American tour. Before I knew it, I was leaving my new home (and the sweet smile on the stairs) and then, in early 1965, was heading back out to the States with The Animals.

Here, as we'd learnt from our last visit, we were always guaranteed more than a smile from the fans and, believe me, we had missed the attention. As Bob Levine had said, all too quickly, we had got used to it.

Even though I wasn't actually a member of the band, my position as a roadie often offered me an advantage over the boys. These girls wanted to meet The Animals but straight after a gig the band would be driven off to their hotel leaving me to pack up and check the equipment, and to comfort the fans who loitered in the hope that their heroes were just backstage. I'd played this situation back in the UK, but in the States The Animals' hotel would be as besieged as the backstage door, with girls camped out and singing vigils to their windows. The Animals were for the most part prisoners in their hotel rooms and, if they wanted a girl, it was often I who would have to go and fetch her. Hence my advantage: I had the freedom to pick and choose and I was the fans' gateway to The Animals. And, with a little charm, I'd found that it wasn't too difficult to convince a beauty to settle happily for the bed of the sixth Animal instead.

That said, we all had our fair share of girls on that first tour. We were young lads who had never known girls like these, and while we were always grateful, the shock soon wore off. In fact, we even started to make a game out of the women and to compete to see who could bed the most.

One night Eric and I were sitting together in a hotel, drinking, smoking and laughing. There was a lot of bragging and calls for proof for some of our more outlandish claims. Then came a plan. I can't remember who had it, but the idea of it brightened our hotel stays considerably over the next month.

Each member of the band would be given a piece of blank paper on which to draw a large smiling face. Then double-sided sticky tape could be stuck along the top lip of our drawing. The challenge? To fill the tape with hair. Pubic hair. One hair from each woman we slept with over the following month. We could all put $100 in the kitty and stick our paper faces up on the wall in the tour bus. The winner would be the man with the bushiest moustache at the end of the month.

I don't think I could have worked any harder in that department. Despite the boasts, we were all getting through a lot of women – about 70 a month. But, confident as we were, there could still be the occasional disappointment of a clean-shaven Brazilian to contend with and, after all, hair harvesting would be the name of the game.

We would all want to beat Eric. Those 'Howlin' Wolf' soul vocals came from trousers straining with the largest cock I'd ever seen. Size doesn't matter, maybe, but I wrapped an elastic band around the base of my shaft and stretched my dick, hoping it would get bigger. Then I put it to use . . .

The band never put that pubic hair plan into action, though; maybe we were all too busy getting laid. It wasn't 'til years later, when I was working with another band, that I remembered that conversation with Eric and tried it out. I'm proud to say that some of that rubber band treatment I gave myself must have paid off because by the end of that month my paper face smiled out from under a grand moustache, far hairier than any of the other lads'. Here was work I enjoyed doing and, pocketing my winnings, I realised that I was good at it. And those years with The Animals certainly gave me more practice than I could have ever imagined. God Bless America!

Eric and Ali

Unfortunately, there were times when our ease with women came back to haunt us. Eric preferred to sleep with black women. Even back in Newcastle in the early Sixties he had a black girlfriend (which was remarkable for its time). But he was to learn that, black or white, it's best to find out who the girl you're bedding is related to before you get round to undressing her. And though, as I said, it was often me that would go out to pick up the girls for The Animals to enjoy, I swear this one had nothing to do with me.

It was late in the summer of 1964 and Hilton and I were enjoying breakfast at the City Squire Hotel in New York. I reached over to take the butter and out of the corner of my eye saw a huge hand descend on to Hilton's shoulder.

'Which one of you Animals is sleeping with my sister?'

The hand belonged to Cassius Clay, one of the greatest boxers who ever lived, now known as Muhammad Ali. Under Clay's hand, Hilton was shaking. We both knew immediately it would be Eric, but there was no way we were going to throw him to the mercy of a furious Clay. We played dumb – what else could we do?

Cassius Clay was staying in our hotel along with his massive entourage of family, friends and trainers. They all sat down to eat. After choking down the rest of our breakfast with the knowledge of Clay's eyes on us, I hurried off to phone Eric's room, trying all the while to look nonchalant.

'Yes, I've got a girl with me, Tappy, and, if you don't mind, I'd like to get back to her.'

'Eric, it's not her, it's her brother.'

'Nope, her brother's not here. Personally, that kind of thing doesn't turn me on. Look, what's your problem, Tappy? What's this all about?'

After I'd explained that the beautiful young black girl that Eric had with him was in fact Cassius Clay's baby sister, witty replies seemed to go out of the window and were replaced by blind panic.

'Please, Tappy, you've got to come get her. Fucking hell, he'll kill me. I mean . . . Christ! Cassius Clay!'

With help from Hilton, I managed to get the girl out of Eric's room and back to the hotel lobby without anyone from the Clay entourage spotting us. Still terrified, Eric locked himself in his room and refused to come out.

In fact, the rest of the time that Clay shared a hotel with us, Eric ate all his meals in his room and barely ventured out at all, just sitting staring out at the huge tour bus that sat in the hotel grounds outside his window, with the legend 'CASSIUS CLAY, WORLD CHAMPION' printed across it. Before gigs, he would only leave his room at the last minute and then make his dash down the stairs, for fear that he could get trapped in an elevator with Clay.

I could see what he was worried about; there was no way that you could meet Cassius Clay without getting an impression of the sheer power, strength and agility of the man. As he crossed a room, people would simply stop and stare in awe. But if he caught sight of Hilton or me staring at him, we were more likely to be impressed by the clenched fists and the animal-like growl that he directed at us. Yes, I could certainly understand why Eric was worried.

Back to Work

While we were charming the girls, and dodging those charming girls' relatives, there was still the real work to be done. We recorded a Christmas TV special, which also starred Liza Minnelli as Little Red Riding Hood and Sammy Davis Jnr as the Big Bad Wolf. They seemed to live up to the characters that they were taking on for the show.

Liza was friendly, always willing to stop for a chat or a laugh or two. Sammy, however, was as scathing about The Animals as he was about all modern pop groups, and he didn't mind letting us know it. He always made sure that one of us was within earshot when he started a rant about these pop stars with 'no talent', that 'couldn't dance, act or sing' and who would have sunk without trace in the 'good old days' that made his career. A real-life Big Bad Wolf if ever I met one.

We'd heard enough about these 'good old days' back in England, but that had been from politicians, from the bowler hat and umbrella carrying crowd, who caught their train in the morning, and always reminded us how they had fought a war for us 'scruffy layabouts'. But Sammy Davis Jnr was working in the same industry as us. We'd worked to get where we were, and we were still working. That didn't seem to occur to him. He ignored us completely on set and snubbed any attempts to pull him into conversation.

I didn't like Sammy Davis Jnr any more than his great buddy, Dean Martin. I met him when The Animals followed up their Christmas special with an appearance on *The Dean Martin Show*. When I say I met him, Dean didn't actually turn up to any of the rehearsals. When he did turn up, on the day of the show, it was only to give us more of the same treatment we'd received from Sammy Davis Jnr. Though when the cameras rolled and the girls started screaming, Dean was careful to play the friendly host and sing the praises of The Animals and Sixties pop.

The great sadness in this was not just the hypocrisy with which we were treated, but that both Dean Martin and Sammy Davis Jnr were names which we had grown up with. These were men, and artists, who we were delighted to meet, who we wanted to talk to and to learn from. The threat that they must have felt from this new breed of music was enough to make them rude and arrogant. It was such a waste of time.

The International Sex Girls

So we were not always among friends, and even with the fun and games with fans, there was a lot of hard graft, but we began our first major American tour due the success of the few gigs we had done previously. We were leaving the towering buildings and wonders of New York and heading out across the USA. Little did we know that the strangest fun and games were right behind us – and it was what was behind him that would be worrying Hilton Valentine after one particular night in San Francisco.

It was in the fall of 1964 and The Animals had just finished a gig at the Cow Palace Stadium in San Francisco. I listened to the usual chants and screams from the crowd begging for an encore. Now, as I think I mentioned before, this was usually the time when I could take my pick of the groupies while The Animals were hurried away to their hotel. But, as it happened that night, The Animals were delayed in their dressing room for a couple of minutes. A couple of girls caught my eye in the front row. A little blonde and a gorgeous dark-haired girl with carefully arranged curls. They were waving desperately and trying to catch my attention, knowing that the roadie was the best route to the band.

I chatted to them for a bit while the stadium was cleared. They introduced themselves as Donna and Susie and seemed like nice girls. In the end, I agreed to make the most of The Animals' delay and take them backstage to meet the band. There was just time for a couple of pecks on the cheek and some autograph signing in the dressing room before the band had to leave.

Now, what I don't think I have mentioned is that sometimes the freedom I had after a gig to meet girls caused some jealousy from the boys in The Animals. I was therefore pretty clear as to what was in the mind of Hilton Valentine when he declined the car to the hotel and offered to stay back with me to help pack up the equipment.

Sure enough, thrilled at finally meeting The Animals, Donna and Susie wasted little time in inviting Hilton and me back to their apartment for a drink. With the equipment safely stowed away in The Animals' bus, we followed them home, Hilton busying himself with a discussion on who should get which girl when we got there. I wasn't entirely convinced by Hilton's optimism. These seemed like nice girls; we'd probably get nothing more than a cup of coffee or a glass of cheap wine followed by a kiss goodbye. I couldn't have been more wrong.

After several drinks in their little living room, the conversation turned to sex. To our surprise, the girls suddenly informed us that they were quite the experts when it came to sex. 'International' sex that is.

'What do you mean "international"?' Hilton asked.

'Well,' Susie said, draining the last of the wine from her glass. 'We're the International sex girls. You should try it; it's a lot of fun. What do you reckon, Donna, shall we show them?'

Donna grinned and ran a hand over her dark curls. 'Sure. Follow us, boys.'

With a quick look at each other, Hilton and I quickly stubbed out our cigarettes and followed them through a door leading off the living room into a much larger room, the like of which I have never seen before or since.

'Welcome,' said Susie, throwing out her arms. 'This is our International sex room. You'll never find another room like this in the world. A lot of research has gone into this, you know.' She smiled at us.

This was unbelievable. By this time, we had seen a lot of things that would have shocked and appalled our parents back home but, believe me, this was something else! The room was littered with strange objects; a bed was pushed up against the wall and in the centre of the room was a table covered with a padded quilt and pillows, above which hung a large basket.

'What's this for?' I asked, swinging the basket on its ropes.

'Ooh, that's my favourite,' said Donna stroking the wicker lovingly and giving me the kind of smile that would melt steel. 'We call it the Mexican basket.'

'Would you like to try?' Susie asked me. 'It could be a kind of thank you gift from us for getting us backstage.'

So much for sweet and innocent. This looked like it was going to be an evening to remember and there was no way I was going to pass up an opportunity of promised pleasure. Even if I was still a little confused about exactly what I was about to let myself in for.

'Hey, what about me?' Hilton piped up. 'Don't I get a try with the Mexican basket?'

'Sure,' Susie said, putting a hand on his arm. 'But after Tappy, he got us in to meet the band after all.'

'I *am* the bloody band!' protested Hilton.

'I know, honey,' Donna said, sliding out of her dress. 'Why don't you just go lie down on the bed and watch for a while? It'll be your turn soon.'

The sight of naked flesh seemed to silence Hilton and he crawled on to the bed to watch the rest of the girls' clothes disappear. But he gave a groan as a pair of neatly-shaven pussies appeared. Hilton had earned the nickname 'Soon-shoot' during his time in The Animals and this was all getting too much for him already.

'You better hurry up, Tappy. I don't think I'm going to be able to wait that long.'

'Shut up, Hilton. This is my turn, son. You'd better close your eyes and think of England, because I'm taking my time.'

The girls led me to the table and undressed me. With my head settled among the pillows, Donna began to pour handfuls of warm oil on to my body. While Susie climbed into the basket, Donna kneaded the oil gently into my groin and then stroked it up the length of my erection. At this point, the main thought in my mind was that I was soon to share Hilton's nickname; I felt like I was about to explode. Donna looked down at me and smiled, seeming to read my thoughts.

'OK, Susie, I think he's ready for you.'

'Hoist me up then,' Susie instructed. 'I hope you're prepared, Tappy, I'm going to give you the screw of your life.'

Donna walked over to the wall and started to pull on a rope. Slowly, both Susie and the basket began to rise until they were right above me. Susie's legs were splayed out over the edge of the basket and through a hole in the centre I had a perfect view of her beautiful shaven pussy. Slowly, Donna lowered the basket until Susie was just touching the tip of my cock, then the rope was jerked and Susie's pussy locked around me. I groaned with pleasure, but they were just getting started. Donna tied off the rope then moved back over to the basket and gave it a spin.

Slowly at first and then gradually increasing in speed until she was like a spinning top above me, my well-oiled cock was 'screwed' until I could last no longer. With a yell I climaxed with such force that it actually hurt.

I lay on the table gasping for breath; I had never felt anything like it. The basket was lifted away and I saw Susie looking down on me and giggling.

'Thank you,' I panted. 'That was amazing. I . . .'

'Me now. For God's sake, it's my turn now.' Hilton was on his feet, his clothes off and pulling me off the table before I could even catch my breath.

He lay down on the table with a wide grin on his face. He knew exactly what he was in for.

'Right, Donna, hoist her up. No messing, just get that girl and that basket on to this prick.'

I crawled over to the bed and watched Hilton receive the Mexican treatment, although Hilton's wait meant that his experience lasted a little less time than mine. These girls were amazing and, as Hilton staggered over to the bed to join me, I felt some of my strength returning.

'Ooh,' Susie cooed, coming over and planting a soft kiss on my cock, so that her short blonde hair brushed my thighs. 'I think this one's ready for more. How's about a little Japanese?'

Donna lay down on the floor and spread her legs wide. I eagerly dropped down on top of her, hoping to prove myself a little longer-lasting this time around. But eventually I couldn't hold on a moment longer.

'Now, Susie!' Donna called, as my cock began to jerk inside her.

Suddenly, I felt two small taps on my shoulder blades and an ice cold liquid began to run down my back to my buttocks. As my orgasm began, the liquid was dripping onto my balls. I gave one last thrust and grunted like an animal before I collapsed on top of Donna. She wiped the sweat from my face and gave me a smile.

'How did you like Japanese eggs then, Tappy?'

'Eggs?'

She was right; I was covered in raw egg and horribly sticky.

'Don't worry about it; I'll give you a wash.'

Carefully, Donna soaped, washed and dried me and I climbed, satisfied, back on to the bed next to Hilton.

'I'm not sure about the eggs, Tappy,' he whispered to me, looking slightly frightened.

'Seriously, go for it. You'll love it.'

Hilton raised his eyebrows speculatively, but moved over to take his turn with Donna. Before he began, though, he turned to Susie. 'Be gentle with those eggs now, won't you, love? I'm very delicate you know.'

Susie laughed and soon I was witnessing Hilton's squeals of delight as the cold eggs slithered down his back.

After it was all over, the girls made us a coffee and we sat talking in the International sex room. Then I noticed that Donna had a long silky scarf in her hand, in which she was tying a series of tight knots. She grinned at me when she caught me watching, put the scarf into her mouth and chewed on it.

Susie glanced over as Donna pulled the wet scarf from between her lips, pulling it taut in her hands.

'A special nightcap for you, boys. Would either of you fancy a Chinese blow-job before you go?'

Hilton slammed his coffee cup down on the floor, nearly upsetting the remaining contents.

'The Chinese blow-job is mine. I'm first this time,' he said, with a warning look at me.

'OK then,' said Susie, laughing at his eagerness. 'You need to lie down on your side here.'

Hilton did as he was told and Donna lay down next to him and began to nibble and suck on his cock.

'No need to be gentle now, Donna,' Hilton said, with a wink at me and a firm hand on the back of Donna's head. 'You go as hard as you like. A firm blow-job is a favourite of mine: English, American or Chinese.'

He groaned as Donna did as she was told. Susie moved round behind him and without him noticing began to insert the damp scarf into his arsehole. Hilton, oblivious, continued enjoying himself with Donna.

As Hilton's pants and groans turned into choked screams and it was obvious he was about to orgasm, Susie suddenly yanked the scarf free. Each knot on the scarf must have torn at his arsehole, because now Hilton's screams were very clear and there wasn't much pleasure in them.

I declined the offered turn at a Chinese-blow job and we left the girls to drive back to the hotel.

'You fucking bastard,' Hilton muttered from his place on a cushion in the passenger seat of the van. 'Why did I have to pick that one to go first on? I mean, I've heard of Chinese water torture, but that was below the belt.'

'Literally.'

'Oh all right, you can laugh . . .'

Believe me, I *was* laughing.

'Just promise me that none of the boys will hear about this.'

I did promise him, but it just so happened that my fingers were crossed at the time. And then it just so happened that it came up in conversation with Eric the next day. And it just so happened that Eric has the biggest mouth known to mankind. And it just so happened that soon all The Animals knew about it. Sorry, Hilton, but you did say I could laugh.

A Different Kind of Animal

Now, I was loving my time with The Animals, but I could never have foreseen how close a chance encounter would get me to becoming a member of another of the best-known acts of the 1960s.

It was our first time in LA, later in that same tour during the autumn of 1964; our West Coast promoter, Al, booked us into the Beverly Wilshire Hotel opposite Rodeo Drive, the most expensive shopping street in the world. Al arrived on our first day and introduced himself. He was tall and confident, with one of those gleaming white smiles they seem to make in America. Along with his short-cropped black hair and brown eyes this guy looked far too handsome to be a promoter to me, especially compared to the rough diamonds we were used to dealing with in England. But this was Hollywood; everyone seemed to look like a movie star here and, despite his good looks, Al was a nice guy and we got on well.

Al loved the Hollywood life and was obviously keen to share some of it with me, an offer I wasn't going to refuse.

'Is there anyone you'd really like to meet while you're here, Tappy?'

I thought about this, listing names in my mind. I knew that Al had contacts and I was keen to test them. This was the chance of a lifetime.

'Well, there is one man . . .'

'Come on, Tappy, this is Hollywood. Name the name.'

'Jerry Lewis,' I said at last, not holding much hope. 'When I was a kid, I watched all his movies. I love that man. He's a legend.' I watched Al.

He looked over his sunglasses and then gave me his movie star smile. 'Sure. I know Jerry well. Leave it with me Tappy; I'll see what I can do.'

I liked Al well enough, and he certainly played at being a big-shot, but I'd seen enough of LA to realise that everyone was beautiful and everyone thought they were a big-shot. It would probably come to nothing. I was certainly not holding my breath until I heard from Al again.

It was with surprise, therefore, that I greeted Al's shouted hello early next morning. Surprise and not a great deal of grace: it was *very* early next morning. How is it that Americans can be so cheerful whatever the hour? I was stomping down the street, returning from an enjoyable night with the latest girl, and trying to shake some wakefulness into my bones.

'Hey, Tappy!' Al called from his car, pulling in next to me.

'What . . . ? Who . . . ? What the hell do you want, Al?'

'Now, c'mon, Tappy. Let's just say Santa Claus has come early this year and you should jump into his awaiting sleigh.'

'Early is right. Have you seen the time? What's this about?'

'I'm granting your wish, so hop in. Columbia Pictures' studio and Jerry Lewis await. Seriously, if you stand there with your mouth open any longer it will fill up with mosquitoes and I'll be late. You coming or what?'

'I'm coming!' I said, closing my mouth and jumping into Al's car. He sped away singing 'Jingle Bells' at the top of his voice.

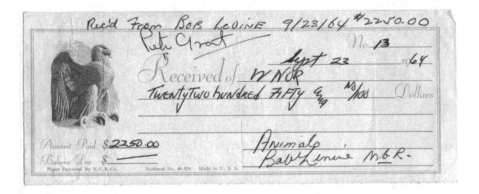

Bob Levine would always make sure he got a signature for money he handed over – this one from Peter Grant.

I hadn't lied to Al when he'd asked who I'd really like to meet. Jerry Lewis was a hero of mine. But I was still nervous about actually meeting him. He had a reputation as the most hated man in Hollywood; how would he react to being introduced to some guy from England he'd never met in his life? I just hoped that Al's assurance that he 'knew Jerry well' was true. Or that Jerry Lewis was a closet fan of The Animals.

When we drove through those famous studio gates, we were told that Mr Lewis was 'on set' with his new movie, *Three on a Couch*. Al had things to do, so he pointed me off into a room to wait for him, promising he'd be back soon to fulfil his 'Santa duties'.

I sat down in the empty room and tried to control my nerves. One minute I was walking down the street, half-asleep and heading home to my own shower, and now here I was waiting to meet Jerry Lewis. I wished I'd had time for that shower.

After a couple of minutes, several more men came into the room and sat down alongside me. At first, I was surprised at their appearance, but then I thought that maybe this was normal. With a big star like Jerry Lewis there must be hundreds of 'friends of friends' who were desperate to meet him. Maybe they had devised this system to get it over quickly and let him meet his fans in batches, rather than having to speak to them all one on one. I was pleased to notice that the other men in the room looked as nervous as me about meeting him. We smiled at each other quickly when we caught each other's eyes, but didn't talk.

Then a woman put her head round the door and looked round at us. She nodded to me and beckoned to follow her. So we were going to see him one at a time after all. The woman led me along the corridors to another room.

'Good luck,' she whispered and squeezed my arm, before opening the door and giving me a gentle push into the room. How scary was Jerry Lewis going to be if I needed good luck to say hello?

Inside the room, two men in suits sat behind a large desk. Jerry Lewis was nowhere to be seen. Confused, I smiled and took an empty chair that faced the desk.

'Hi there, I'm Bob Rafelson and this is Bert Schneider,' one of the men said, nodding at his companion.

'Hi, I'm Tappy Wright,' I said and reached across the table to shake their hands.

'OK, Mr Wright. Let's start by asking what kind of singing and dancing experience you have?'

'Sorry?'

'Singing and dancing,' Bob repeated.

'Erm, I can't sing or dance.'

'Do you mind me asking what the hell you're doing here then?' Bert asked.

'I came to meet Mr Lewis.'

'Mr Lewis? Do you mean Jerry Lewis?'

'That's right.'

The two men looked at each other. 'There seems to have been some kind of mix-up. This is an audition, Mr Wright. You are currently auditioning for a new band we're putting together. I'm guessing that this was not your intention?'

'No. I thought . . .'

At that moment there was a knock on the door and we turned to see Al entering the room.

'Excuse me, I was just . . .' Then he saw me. 'Tappy, where the hell have you been? I've been looking for you everywhere.'

Amidst some laughter, the confusion was quickly sorted out. As we left the audition room Al explained that I'd been mistakenly directed into Screen Gems, the television production side of Colombia Pictures, and I'd nearly been part of a new band that Bob and Bert were putting together – The Monkees. If I'd known then how huge

The hotel extras bill for all members of the Animals on the first night of their US tour. No room service charges then!

The Monkees were to become I would have put more effort into the meeting. Tappy Wright could have been Davey Jones!

But the day's excitements were not yet over. We headed for Studio 3, where Jerry Lewis was working. I watched nervously as Al sauntered over to my teen hero, but almost forgot all about Jerry Lewis when the most beautiful woman I had ever seen wandered past me and smiled. A very young Janet Leigh, wife of Tony Curtis and future mother to Jamie Lee Curtis, was within touching distance, and even more dazzling in the flesh than she was on screen.

'Mosquito-catching again are we, Tappy?' Al said into my ear, forcing my attention back to my purpose. 'Come meet Jerry.'

Jerry Lewis was walking towards us. I wiped my hands down the leg of my trousers (I did not want to give Mr Lewis a sweaty hand to shake) and swallowed.

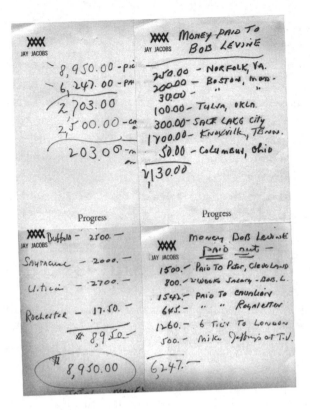

Bob Levine was meticulous in his keeping of accounts – even if it was on scraps of paper . . .

'Hi, I'm Jerry Lewis. How ya doin'?'

I mumbled something and grasped his offered hand enthusiastically, pumping it up and down.

He smiled. 'You work with The Animals, I hear? The group from England?'

Jerry Lewis *was* a closet fan of The Animals! Who would have believed that?

'That's right,' I said, feeling more confident and releasing his hand.

'Hey look, I have about 30 minutes before I'm back on set. Why don't we go and have a coffee?'

We all sat in the coffee shop and Jerry asked me about England. His son, Gary Lewis, was over in England on tour with his band, The Playboys, and Jerry was worried about him. I reassured him that Gary would have a great time, and we chatted about this and that until it was time for Jerry to return to the set.

'Nice to meet you, Tappy,' he said, shaking my hand before he left. (I let him have his hand back more quickly this time).

What a day! Half an audition for a band, Janet Leigh and then a coffee with Jerry Lewis. I couldn't thank Al enough, although he brushed any attempts away with 'Hey, it was nothing.' Al was a great guy, a Hollywood big-shot who kept his word, and I've always been grateful to him for letting me meet one of my greatest heroes. Still, every once in a while, I do wonder what would have happened if I had become a Monkee . . .

My Big Simple Chance

The Animals' tour, meanwhile, was a success. Remember that short, fat, bald man I met at New York airport, back in that first visit to America for Ed Sullivan? Well, Bob Levine had been with us through it all, and by now he was a close friend. Our first American tour had in fact proved so successful that plans were already being made for a second and so, towards the end of the first tour, Bob Levine announced that he had to get back to the New York office. The next tour was going to be huge and he had to be there to help with the preparations.

'I'm putting you in charge, Tappy,' he said, laughing at the panic in my face. 'I've got a lot of faith in you. Look after the band and collect the money, but don't take any chances. Always make sure the money is put up front. If the promoter refuses, the band don't play. Simple. Just stick to that and you'll be fine.'

Bob could be a lot of fun, but when it came to work he was a true professional. He explained that bands were in danger of getting ripped off. Shows weren't promoted sufficiently and then the promoters lost money on ticket sales. If the band hadn't got their money in advance of performance then the promoter was likely to tell them that they had not made enough money to pay them. Hence Bob's simple rule.

Simple? Yeah, right. But this was a big chance for me. Tour manager in the USA, sounds wonderful doesn't it? Well, Bob left us to finish the tour on our own. He went to New York and The Animals set off for Albuquerque in New Mexico with me in charge.

We arrived in New Mexico and I introduced myself to the promoter of the Albuquerque venue and asked for our money. This
promoter was nothing like the smiling Al I had met in Hollywood. He
refused to give me any money, telling me the band would be paid
when they had performed. I insisted, remembering my orders from
Bob. This was my big chance. I must have sounded just as naïve as I
was. In the end I phoned New York, but Bob just repeated what he
had told me before he left. I repeated it back to the promoter.

'No money, no performance.'

'You will only be paid after . . .'

'Then we're leaving, now.'

The promoter went berserk. He started screaming about contracts
and law courts and finally said if we didn't go on stage he would shoot
me. I'd met American girls; I knew that Americans were crazy, but
this guy was serious. Terrified, I muttered something about the
Sheriff.

Seconds later, and now hysterical, I was back on the phone to Bob.

'Bob, get us out of here! The promoter's gone fucking mental. He
won't pay and he says he's going to shoot me if the band doesn't go on
stage. And Bob, the Sheriff . . . the Sheriff is his brother . . .'

'Get back to the hotel and stay put. I'll sort it.'

I fobbed off the promoter with some lie about our New York office
being more than happy to work with crazed gunmen and managed to
get back to the hotel. Within half an hour, the State Police arrived
to rescue us. They provided an escort over the State line and we were
free from New Mexico and the death threats it contained. I've never
been back there and The Animals never returned in their time
together as a group.

Back and Forth and Best Forgotten

The second American tour was to follow hot on the heels of the first,
with only a short stop-over in England where there were more
bookings to complete. We were incredibly busy. The world was now

the playground of The Animals and they were playing hard. Looking back, those years seem a blur of different countries, accents and hotel rooms. There were more girls along the way and, despite the glimpses of my pretty neighbour in London, it was 1964 and I was still only 20 years old; not yet ready to settle down. Besides, I was popular and I had fast discovered that, when it came to women, I was able to take my pick. Unfortunately, it was not just ladies lying in wait for Tappy Wright, as I found out a few months later in New York.

I was pleased to see Bob again after our time in England. That little man became something of a father figure to me over the years. Any tricks of the trade I know, I learnt them from Bob Levine. He took care of me during my time in New York, although he was not above playing a few practical jokes on me.

New York was proving as exhausting as London, but after Bob's rescue effort back in New Mexico, I was determined to impress him. My hotel faced his apartment over West 57, near Central Park. This was convenient, as it meant that we could easily meet every morning in the coffee bar downstairs and discuss the business of the day.

It was the business of days and long nights that were tiring me out, though. One night, very late, after we got back from a gig I was desperate just to find my bed and get some sleep. Bob, however, was tireless.

'Fancy a nightcap, Tappy?'

I shook my head and rubbed at my eyes, too tired even to answer him.

'OK then, you go get some rest. But make sure I see you bright-eyed and bushy-tailed tomorrow morning. Don't, for God's sake, go and sleep in on me. I've booked a wake-up call at your hotel to make sure, but tomorrow's important. Don't let me down, Tappy.'

I murmured a reply and headed back to my flat. Totally exhausted, I think I fell into bed fully clothed. In what seemed like minutes, the telephone was ringing. It was Bob and he was furious.

'You stupid bastard,' he screamed down the line. 'I give you that big talking-to last night and you've gone and slept through your wake-up call. If you don't want this job, Tappy, you only have to say. I can easily find a replacement!'

Shit! What time was it?

'No, Bob. Of course I want the job. I'm so sorry. I'll be at yours right away.'

'You'd better fucking well be.' He slammed the phone down.

Without so much as a wash, and still in the clothes that I had slept in, I grabbed my jacket and made for the door. I tried the elevator, then decided I couldn't wait and ran down the stairs of my apartment block across the street and up the stairs to Bob's. Christ! Bob was going to kill me. Finally, I reached his door, my sides ached and I was gasping for breath.

'Bob,' I panted. 'Bob, I'm so sorry. Please . . .'

Bob was standing there laughing, tears rolling down his round cheeks, a glass in his hand.

'Nightcap, Tappy?'

I looked at my watch. What had seemed like only a few minutes' sleep *was* only a few minutes' sleep. The bastard had got me.

Admitting defeat, I had the nightcap and then another. In fact, we drank through 'til the next morning and our 6.00am leaving time. This, as Bob pointed out, saved any chance of me sleeping through my wake-up call.

It wasn't all jokes and laughter, though. Well, maybe it was, just not the type that I was expecting. I'd been in New York two months in the Spring of '65 and Bob, when not torturing me with his practical jokes, had shown me a good deal of the city.

One night, we were sitting in a very fashionable restaurant in the Village when my eyes did the best piece of sightseeing they had done since I got to New York City: there in front of me were the best pair of tits I had ever seen. The tits were attached to a redhead, and they, along with her, obviously had a date. She threw her head back as she laughed at something he said. Christ, she was gorgeous and a more mature woman. I could feel my groin stirring. The date had one hand firmly planted on her backside, and who could blame him. Pulling my eyes away from the obvious, I checked her fingers. No wedding ring. Well, that meant fair game, I thought.

I was trying not to stare, trying to hear something that Bob was saying, and trying (and failing) to keep my cock under control, when the redhead, with those beautiful breasts sailing ahead of her, walked past our table. I excused myself from Bob and followed her. By the time she reached the door to the ladies', I was right behind her.

'Excuse me, madam,' (use the accent, don't all American girls love a British accent?) 'this may sound very corny to you, but I felt I just had to tell you something.' (Christ, I hope this is a sexy smile I'm giving her. I don't want her to think I'm leering, even though I am leering.) 'I hope you know that you are the most beautiful woman in here tonight.' (Probably wise to leave the tits out of it for now.)

A smile and she was gone. A smile. Was that all I got? Somewhat disheartened, I returned to my table.

'No luck, huh?' Bob said as I sat down. 'The redhead you were gaping at? Dream on, Tappy. Knock you back, did she?'

'No. I just told her she was beautiful.'

'Fucking hell, a girl like that should know that she's beautiful without you to tell her!' Bob laughed and returned to his drink.

But I waited. She'd have to walk past our table to get back to her date, and she had smiled, hadn't she? I'd almost given up hope when a hand reached over my shoulder and dropped a note into my lap. She didn't turn round or say a word to me, just kept on walking over to the man waiting for her on the other side of the restaurant.

Bob's mouth fell open. 'You son-of-a-bitch, how did you swing that one? She's already on a date! Well, c'mon, Tappy, open the note. What does it say?'

The note contained a slip of paper with her name – Rhonda – and her telephone number. There was also a ticket for Anthony Newley's new Broadway show, *The Roar of the Greasepaint – The Smell of the Crowd*. I looked over at her, but she seemed completely engrossed in her date.

'I think we'd better head off, lover boy,' Bob said. 'Before that poor fella over there realises what's going on.'

We paid our bill and, with Rhonda's note safely stowed away in my inside pocket, left the restaurant.

I wasted no time giving her a call. The next night, using my 'British accent' for all I was worth, I telephoned the lovely Rhonda and we arranged to meet that night after I had watched her perform in *The Roar of the Greasepaint*. There was going to be a cast party after the show and she told me to come along.

The play was great and, after watching her move on stage, I was in the mood for seeing a bit more of Rhonda close up. I just hoped that my gentlemanly behaviour in the restaurant wouldn't count against me getting a little action. Still, it was best not to push my luck at this stage. I had a feeling that this woman would be worth waiting for. As it turned out I needn't have concerned myself about Rhonda's virtue, but as I met her at the stage door and got into a waiting limousine alongside her, I was the perfect gent. Maybe she took *me* for a challenge.

When we arrived the party was in full swing. Otis Redding was blasting out of the record player and couples were dancing under a fog of cannabis smoke. This was some party; even without Rhonda, there wasn't a woman present I wouldn't ordinarily have crossed the room for.

But that redhead soon had back my full attention. As soon as we took to the dance floor she started to kiss me, those beautiful tits of hers pressed hard against my chest. As she gently nibbled my lips, she began to moan softly and rub her body against mine, grinding her hips against my predictable hard-on.

Eventually, and feeling like I had to have this girl right now or come in my trousers, I grabbed her hand and pulled her down on to a sofa. It seemed that this was the expected route of all guests at the party. Apart from a few couples who still stood coiled together gyrating to the music, all available floor space seemed full of a tangle of bodies. Bare white arses hammered away, and I stared out over a sea of naked breasts and long polished legs thrown up to trip the dancers. Otis Redding was now competing with a rising crescendo of screaming, moans and laughter. This was indeed some party, and it seemed that I was not going to be left out of a full appreciation of it.

Rhonda, the inaccessible beauty who had now transformed into my own personal sex kitten, pushed me off the sofa on to a patch of spare carpet. With a grin she hitched her dress, pulled her panties to one side and lowered herself down on my face. Now if any women reading this have had a 20-year-old boy crawl between their legs, they will well know that we usually have a fair bit to learn. But this girl was beautiful and she was soaking wet and sitting astride me, so I concentrated hard and did my best. As her groans got louder and faster, I figured that I was doing something right and began to enjoy myself.

There is nothing quite like the pleasure you get from pleasuring a woman and, as Rhonda rocked herself towards another climax, I barely noticed my fly being unzipped. Suddenly, I felt my already swollen cock stiffen like it had never stiffened before. Someone else had taken it into their mouth and was sucking furiously. Fucking hell,

I was in an orgy! This party was fantastic, but this blow-job was something else. My cock was nibbled, sucked and teased, and I'd never felt anything like it. During my time with The Animals I'd had more than a few girls get down on their knees for me, but none of them had managed anything like this. It was incredible.

I felt my balls tighten and my orgasm begin just as Rhonda shuddered for the final time and rolled off me. She lay panting beside me and stroked my face as I gave a choking bellow of pure satisfaction and came. I lifted my head, exhausted, to look down at the face that had been responsible for all that pleasure. The room swam into black and then white. The mouth still moved over me, licking me clean.

'What the fuck!' I sprang to my feet, pulling up my trousers with shaking hands.

A man squatted on the floor at my feet. A man. A great big hairy fucking man! He smiled at me, still licking my juices from his red lips, then laughed and rolled over to join another group on the floor.

I stood and stared after him, feeling a nausea creep over me, all pleasure forgotten. I shook off Rhonda's enquiring hand and left the room. What should I have done? I thought as I walked away down the street. Maybe I should go back and hit the bastard? I just couldn't believe that I'd just received the best blow-job of my life from a man. Did this mean I was gay? No. Just forget about it; it never happened. Just forget all about it.

I got back to my hotel room and did just that. I ripped up Rhonda's phone number and flushed it down the toilet. I avoided the restaurant where I had first seen her. I never saw her again; I returned to England soon enough not to run any chance of that. For years after that night, though, I felt strange during oral sex. I kept seeing that face smiling up at me with my semen running over his lips. But I did believe I had managed to forget it. That was until one night by the North Sea, back home in Whitley Bay.

CHAPTER 4

England Swings, but The Animals Rock: Back in the UK with The Animals

Not So Rock 'n' roll

The Drugs Don't Work

Meanwhile, there was work to be done and we were doing it. Despite the odd days spent catching up on sleep back in London, I began to feel that all I ever did was drive that van with the lads sleeping soundly in the back. By the late summer of 1965, I'd abandoned my own little flat in Earl's Court, with Lady Fate on the stairs, and had moved in with Eric and Hilton. One night, Eric convinced me to come with him to the Flamingo Club in Soho, London.

When I say *convinced*, what I really mean is that Eric exhibited another amazing talent of his: not hearing what he didn't want to hear. I was really exhausted, but Eric wasn't taking no for an answer. We were soon sitting down at a table. Georgie Fame and the Blue Flames were playing and that guaranteed a full house. He was fantastic and Eric was a huge fan, but I was hoping to bed down on the table once the band started. Then Rik Gunnell swung over to our table.

Rik and his brother John owned the Flamingo along with their own agency, which supplied most of the acts they booked to perform at their club. Both Rik and John were good friends of mine, which I knew was lucky for me. They were a couple of men that ruled over their part of London. They had a kind of vicious, West End-flavoured humour, but depending on the way you dealt with them this could turn itself into something heavy and very ugly. The long scar running down John's cheek was testament to the fact that these were a pair of men not afraid to face a fight. I was sharing The Animals' charmed luck with dangerous men, and was grateful for it.

'Hello, Tappy, nice to see you again,' Rik said, shaking my hand. 'Mike (Jeffery) was on the phone earlier. He said that it was important. You can use the telephone in reception if you want to call him back.'

'What could he want now?' I said, smothering a yawn and making my way back into the club's reception.

'Mike. It's Tappy. What's up?'

'At last, I've been trying to get hold of you everywhere. I need you to drive up to Newcastle for me and pick up a suitcase from my office.'

'Newcastle! Can't this wait until tomorrow, Mike? I'm really tired.'

'This is important, Tappy. I'm sorry to interrupt your evening, but I need that case by nine o'clock tomorrow morning. You understand?'

I agreed and hung up, silently cursing Mike Jeffery. But when Mike gave me an order, I obeyed. Simple as that. He was The Animals' manager, my boss and, while I liked him, I certainly didn't want to get on the wrong side of him. I returned to Eric in the club and explained. 'So basically, I have to leave now. The thing is, Eric, I don't know how I'm going to do it. I'll have to prise my eyelids open with matchsticks to make this journey.'

'I've got just the thing for you,' Eric said, lowering his voice to a whisper. He placed a small pink tablet on the table in front of me. 'One tiny pill, Tappy. This will keep you live and kicking all the way to Newcastle and back.'

Now, they say that if you can remember the Sixties, you weren't there. I was certainly there, and I did my fair share of stupid things, but drugs were never one of them. The roadie stereotype didn't fit for me when it came to drugs. They had slowly crept into our lives, almost without me noticing: dope, purple hearts (what's now known as Speed), LSD. Many of the bands we knew and worked with took drugs as a release from the pressures that they were under, but I'd never been tempted. Until now.

'What is it, Eric?'

'It's called a purple heart,' Eric grinned. 'The answer to all your prayers.'

Without giving myself time to think about what I was doing, I picked up the pill and swilled it down with a glass of water. 'It's the only way I'll do it. How long will this thing take to start working, Eric?'

'A matter of minutes, my friend. You can leave now and you'll be fine.' Eric grinned at me again as I grabbed my van keys and left the club.

Minutes was right. Heading north with my foot pressed on the accelerator, I felt great. My eyes were open and I was wide awake and alert. This was great stuff that Eric had given me. As the cool night breeze swept in through the car window, I made a mental note to ask him to get me a supply of these purple hearts, to keep at the ready whenever I had to drive long hours with the band. I hadn't felt this good for weeks.

I arrived at Newcastle in record time, collected the suitcase from Mike's office at Club A Go Go and, without so much as stopping for a cup of coffee, turned the car round and headed back down south to London. I felt fantastic, not drugged at all, but wide awake and happy. I switched the car radio on and sang along to all the songs at the top of my voice. Before I realised it, I was back in London. The journey had flown by.

I parked my car outside Mike's apartment and lugged the suitcase to his door. I hadn't thought what it contained. It was heavy and obviously packed close with something, probably papers or contracts Mike needed for a morning meeting. Any curiosity had been lost in my delight at the wonder of Eric's magic pill.

Mike opened his door before I could reach for the bell.

'Thank God, you're a life-saver, Tappy.' He grabbed the case and opened it.

I whistled at the contents. Thick, fat wads of notes, bundled together filled the suitcase. I knew Mike well enough not to ask questions, or to expect any answers, so I said my good morning and goodbye and left.

Now to find Eric. He'd obviously been having a better night than me; I found him lying in bed with a beautiful black girl curled round him.

'Eric, that pill you gave me was bloody marvellous!' I shouted, as I burst in on them. 'Where did you get them? I haven't even been to bed yet and look at me. You'll have to get me some more, I was thinking if I could get a supply . . .' I trailed off as I looked down at the pair of grinning faces. 'What's up with you two?'

'Tappy, my best mate, come and sit down,' Eric said, patting the edge of the bed. 'I'm afraid I've got a little confession to make to you.'

'What have you been up to now?' I asked suspiciously as the girl picked Eric's shirt from the floor and, wrapping it round her naked body, headed laughing out of the room.

'Well, it's like this. That pill I gave to you, Tappy, it wasn't exactly a purple heart.'

'What was it then? Seriously, it worked, I mean look at me . . .'

'Tappy, I gave you a contraceptive.' Eric was laughing so hard that he had to wipe tears from his face.

'What do you mean contraceptive?' But Eric now seemed incapable of speech. 'Eric, I definitely did not swallow a rubber johnny, mate', I said, not finding this situation funny.

Eric breathed hard and finally managed to control his laughter enough to speak. 'It's a woman's contraceptive pill. You know, *the* pill. I gave you a pill and you drove to Newcastle and back thinking you were buzzing on a purple heart. Tappy, you're the best! Rik and John were hysterical after you left last night. Bright-eyed and wide awake. Christ, I don't think I've ever laughed so much.'

The sound of Eric's laughter was now joined by that of Hilton and Eric's girl, both obviously listening in the kitchen. What an idiot. So much for crazy days on drugs in the Sixties! I was suddenly struck by the thought that I had all these female hormones raging around in my body. I felt sick. Silently, I left Eric and walked into my bedroom. What I needed was sleep and finally I got it. My first, and last, experience of drug taking ended with a fitful doze in a darkened room, waking every few hours to run my hands over my chest to check that I wasn't sprouting young girl's breasts.

Clap, But No Applause
Time passed. I was still, thankfully, flat-chested and exploiting my manhood for all I was worth. It would take more than a dose of female hormones to put Tappy Wright down! Then Hilton announced that

he had the clap, not only that but he was convinced he'd caught it from a girl we had both bedded.

I declined the offer of a look and took his word for it, running to the bathroom to check myself. Everything seemed fine, but I wasn't sure what I was looking for. Bloody hell, please, not a dose of the clap!

We headed down to the Hammersmith Hospital. This was my first visit to a VD clinic. I silently vowed it would be my last, but in a business that required me to take care of rock stars, there was fat chance of that. Hilton sat next to me, nervously clutching his ticket – 42. I was 41. What is it about waiting rooms that make you think you're going to die?

Our numbers were called out together and we both went behind our separate screens. Now, I was brought up well; I knew that I'd probably have to give a urine sample and my mind was full of Mother's advice: don't go until you get there, so you can give the doctor what he needs. Although what my mother would have thought about her advice being needed here, I dreaded to think. Anyway, I'd avoided the bathroom all morning and was therefore absolutely bursting before our numbers had even been called. The nurse handed me a glass bottle and then left me to it. I could hear her telling Hilton to do the same on the other side of his screen.

Finally. The floodgates opened and I quickly filled my bottle. The problem was that now I'd got going I couldn't stop. Piss poured over the top of the bottle, on to my hands and the glass slipped out of my fingers. The bottle fell to the floor and smashed.

A furious nurse pulled back the screen to face me, trousers down and soaked in my own urine.

'Mr Wright! What are you doing?'

I garbled an apology, but the screens were thin and hardly sound proof. I could hear Hilton's distinct laugh ring out.

'And you, Mr Valentine,' the nurse shouted indignantly. 'Will you please be quiet!'

Fantastic. Now the whole clinic knew that one of The Animals and his road manager had the clap. Mr Wright we could have got away with, but how many Valentines have you met? I felt my ears burn as a murmur of interested voices rose up after our names were shouted. After the result of that incident with the cows in Newcastle, I should have known better than to piss in public with Hilton Valentine.

As it turned out, I had the last laugh over Hilton. When our results finally came back from the clinic I was in the clear. Hilton, however, was simply described as 'rancid'.

Back on Track: Big Day with Big Names

Putting these embarrassments behind me, on 22 December 1964 I turned 21. It seems strange, looking back, to realise just how young we were back then. I'd escaped a life of working-class poverty; I'd travelled most of the world; I'd bedded more women than most men see in a lifetime; I'd managed to get myself a job I loved and was good at; I'd done all this with a group of good friends, and it was only now (in the Scotch of St James, a nightclub in the West End of London) that I was becoming a man.

The party was organised by The Animals. They wanted to see me into my 21st year in style and so the guest list was to be something a little bit special. To be honest, the party itself was everything that would be expected of the plans of over-excited young men in their early 20s. And, although we were surrounded by London glamour, they had made sure that that there was more than a flavour of the North-East to my 21st: men swigging Newcastle Brown Ale, the women sipping at their glasses of rosé and Babycham.

Girls packed the room. I will always miss that passion for the mini-skirt that reigned in the early Sixties. Bare legs and painted faces seemed to line every wall – and I was loving the décor. I was aware that there were some faces in the crowd that I recognised, but with all those long black eyelashes blinking at the birthday boy, I barely glanced at the lads I was talking to.

Then the music and the lights were turned down and a huge cake was brought in, covered in candles. I stood to attention by a large table while the crowd sang me 'Happy Birthday'. The song descended into 'hip – hip – hoorays' and Eric ordered me to blow out the candles.

'One blow, Tap, for the wish.'

I filled my lungs and leant forward. Just then a hand grabbed the back of my neck. With one swift push, my whole face was in the cake. I pulled myself free, wiping icing and cream from my eyes, as the room burst into applause and laughter. Laughing hardest was the culprit standing next to me.

'Happy birthday, Tappy,' said John Lennon. 'Nice cake?'

'Yeah, John, you should try some.'

I put my hand into the splattered remains of my birthday cake and heaved out a fistful. Before John could stop laughing I'd plastered a sticky layer over his face. I caught sight of Eric and wondered if he would really appreciate me covering his famous friend in birthday cake. John Lennon stood there a moment, then stuck out his tongue and licked his lips.

'Yeah, it's good,' he said appraisingly.

'Fight! Fight!' Hilton shouted as he ran forward, scooped up a handful of cream and threw it at Eric. His aim was a bit off and he caught Brian Jones from The Rolling Stones, snappy suit and all.

Soon, the whole club was a riot of thrown birthday cake and cream. All those bare legs and carefully made-up faces were splattered with white icing and sponge, and none the worse for that. By the time the party finally came to an end, nothing but a few greasy smears remained on the birthday cake platter, but cake was highly in evidence on my guests and all over the room, hanging in wet handfuls from the lights and chairs.

The owner of the Scotch of St James didn't seem to share our amusement as he came to see us out. But with many apologies and promises to pay for the damages, The Animals and I finally left, still laughing about the most original 21st we'd ever been to, but then it was our first with John Lennon.

Ready, Steady, Go!

So 1964 came to its close with all of us covered in birthday cake, but I should have known that Eric was not going to be outdone by anyone when it came to practical jokes; not even John Lennon.

Before the end of the year, The Animals were booked to perform on *Ready, Steady, Go!* This one of Britain's most popular, and one of the best, television pop shows. Whereas the acts on *Top of the Pops* mimed their way through songs, on *Ready, Steady, Go!* everyone performed live. This made a booking for the show much more of an event, much more like the tours we were used to. And Eric was ready to use the atmosphere to his advantage.

The Animals shared their dressing room with The Rolling Stones. We knew the Stones, of course; poor Brian Jones had left my birthday party as coated with cake as the rest of us, and we were happy to share space with them.

It was while The Rolling Stones were performing that Eric noticed that Chrissy Shrimpton, Mick Jagger's girlfriend at the time, had left her camera behind in the dressing room. This was understandable as cameras were forbidden on set whilst the bands were being filmed, but it gave Eric the idea to give Chrissy a gift that would let her remember 1964 for ever.

'Here, Tappy, catch,' Eric said, throwing the camera to me.

He dropped his trousers to his ankles and grabbed hold of his cock. Now, I know I've mentioned Eric's cock before, but believe me it deserves a second description. Eric had a monster in his pants and no mistake. After a couple of hard yanks it was with us, standing erect and putting all other men to shame. I'd known Eric long enough to realise what Chrissy was in for and, laughing, I knelt down and took a couple of snaps of Eric's raging hard-on.

'And, just for good measure,' laughed Eric, turning round, 'let's give her one of my arse as well.'

He bent over and pulled his cheeks apart; I added a close-up of Eric's hairy arsehole to Chrissy's collection. The camera was back in position, and Eric's trousers back on, when Chrissy and Mick returned.

We were hysterical. There was no way that even Mick Jagger could compete with that, but we were sure that when Chrissy innocently handed her film in to the local chemist to be developed, it would be Mick that would be blamed for the pornographic content. Maybe she'd have him drop his trousers to compare?

Luckily for us, Mick saw the funny side. But, from what he said about Chrissy's reaction to being pulled to one side for a quiet chat about the contents of her film when she went to collect her photographs, we guessed that it would probably be a good idea to avoid Chrissy Shrimpton for a while.

Partying Up North: Doubles, Memories, Danger and the Man from the NME

So, welcome in 1965 and we were back in Newcastle. Our home-coming was just the tonic we needed; it seemed like we had been away so long. Though we always tried to head up North as much as we could when we were in the country, I didn't feel like I saw my dad nearly as much as I would have liked to.

We played the City Hall and I think that this was the best performance that I ever saw from The Animals. They were as happy to be home as I was, and the crowd were certainly happy to see us. The girls went crazy for Eric; all I could think was how much they'd like to get their hands on the contents of Chrissy Shrimpton's camera.

After the gig, there was a party held for us at The Sands nightclub in Whitley Bay. The Animals and I did the usual: a circuit of polite handshakes and introductions, to be got out of the way before the party got into full swing.

I approached one group and introduced myself. They just stared at me. 'You're not Tappy Wright,' one woman said.

'Yes I am. Well, I was last time I checked,' I laughed, but this was getting uncomfortable.

A man shook his head. 'Look, I don't know who you are, but Tappy Wright comes to The Sands nearly every weekend. He works with The Animals, you see, and there's been a bit of trouble with . . . well you know . . . all the women.'

This was unbelievable. Eventually, after producing members of The Animals and Keith Altham, a *New Music Express* journalist, willing to testify that I was indeed Tappy Wright, they told me more about my impostor. This man had a bigger appetite for women than I did! He'd been striding the streets of Whitley Bay cashing in on my name for all it was worth. And it seemed that was worth a fair bit. He was never seen with fewer than two women on his arm and had angered a few boyfriends by stealing their girls out from under their noses. This guy was doing better than me! I have to say, though, he has come in useful in later years. Whenever I'm back home and some story comes out about me, I can always lay the blame on that 'other' Tappy.

After the party some members of The Animals and I decided to head down to the sea with a group of girls. There's nothing like the icy North Sea to cool high spirits, but thanks to the alcoholic spirits supplied at the party, the call for skinny-dipping was soon in the air. We all stripped and ran, laughing, towards the black sea. A girl next to me slipped and fell. As I reached down to help her up she smiled and pulled me down next to her.

What the hell, I thought as she kissed me. I certainly wasn't going to knock back a naked girl on her back, whatever the temperature.

The beach was in total darkness by now, but I could hear Hilton calling my name. The girl wound her legs up and round my waist – Hilton could wait. I had started to bang away when I felt the weight of a body fall on top of me. I screamed out in shock. Hilton, naked and wet from his brief swim in the sea, had stumbled up the beach to find me and quite literally fallen over us.

The thing was that, as he fell, his cock had seemed to ram up against my backside. That memory of the blow-job in New York, the memory I'd sworn to forget, flooded my mind and suddenly I was furious. I pulled myself off the girl and screamed abuse at Hilton. I grabbed him round the throat and pushed him hard against the sand.

'Tappy, for fuck's sake!' Hilton choked. 'What is wrong with you?'

And just like that all that fury was gone. I let Hilton go, and with one silent look at the girl, walked off up the beach towards home. How could I tell my best friend that I had nearly given him a beating because I'd let a man suck my cock?

I'd lost Keith Altham (the *NME* journalist) after the party at The Sands. I'd offered him a bed for the night at my dad's house, but he hadn't come down to the beach with us and I'd forgotten all about him. It was a bit of a surprise, therefore, when I finally got back to my room, covered in sand and still feeling ashamed of what had happened with Hilton, to find Keith (whom my father had let in to the house earlier) and a young girl in my bed. 'I'll not be long,' he shouted as he heard me open the bedroom door.

'Carry on, mate,' I said with a grin. At least someone was having a good night. 'I'm going to have a cup of tea, anyway.'

I closed the door and went down to the kitchen to boil the kettle.

Keith was a young, hotshot reporter, who had travelled up to Newcastle with us to write about the gig. He was a walking success story, good at his job (the *NME* was then, as it is now, one of the best music papers in the country) and tall, dark and handsome enough to be good with the ladies, too. As he was proving right now in my bedroom.

I'd just set about making myself a cup of tea when there was a loud hammering on the front door. Fucking hell, it was Dave Finley! Without doubt the toughest hard man in Newcastle.

'Where is she?' Dave growled.

'Who?'

'My girlfriend, that's who,' he said, pushing his face up against mine, as if he could smell her on me.

'She's not here, Dave, honestly. I saw her at The Sands earlier, but I've just got back. Sorry, mate, but I was just off to bed.'

'She's with a bloke, I know she is. I'll kill the fuckin' bastard when I catch him.' With that he turned and stomped off down the path.

I closed the door and glanced up at the ceiling where the noise of my bed springs squeaked faster and faster through the floorboards, and groaned. Dave Finley. He was known locally as 'Hammerhead' because of his ability to knock people out cold with one swift headbutt, and that was if they were lucky enough to merit a quick knockout. And above me my charming, well-dressed journalist friend from London was shafting way, without a clue as to the identity of the girl beneath him.

I recognised her quickly enough, when they finally emerged from my bedroom and came, looking smug and dishevelled, into my father's kitchen. The smug look quickly fell from Keith's face when I explained Dave Finley's visit, and what the man was capable of.

'I'm off,' he shouted, panic stricken.

'You're not going to leave her here with me, son. If Finley comes back and finds her, he'll think it's me that's fucked her.'

Dave's girlfriend, apparently unconcerned by our dispute, sat calmly at the kitchen table with her compact, applying a fresh coat of lipstick. Finally, she snapped her mirror shut and stood up.

'Oh, stop your fussing. He's not that bad.' She smiled at us and fluffed up her hair. 'I wouldn't mind a cup of that tea, if there's one going spare?'

'You listen to me, lady, you're going with him. And both of you are going now. Seriously, Keith, you're taking her. Drop her off somewhere. Anywhere. She's not staying here.'

I called them a taxi. After a quick check of the empty street for the lurking boyfriend, I bundled them out of the house and they made their escape. Dave Finley was none the wiser. With a sigh of relief I made my way upstairs and, tearing the soiled sheets off my bed, finally sank down to sleep on the bare mattress. What a night!

The next day, after a few hours' precious sleep, I awoke and prepared to set off back to London. I said my goodbyes to my father, who was happily oblivious to the night's events, and hit the road once more.

Daddy Cool

My father, Joseph Wright, was a fantastic man. He had always worked hard for us and loved us. With his working life spent down the coal mines, he was proud of the life that I had created for myself. I can honestly say that there was never a harsh word between us. Despite my hectic schedule, I tried to get back to Whitley Bay as often as I could to visit him.

One of the remarkable things about these visits was how unchanged our home remained. Living in London and touring hard, it was easy to get the impression that the whole world was caught up in the same musical fever and free-living craziness as we were. But, in the north-east of England, Sixties freedoms were slow coming. Tradition and normality ruled. Even with all those famous faces passing through his house, I think my dad still saw them as 'young Hilton from down the road' and 'some friend of our Tappy'. Once or twice, though, even he experienced some favours of swinging Sixties' London. Even if he wasn't aware of it at the time.

One of these occasions was thanks to Hilton Valentine. Dad's relationship with Hilton remained strong and he loved him like a fourth son. When we were up north, Hilton would often stay at our house for the night, taking advantage of the bed and the chance to catch up with my dad. One day, though, when I was up visiting, Dad asked if I could get hold of some of the tabs that young Hilton smoked. (A 'tab' is the Geordie expression for a cigarette.) Now, Hilton was the first of The Animals to start experimenting with drugs, and I knew that he rarely smoked anything but joints.

As it turned out, Hilton had left a cigarette packet behind. My dad, short on tabs, had found it lying around in the living room and had taken them to the pub with him. But Hilton just used the cigarette packet to store his hand-rolled joints in, and my Dad had been passing them round the pub!

'Lovely they were, some foreign brand by the smell of them. Ask Hilton to get hold of some more for me. All the lads down the pub loved them.'

Yes, my dear old dad had become the first druggy of Whitley Bay. He'd even taken orders from all the old boys at the pub, after getting them all stoned. My dad was a drug-pusher! I did try to explain, but eventually decided that he was best left in blissful ignorance.

My dad's other brush with London glamour came after Keith Altham's swift exit from his house on the night of The Animals party at The Sands. So how did my father become the best-dressed coal miner in Newcastle? Well, when I got back to London after my drive from Newcastle, the phone in my flat was already ringing. Keith at least sounded a lot calmer than he had the last time I saw him.

'Hey, Tappy. Look, thanks for your help last night,' he laughed. 'I'm glad I escaped with my skin. The thing is, in running for my life and all that, I left my new pair of Hush Puppies behind.'

'Blimey.' Hush Puppies may not rate highly on the fashion stakes nowadays, but in the Sixties they were the height of cool. 'Don't worry, Keith, I'll get them the next time I'm up there.'

'OK, but make sure you do, mate. They cost me an absolute fortune.'

'Don't panic, I'll get them. It'll be a couple of weeks before I'm back up North, though.'

'That's fine, just so long as I get them back.'

Just over two weeks later I was back at my dad's and I didn't forget my promise to Keith. I asked him if he'd seen a pair of brown suede shoes lying around.

'Oh yes, are these them?' He pointed to a pair of battered shoes, blacked and encrusted with mud and coal dust. 'I found them in the kitchen. They fit perfect. Just the job for work; nice and comfy. Some of lads have been asking about them,' he added proudly.

'I bet they have.'

My dear old dad had been wearing fashion's finest down the coal mine. Well, that would teach Keith Altham for mucking around with Dave Finley's broad. Seems he'd got his revenge after all, and hit Keith right where it would hurt the most.

I broke the news to Keith when I got back to London a couple of days later, the good news that his precious Hush Puppies were in my house and the bad news that they now belonged to a coal miner, who'd worn them out in the space of two weeks. Dave Finley couldn't have done better, but it was hard not to laugh at poor Keith. To this day, when I run into Keith Altham, I still occasionally hear the mutter of 'those fuckin' Hush Puppies'.

Pay Back

Maybe it was revenge then, which caused Keith to reveal rather too many of my trade secrets in a piece he did for the NME later that year. He'd frequently interviewed all the members of The Animals, though he'd obviously worked more with Eric, and he had become rather like a part of the scenery of both our professional and social lives. We'd always got on well, and when he told me that he wanted to write a series of articles about a day in the life of a road manager, I readily agreed to be a part of it.

He wanted to use the road managers of the top three bands in Britain. He proved that his charm didn't just work on the girlfriends of northern thugs by getting all of us to agree:

1. The Rolling Stones, with road manager Ian Stewart.
2. The Beatles, with road manager Malcolm Evans.
3. The Animals, with road manager Tappy Wright (. . . but you knew that one already).

Though I didn't know it at the time, I was one of a very small group of men who would pioneer the way for modern-day roadies. Whereas, nowadays, a big act would have hundreds of roadies working for them during a tour, in the early 1960s it would literally be one man and the band. This meant that, for example, with The Animals, it was me, and me alone, who was responsible for organising, setting up and clearing out the band and equipment before and after a gig. There were not many men who could do what I did back then. That was why Keith's article was such a good idea; it finally documented what we achieved.

But it was odd being the subject of Keith's investigations. I was used to watching him interview the lads and scribble away during gigs, but this was different – this was all about me!

Keith phoned and we arranged to meet before a concert in South London. The Animals were due on stage at 8.00pm. The boys were making their own way to the venue and I would ordinarily be there an hour before to deliver and set up the equipment. I parked the van and met Keith at a local pub a couple of hours before the set.

We sat and talked. I ordered us another round from the bar, but as I brought them to the table I could see Keith was getting fidgety.

'Are we going to have time for these, Tappy?'

'There's plenty of time yet.'

He pulled back his shirt cuff and showed me his watch. 'It's gone seven. Isn't the band on at eight? By the time we get there and set up all the equipment, well . . .'

'Relax. I said there's plenty of time. It's all under control Keith, calm down.'

We finished our drinks, Keith still glancing at his watch every five minutes and looking anxious. We were friends, remember, and no matter what my father had done to his shoes, I don't think he fancied having to write up Tappy Wright as the biggest disaster in the music industry.

At 7.40pm we arrived at the gig in Croydon. The promoter was standing outside, with a look on his face very much like the one Keith had been wearing for the last half hour. They should have just trusted me. All that worry can't have been good for their health.

'Sorry I'm late,' I panted. 'We had a flat tyre on the way. Nightmare.' I winked at Keith, who was staring at me in disbelief. 'Come on, Keith, you'll have to help me with this lot, son, or we'll be late.'

I wish I'd always had Keith Altham with me for this scam. Even without his precious Hush Puppies, he looked so polished standing there in his immaculate suit that no one would have mistaken him for a roadie.

'It's all right,' one of the doormen said, with an appraising look at Keith. 'We'll give you a hand.'

Within five minutes, thanks to four bulky doormen and a panicking promoter, all the heavy equipment was up a flight of stairs and ready to go. I hadn't even broken a sweat. The Animals appeared on time.

'You're a fuckin' liar,' Keith said, when he caught up with me later.

I shrugged. 'Beats carrying it myself, don't it? Works every time. Hey, I'm the best in the business, you said Keith. Have to have a couple of tricks of the trade up my sleeve to save wearing out all that talent, don't you reckon'?'

Keith laughed, but it was soon clear that I was going to pay for those comfy working shoes of my dad's with an aching back. Keith printed an entire page on Tappy Wright's amazing scam of turning up late for gigs. Even a genuine late arrival was now greeted with the same six words: 'Fuck off, Tappy. Carry it yourself.'

CHAPTER 5

Animals will be Animals: The Beginning of the End

Finding the Help

After Keith's revelations about my favourite scams had hit the press, I decided that it was time that I got some real help. The Animals were busier than ever. By this time we were based for about six months in New York and six months in London, and although Keith Altham's article had not yet reached a US readership, I was feeling the pressure.

This was how I met Alex Taws. Alex was a nice, red-headed guy from Newcastle, he looked strong enough and I took him on as my assistant. This way I hoped that I would have someone else to help me with the donkey work whilst I took care of the demands of the increasingly fractious band and I might even be able to catch up on some sleep during the long drives through the UK and the States. Unfortunately, it didn't quite work out that way . . .

The first and only time that Alex took the wheel of The Animals' van, I realised that we were going to have problems. It seems that Alex's easy-going manner came from a very artificial source – the guy was always completely stoned! Approaching a roundabout, Alex, in his fuddled state, decided not to waste time driving around it and instead, bucking and rearing all the way, drove us straight across the thing.

Alan Price's nervousness concerning travel is well documented, and an off-road trip with a stoner at the wheel was enough to tip him over the edge. Alan's screams from the back were enough to stop even Alex in his tracks and, after hysterics at the side of the road, I realised that the only way I was ever going to get Alan to step in that van again was to promise that Alex would never drive again.

So much for the hired help. Instead of a helping hand, I had simply acquired another passenger, and the hours of leisure in the back of the van did little to help Alex's smoking habit. He didn't last long. During our first tour of America with him in tow, he was arrested and jailed for five years as a drug-dealer. A life alongside pop stars can be confusing. Alex didn't even have that many drugs on him (particularly compared to the other members of The Animals at the time), but he was just a roadie and not a pop star. It was a hard lesson for the kid, but living the life does not make you a member of the band.

Still, I do sometimes wish that the hypocrisy had not stretched so far. On my own with The Animals once more, the drug-taking that had leached into our lives continued to have an effect that perhaps the shock of arrest could have done something to remedy.

Hilton in the Sky

Much as I had come to love and trust each of the members of The Animals (even though they could drive me crazy a lot of the time), Hilton Valentine remained one of my closest and most treasured friends. That was why it was Hilton's experimentation with drugs which affected me the most. He is a sweet soul, Hilton, but sometimes his quest for answers caused him more harm than good.

Hilton was probably the first member of The Animals to start using drugs, so I think that by 1965 I had become used to him being stoned the majority of the time. But it wasn't until a night in New York that I realised how far things had gone.

We were staying in a hotel and, due to a shortage of rooms that night, Hilton and I were sharing a suite on the 52nd floor. I woke up in the middle of the night, aware of a cold breeze blowing through the hotel room. I fumbled for the light switch and then stumbled towards the window. What kind of idiot leaves a window open this high up? Then I saw him: Hilton was sitting perched on the window ledge with his feet hanging down into the void below and his arms outstretched.

For a moment I was simply paralysed with fear. 'Hilton,' I said finally, speaking quietly so as not to startle him. Was he going to jump? 'What are you doing, son?'

He turned round to me and frowned. 'C'mon, Tappy, you've got to help me. It's the clouds – we've got to get them in. They're freezing out there, Tappy; we've got to help them.'

He shifted closer to the edge of the window ledge, his arms flailing around in front of him. My heart leapt into my throat. I moved over until I was leaning out beside him and mimicked his catching motions. If I tried anything now, he could go over the edge and it was a long way down.

'Look, Hilton,' I said, trying to sound efficient and calm. 'You move back a bit, I can't reach them with you in the way. Move back now.'

Hilton looked at me and then pulled himself back slightly. This was my chance: as he moved, I grabbed at him and pulled back, tipping us both back on to the carpet and into the safety of the room. He didn't struggle but he was freezing cold.

'It's OK, Hilton,' I said, wrapping my arms around him and hugging him close, as you would to a small child in distress. 'It's all right now. Let's just keep you and me warm. Don't worry about those clouds, they'll be fine now.'

We spent the rest of the night like that, wrapped up in blankets on the floor, while I talked Hilton through the various hallucinations that he suffered. Drugs may give some people a lot of fun and they have certainly helped to write a fair few brilliant pop songs, but when you have seen the effects first hand, they really don't seem worth the trouble.

Hilton Hypnotises

But I'm sad to say that hanging out of a 52nd floor window did little to calm Hilton's love of drugs. Maybe it was due to the early death of his mother? This was a tragedy that both Hilton and I shared, but whilst my mother had died in an accident, Hilton's mother had died tragically and he hadn't had his father around to support him. Maybe it was this lack of parental guidance that caused Hilton's need to escape from reality? I really don't know. But Hilton took further steps than drug-taking to create an unreal world, and one of those was a passion for hypnosis.

Now, this particular interest was not nearly as disturbing as the drugs to me. In fact, Hilton mostly used it as a tool to combat his nickname, 'Soon-shoot'. He'd hypnotise groupies into the belief that they had just experienced the greatest night of passion of their lives (whereas, to be honest, he would have been lucky if his cock had managed to keep them entertained for more than a couple of minutes). The whole thing had become a joke amongst The Animals, a joke which was to come to an abrupt end one night in Los Angeles.

We were all staying at The Beverly Rodeo Hyatt House Hotel (now called the Luxe Rodeo Hotel) at 360 North Rodeo Drive. I'd picked up a rather cute little blonde and was endeavouring to give her the kind of night that Hilton had to hypnotise his girls into believing. We were just aiming for a rather awkward position when there was a hammering on the door. Cursing, I left the girl and opened up.

'Tappy, you've got to help me!' Predictably, it was Hilton.

'I'm a little busy here,' I said, pulling up my trousers and nodding my head towards the bed where my girl was waiting.

'Oh never mind that,' Hilton replied, dismissively. 'This is serious. There's a girl in my room . . .'

'And there's one in mine. I don't see why I should be interested . . .'

'No! Shut up and listen. This girl, well . . . I was practising the hypnosis and now I can't bring her round. She's just sitting there. Tappy, you've got to help!'

Reluctantly I made my apologies to the blonde and followed Hilton back to his room. Sure enough there was the girl, sitting rigid and upright in a chair next to his bed.

'What are we going to do?' Hilton pleaded, sinking down on to the bed and letting his head fall into his hands.

'Now, don't go getting like that Hilton, there's got to be something . . .'

We tried everything: clapping our hands, splashing water in her face, shouting in her ears, pinching and even (in growing desperation) shaking the poor girl. Nothing. She just sat there, as silent and unresponsive as she had been when I first came into the room. Hilton looked close to tears. We sat on the bed and watched her. There had to be something that could shake her out of this trance.

'Hang on a minute, Hilton. I've got an idea.'

Leaving Hilton to keep an eye on his victim, I dashed to John Steel's room. After a quick search through his bedside drawers, Johnny found what he was looking for: his .38 pistol, already loaded with blanks. If the girl thought that he was going to shoot her, then surely her survival instincts would pull her back into consciousness. Johnny wasn't particularly happy with pointing a gun at someone, but it was the only plan we had. So, Johnny shoved the gun into his belt and we ran back to Hilton's room.

What we hadn't counted on was how Hilton had dealt with the stress of the unconscious girl before he'd come knocking on my door. True to form, he'd managed to get himself stoned. So, when we appeared in his doorway wielding a gun, he was in no mood to listen to my idea.

With Hilton holding on to my knees, begging and pleading with us not to kill the girl, Johnny raised the barrel and fired a blank towards her. Hilton screamed but, due to the shock of gunfire or just the loud noise, the girl came to. Unfortunately, being greeted back into reality by the sight of a half-naked man holding a gun with Hilton weeping at his feet and screaming made the poor girl believe that she was indeed about to be shot. Now I had two hysterics to deal with.

Thankfully, just then Chas Chandler burst into the room. He'd heard the gunshot and come to investigate. Over the shouts of Hilton and his 'patient', I managed to tell him what had happened and between us we got rid of the girl and calmed Hilton down. Needless to say, that was the last time I ever heard of Hilton using hypnosis.

Alan and Bugs

But it was not only Hilton who had developed strange habits when it came to groupies. The Animals were one of the biggest bands in the world and girls were never in short supply; and as I was often the one sent to pick up the girls for them, I soon noticed that I was being sent out with what increasingly looked like a shopping list.

We used to call it 'catching a fish'. The lads would have just managed to dodge the fans and get back to the hotel in one piece, when the call would go out for me to go 'catch a fish'.

The bait was simple enough; all I had to do was take out The Animals' van, which was by this time covered in messages from fans, written in lipstick and marker pens. I'd park up in a square some-where, sometimes for good measure draping the drum skin (with the band's name printed across it) across the back window, light my cigarette and wait. Soon enough, girls would be knocking on my window, asking if I knew The Animals and how they could get to meet them. The prettiest would be reeled in and the fish caught.

But when it came to Alan Price it was never a pretty face that he was interested in, it was what was sitting a little due south. Alan had a passion for breasts, the bigger the better. Nothing else mattered to him, just so long as the breasts were huge.

Often, I would deliberately hunt out the ugliest girl I could find and, so long as she had a large chest, I'd deliver her back to Alan. It became a kind of challenge. But each time I thought I'd found a girl that not even he would touch, he'd prove me wrong and emerge, looking exhausted and happy, thanking me for finding a wonderful pair! The expression 'Never look at the fireplace when you're stoking those two hot smouldering coals' became his motto.

Though Alan's commitment to his fetish was a source of constant wonder to me, the other great delight of his sex life was something that I couldn't even *begin* to understand.

We'd heard rumours about what Alan was doing with his big-breasted ladies and one night curiosity got the better of us. Hilton and I crept up to his room to hear what was going on inside. We'd seen Alan go upstairs and had just caught a glimpse of the buxom, dark-haired girl who accompanied him. Each of us pressed an ear to a glass and lent against the bedroom door, hoping to finally find out the truth behind the talk.

At first there was nothing. Utter silence. I was quite disappointed, but Hilton just shrugged and lit up a cigarette.

'He hasn't got started yet. Be patient.' He grinned.

Then the panting started and we could hear the girl begging Alan for more. Well, I thought, good work, Alan. I was beginning to feel a bit odd about the spying. After all, it now seemed as if Hilton and I were just stuck out in a corridor with glasses to our ears listening to two people have normal everyday sex. We were the perverts, not Alan. Maybe all that talk was just vicious rumour? And then I heard it . . . an echoing, unbelievably loud fart.

This was what the rumours had been about: Alan's version of foreplay. It appeared that the one thing guaranteed to turn Alan Price on, apart from the necessary gigantic breasts, was a 'fanny fart'. He would blow into a girl's vagina and then listen to the noise as the air rattled back out. The louder the sound, the greater the effect on Alan.

Well, he must have been pretty happy after what we had just heard. It was like an earthquake. The glass actually trembled against my ear! And then Hilton's glass slipped through his fingers and smashed. There was a terrible silence behind the door and Hilton and I froze, struggling to contain our laughter. I pressed my ear against the door again, thinking that maybe Alan was so caught up in what he was doing that he hadn't heard. But, with perfect comic timing, Alan chose that moment to fling open his door and, astonished, I fell at his feet. We were caught red-handed – or rather, red-eared.

Alan was understandably furious and, with a yell of rage, aimed a kick at me, which I probably deserved. But Hilton just stood there staring into the room and, as I rolled away from Alan's attack, I got a look at what had caught his attention. There on the bed lay a naked girl, her immense tits bobbing like two giant landed jellyfish. Both her legs were elevated and spread wide, one ankle securely tied by a dressing gown cord and one by a black tie. Surely not bondage as well, Alan! At the sight of us, she began to scream for someone to untie her.

I couldn't believe it. Even in my mission to beat Alan's love of breasts with the ugliest girl I could find, I would never have picked up anything like this. The girl had the longest protruding front teeth I had ever seen in my life. Hilton and I just burst out laughing. The whole situation was incredible. But, with a couple more kicks Alan managed to get us out of his room, telling us in no uncertain terms what would happen to us if we ever came back. But we had all the ammunition we needed; there was no way that Alan was going to get away with this one.

Still, being greeted the next morning by a chorus of, 'What's up, Doc?' from the rest of The Animals, didn't seem to lighten his mood. I can't think why. Though I have to say that after the long drive to the Manchester gig that day, with Alan's eyes boring into my back, I wasn't much in a laughing mood, either.

Eric and Chas: Egos at War

Part of a life with The Animals was to expect to be the subject of practical jokes; to expect that the band would know everything about you and that they would probably use that knowledge to entertain themselves as best they could.

It's hard to explain the claustrophobia of a life on the road. We were travelling from city to city, hotel to hotel, sometimes not even stopping long enough for a change of clothes or a shave. We were each other's constants in a world of ever-changing landscapes, girls and venues, and although that could often be a comfort, it could also be a curse.

After that conversation in the back of the van, over a year ago now, Chas Chandler had done a lot to remedy his ways. Seeing each of The Animals vote to throw him out of the band seemed to have been the shock he needed to calm his bullying and intimidating behaviour. But Chas was still a big personality and he was in good company with that. Eric Burdon, Alan Price and Chas Chandler sharing limited space was no picnic and, with Hilton disappearing into his own drug-fuelled world and quiet John Steel hiding away whenever a row seemed to be brewing, I was beginning to feel more like a referee for constant arguments than The Animals' road manager.

There was one argument in particular, while The Animals were on tour in Sweden, when Chas pushed Eric that bit too far and caused a tirade of abuse. Now, Eric has a big mouth but, if I hadn't already had to fence a dozen similar rows, the situation could have been funny. There was Eric, propped up on his toes, screaming that he was going to have Chas beaten up, or murdered, or whatever threat he'd come up with that day. Chas simply towered over Eric's tiny 5ft 6in (1.62m) frame and Eric had to jump up in order to meet his eyes. I wasn't, therefore, that worried about Eric getting any further than threats and as Eric saw Chas's temper start to fray, I think even he began to feel the height difference and scuttled off back to his hotel room. That, you would think, would be the end of it. Well, you wouldn't think that if you knew Eric as well as I did.

At breakfast the next morning I sincerely thought that Eric was going to prove me wrong. Chas and his girlfriend came down and joined us; Eric was all smiles and good mornings. Maybe mighty-mouth Burdon had finally learnt to bite his tongue?

'Actually, I think I'll go and get ready now. Early start, you know?' Eric said suddenly, standing up and draining his coffee cup. 'I'll just take a slice of this for the walk.'

He leant over towards me and grabbed a slice of toast, taking the opportunity to whisper into my ear, 'I'm gonna get that fat son-of-a-bitch once and for all.'

With a wink and a smile at me, he was gone. Oh well, so much for water under the bridge. With growing concern for what Eric could be getting up to in our absence, I finished my breakfast and went in search of him. When I finally caught up with him he was looking very smug and, worse, telling me nothing of what he'd done while we finished our breakfast.

'Don't worry about it, Tappy. Let's just say that I've sorted out Chas Chandler and leave it at that. The less you know about it, the better.'

'For Christ's sake, Eric, I need to know. It'll be me that has to clean up the mess afterwards. What have you done?'

'All will be revealed,' he said, giving his nose a tap. 'I'd hate to spoil the surprise.'

Fantastic, this was all I needed. But after a couple of days of worry, I forgot all about Eric's secret masterplan. The tour continued and, for the moment, there was peace. That was until Chas's girlfriend had her photographs developed.

'You dirty fuckin' bastard!' Chas screamed, as he charged on to the tour bus a week later. He lunged at Eric and grabbed him by the throat. 'How dare you! I'm gonna fuckin' kill you, you dirty little pervert!'

I jumped up and ran to prise them apart. I had never seen Chas this angry before and, not even in his blackest days back when The Animals were starting out, had I ever seen him so violent. Even using all my strength I couldn't shift his hands from round Eric's throat. Chas didn't even seem to know I was there. Finally, with Hilton's help, I managed to ease his grip and Eric took a shuddering breath.

'Let go, Chas,' Hilton shouted. 'For Christ's sake, you'll murder him.'

'That's all he deserves, filthy bastard!'

Between us, Hilton and I pulled him off and Eric slumped to the floor. I crouched down to check that he was OK and to my amazement saw that he was laughing. This was not what a furious Chas needed to see right now. I twisted round, shielding Eric from view, and turned to face Chas, who was still being held back by Hilton.

'What the hell is this about? What's happened?'

'I'll tell you what's going to happen,' Chas yelled, shaking off Hilton's restraining arms. 'That dirty little bastard isn't going to see the end of this tour. That's what's going to happen.' He spat down at Eric's protruding feet and stormed off the bus.

Hilton and I looked at one another and then down at Eric, who was rubbing at his neck and laughing fit to burst.

'Oh, that is fucking brilliant! Has he gone?' Eric asked, peering between our legs to the bus door. 'Brilliant. Chas fuckin' Chandler, who the hell does he think he is? Thought he'd got the better of me, didn't he?' Again, he burst out laughing.

'Eric, what is this? What's so funny? He nearly killed you there, son.'

'I'm fine, Tappy. In fact, I'm great. If you want to do me a favour then just go and ask Chas for the photographs. It would truly make my day if you'd do that.'

'What photographs?' Hilton asked, obviously as confused as I was.

'Just go ask for them,' Eric said, pulling himself to his feet and wiping tears of laughter from his eyes.

Hilton shrugged and went off in search of Chas. Meanwhile, I cleaned Eric up, though I still couldn't get any sense out of him as to the cause of the row. He just kept laughing and laughing every time I mentioned it. Perhaps he was hysterical? In shock after a near choking?

A couple of minutes passed and Hilton returned, looking shaken. In his hand was a pack of photographs, but he also sported a large red mark across his face.

'Present from Chas,' he said, patting his swollen cheek, gingerly. 'It's like he's lost his mind. He completely freaked out when I mentioned the photographs and punched me in the face. I got them for you, Eric, but Chas is not a happy man.'

This was getting completely out of hand. I was meant to be looking after The Animals and I had a bassist who was either trying to kill or injure every member of the band he came in contact with, a hysterical lead singer and now a bruised lead guitarist. What the hell was happening to The Animals?

'Oh, stop looking like that, Tappy,' Eric cut in. 'Just take a look at the photographs.'

I took the pictures from Hilton. Now, you remember that little prank that Eric played on Mick Jagger's girlfriend, Chrissy? Well, here was Take Two. Photograph after photograph of Eric Burdon's hairy arsehole, only this time there were props: Chas and his girl's toothbrushes. Yes, you've guessed it, while we were finishing our breakfast the day after Eric and Chas's argument, Eric had been upstairs with Chas's camera and both their toothbrushes. Pink and blue stems were all that was visible, the rest of the brushes securely tucked up Eric's arse! Not only that, but in the week before the photographs were developed, Chas and his girlfriend had been using those brushes every day to clean their teeth. No wonder Chas was angry!

I must admit that Hilton and I joined Eric in a laugh at Chas's expense. Later, in one of my greatest achievements in pop band diplomacy, I even managed to calm Chas down enough to stop him murdering Eric. I also promised never to tell his girlfriend about the contents of the camera, and I was more than happy to spare her that particular truth. In fact, things even quietened down for a while. It seems that even Chas was willing to lay off Eric if it meant a clean toothbrush in the morning.

Saying Hello to The Hollies

I had no way of knowing how far apart these arguments and petty squabbles were going to drive The Animals in the coming year. All I knew, in the April of 1965, was that I was tired of it. We were back in the States and I was grateful for Bob Levine's company, and his help in placating The Animals' various tantrums.

I think that Bob must have guessed my state of mind because when The Animals reached New York, I had a call from Frank Barcelona (The Animals' agent at Premier Talent and Bob's boss). Frank wanted me to pick up a band on 16 April from Kennedy Airport: The Hollies. They'd started to make it big in the UK and this was to be their first trip to the US. I'd heard about The Hollies, obviously; I'd even met them a few times back in the UK on tour with The Animals. I liked their music and was happy to do Frank a favour and take a break from The Animals for a while.

It was odd meeting them like that although; it was like seeing The Animals and me arrive on our first trip (they even had gigs at the Paramount as their first stop, just as we had before them), only this time it was me, and not Bob, who'd escort them through the crowds to their stretch limos. They looked terrified; I stood there smiling and waving, trying to look reassuring and finally they spotted me.

'Hey there, Tappy. This is bloody crazy. Don't suppose you've seen our ride hanging about, have you? I haven't seen your boys round here.'

Great. They thought I was here to meet The Animals. Was I never going to escape those lads?

'I'm your ride, idiot. Frank sent me. Get a move on, your limos await.'

It was nice to be helping out some fresh faces, and it brought back memories of happier days with The Animals, so when Frank asked me if I'd mind working with The Hollies during their American visit I jumped at the chance. It's strange how decisions that seem so small at the time can lead to connections that influence your whole life. It was because of that decision to help out The Hollies that I ended up sitting alongside Bob Levine backstage in the Paramount Theater at the *Soupy Sales Show*. And it was at this gig, although I didn't realise it, that I would meet the man whose life and death would change me for ever.

Paramount Coincidence with a Little Disruption

The *Soupy Sales Show* was The Hollies' first American gig. Soupy was a fantastic comedian, very popular with kids. He televised his own show every week, but the Paramount Theater was a big venue and Soupy had organised acts to match. It was a great chance for The Hollies and they knew it.

Bob Levine had been assigned as stage manager and, although I was primarily there as The Hollies' tour manager, I knew that he could do with my help. When it came to work, Bob was a perfectionist. He spent a great deal of time running over the details of the show with me: each band or artist had been allocated four songs apiece and under no circumstances were there to be any encores. Time's precious on a televised show and Bob was in no position to entertain egos, no matter how famous the act may be. My job was to make sure that, after they had performed, the artists were swiftly moved off stage and into a waiting elevator to their dressing rooms. True to Bob's working style, everything seemed to have been organised perfectly: on stage right – four songs – off stage left – into elevator – back to dressing room. What could go wrong?

Soupy could always draw in the crowds and the theatre was packed. When I heard the deafening roar of cheers and applause from the audience, I even began to worry that our sound system wouldn't be able to compete. It wouldn't be much of a US television début for The Hollies if all you could hear was the crowd screaming. What would Frank Barcelona have to say about my tour management skills then?

But I needn't have worried, The Hollies pulled off a flawless performance and the crowd loved them. I relaxed as I saw them into the elevator after their set. A success if ever I saw one.

'Hey, Tappy,' Bob shouted from the other side of the stage. 'You've got to check out this next lot. They've got to be seen to be believed.'

The announcer's voice boomed through the microphone as I leant out to see what Bob was talking about. 'Ladies and gentlemen, please put your hands together for Little Richard and his band, the Upsetters and Kingpins . . .'

Although they weren't at the top of the bill, Little Richard with the Upsetters and Kingpins were one of the major attractions of Soupy's show but Bob was right; what I was seeing on that stage had to be seen to be believed. Little Richard had just returned from a very successful tour of the UK and he'd obviously enjoyed it so much that he'd decided to bring a little bit of England back with him. That is, England – Little Richard style.

A group of roadies were struggling on stage; one of them carried a huge gold-painted throne, the other a roll of red carpet. With these in place, Little Richard, his head held high, stepped out on to the red carpet and approached his throne, a great red-and-white velvet cape flapping around his legs. There he was in front of a packed house at the Paramount and with all the cameras trained on him playing at being a King. I was already having difficulty smothering my laughter when the Upsetters and Kingpins followed Little Richard on to the stage. How in hell he had convinced them that this was a good idea, I'll never know. Each member was strapped into a red military uniform and, as the icing on the cake, he'd got them all wearing huge black bearskins. The Upsetters and Kingpins had become Little Richard's royal guardsmen.

I walked round to Bob as they started to play.

'What you reckon Bob – King or Queen?' We both laughed.

The ludicrous set continued as his royal majesty Little Richard thumped out the hits and his poor band got hotter and hotter under the lights. One black guitarist seemed to be having more trouble than the rest; his bearskin hat kept toppling over as he tried to play. I caught his eye and grimaced my sympathy. The poor lads were all sweating under their fur hats, the recently applied make-up running down their faces. They had to keep totally still or lose their hats, so as Little Richard threw himself around the stage, the miserable band kept up their roles as a royal guard, barely twitching as they played.

Soupy Sales was unimpressed. He knew exactly what Little Richard was doing: trying to upstage him on his own show. And as the final song came to an end, he was proved right.

'Get ready, Tappy,' Bob said, pulling the next act into position. 'Let's get those poor guys off and get this lot on as quickly as we can.'

But Little Richard had other ideas. As the song came to an end, it became clear that he had no intention of leaving the stage.

'What's that, New York? You want more? I can't hear you; did you say you want more?'

The crowd screamed their approval and, with a quick smirk at Soupy standing next to us in the wings, Little Richard launched into his fifth song. The crowd went wild and Little Richard strutted back and forth on the stage. Soupy went purple with rage.

'Get that guy off my stage!' he shouted to Bob and me. 'Pull the goddamn plug!'

With one swift jerk Bob pulled the power lead out of its socket. Silence fell across the theatre. Little Richard, still mid-song, found himself mouthing words into a dead microphone. The audience began to laugh and he threw down the mike and stormed off stage. As I struggled to corner him into the waiting elevator, Bob pushed the power back on and the compère announced the next act. But then Little Richard spotted Bob.

'You!' he screamed, running over and grabbing Bob by the throat. 'No one ever pulls the plug on Little Richard!'

It took me and several roadies to drag him off Bob. I was pleased to notice that we were also helped by that guitarist in his band, who'd now finally thrown off the unstable bearskin. Between us, we half-shoved, half-lifted Little Richard into the elevator. But as the door slid closed behind him, Soupy Sales came over.

'I think it's about time that someone taught his majesty a lesson,' he said and hit the brake button on the side of the elevator. It screeched to a halt between floors and Little Richard screamed, banged and cursed from inside. 'Tell everyone to use the stairs from now on, Tappy. We'll leave him there for a while; won't do him any harm to sweat it out. Goddamn pop stars, don't know why I put up with them.'

So, with our orders intact, Bob and I settled down to watch the rest of the show, which thankfully drowned out the language coming from the elevator above our heads. After his attention seeking (and air-time stealing) performance on stage, none of the other bands seemed to find much sympathy for Little Richard's imprisonment. In fact, I've never seen pop stars so happy to use the stairs. It all went without a hitch from then on. In fact, after a couple of hours trapped in an elevator it was a rather meek Little Richard who was finally released. He even managed to summon up an apology for Soupy Sales. Now, that did have to be seen to be believed.

Unfortunately, Little Richard's new attitude didn't last long and he lost the gig with Soupy a few days later. He left the show and took with him the black guitarist who had helped me stuff his boss into an elevator. I was still yet to learn the name of that guitarist, but after a few short years in the spotlight, the world would never forget it.

Elvis is *in* the Building

Before I returned from my holiday away from The Animals, I took one other little trip with Bob and moved from an encounter with a future King of Rock 'n' Roll to *the* greatest of all time. Although I didn't realise it right away.

Bob was working with Herman's Hermits, a band who were taking the world by storm in 1965. I'd met them a couple of times and I liked their young lead singer, Peter Noone, a great deal. Bob asked me to come out to Hawaii to help out on a short tour that the Hermits were playing there and, with some more time to play with, I wasn't going to refuse a trip to one of the most beautiful places on earth.

We were staying in the Hilton Hawaiian Village, a luxurious hotel, which consisted of a complex of tower-blocks right on the widest stretch of Waikiki Beach. I shared a suite with Peter and Bob, which had an adjoining lounge. Peter Noone had settled down to rest and Bob had popped out for a couple of minutes, when the telephone rang. I hurried through to the living room and pushed Peter's door closed, so as not to disturb him. The kid had been working hard and needed some sleep.

'Hello, yes?'

'Hi there,' a rich American voice drawled down the phone line. 'Is this the right number for Peter Noone of Herman's Hermits?'

It may have been a male voice, but I was used to groupies' tricks. They'd do anything to locate their heroes and I wasn't going to give Peter Noone away that easily.

'Who's speaking, please?'

'Oh, sure. This is Elvis Presley; I wanted to ask Peter if he could drop by and say hi? Maybe, hang out with us guys for a while?'

'Yeah, right! *Elvis Presley*!'

'That's me, sir.'

'And I'm the Queen of Sheba! Listen, pal, I don't know who you are and I don't care. Mr Noone does not appreciate jokes like this and neither do I. Goodbye.'

I slammed the phone down and sat there fuming. I couldn't believe that, even in a high-class resort like this one, we were still at the mercy of practical jokers. I checked that Peter was still sleeping and then marched down to reception to give the hotel staff a piece of my mind about their security practice.

The girl behind the desk looked up as I approached and gave me a glossy smile.

'Excuse me, ma'am, I work for Mr Noone. Could you make sure that no more calls are put through to his suite without being properly checked? I've just had to deal with a hoax call and not even a very imaginative one. I would have expected you to screen out Elvis Presley impersonators. Mr Noone should not have to deal with this.'

'Actually, sir,' the receptionist cut in, her eyes hardening into a glare. 'We are always very careful about the calls that we put through to our guests' rooms. Mr Presley is staying at one of our sister hotels and he personally requested Mr Noone's number.'

'You mean that I was actually speaking to Elvis Presley . . . *the* Elvis Presley.'

'Yes, sir. *The* Elvis Presley. Are you all right, sir?'

I put my head in my hands and stared down at the polished surface of the reception desk. What had I done? The King of Rock 'n' Roll had been on the same phone line as me and I'd hung up on him. Such. An. Idiot.

'Please don't hit yourself, sir.'

I stopped beating my head against the desk and looked up at the receptionist.

'Would you like me to put you through to Mr Presley's suite?'

'Yes, please.'

With help from the now sympathetic receptionist I finally got through to Elvis's staff. After numerous apologies, I arranged for Peter to meet Elvis on the set of his new movie, *Paradise, Hawaiian Style*, that afternoon and then hurried back to the hotel room to explain to Peter.

Bob was already back and, although he rolled his eyes when he heard about my mistake, he was as excited as Peter and me at the prospect of meeting the King. We piled into the car and drove to Elvis's latest location shoot.

Sitting outside, Peter began to feel nervous, and he wasn't the only one.

'Listen guys,' I said, laying my hands on the steering wheel. 'Elvis wanted to meet you, Peter, and I nearly stopped it happening. If you want me to wait here, then I'll understand.'

Peter laughed. 'You know what, Tappy? What's worrying me is that this could still be a hoax and if we're about to be thrown out on our ear, then I couldn't think of a better guy to do that for me.'

But, as we got out and headed over to the set, Peter caught my arm. 'I'm just joking, mate. You wouldn't want to miss this, would you?'

I grinned. 'No way! Thanks, Peter.'

It wasn't a hoax and soon we were sitting at a large wooden table with various members of the crew from *Paradise, Hawaiian Style* waiting for Elvis to finish a scene. The stunning Marianna Hill, who was co-starring with Elvis, wandered through the room and smiled at us. I nearly lost all the breath left in me, but nothing could prepare me for finally meeting the man that followed her.

It's a strange thing to meet famous faces, but during my years with The Animals I had gradually become desensitised to working with the biggest names in the business. All too quickly, they just became people. Flawed or special, nice or nasty, they were just another personality met on the road. But this was different; this was *Elvis Presley*!

I'd grown up with his music and his image; watching him walk into that room was like watching a photograph come to life. The man was just so beautiful.

'Hi, Peter,' Elvis said, walking over to greet the singer. 'I'm so glad that you could make it. And, these must be your buddies.' He leant over to shake mine and Bob's hands. 'Pleased to meet you, sir.'

Elvis Presley just called me 'sir'!

He settled down to talk to us. He was so polite, anxious to make sure that we were all supplied with sodas and offering us food. He was still in the clothes that he'd worn for the shoot and after a couple of minutes he had to ask for a towel to wipe off his make-up. He was sweating. Could it really be that Elvis was as nervous to meet us as we were to meet him? Peter and Elvis chatted a little about the music business and Herman's Hermits' success, then he talked to Bob for a while about gun culture in the UK. It seemed that Elvis was a keen gunman and passionate about rare styles and designs.

All too soon it was time to leave and I took my chance to apologise for my blunder on the telephone earlier.

'Please, don't worry about it. It happens all the time. You should hear what people say when I try to order pizza!'

We said our goodbyes and Elvis invited us to join him in Graceland if we were ever in the area. He may have been the King of Rock 'n' Roll, but he was also a true Southern gentleman and couldn't have treated us better.

The Plastercasters

Still reeling from my encounter with my greatest musical hero, it was time to return to The Animals and, although I'd enjoyed my time with The Hollies and the holiday with Peter Noone and Bob, I have to say that I was pleased to see them again. Maybe the taste of Little Richard's tantrums was just what I needed to make me appreciate what I'd got. So, in late '65, The Animals hit the American road once again, with me back in tow as their tour manager. Little did we know that we were also heading towards an encounter with the most famous groupies of the 1960s.

Chicago was the next location on The Animals' agenda and I had hired a small plane to get the lads to the venue. I got the band on board along with all the equipment and finally we were all sitting waiting for clearance for take-off. Then the pilot made the announcement that there would be an hour delay. While the boys started to moan and fidget in their seats, I made use of the time to check that all the equipment was there and in the proper order. I was still pleased to be back with The Animals and wasn't keen to remind myself how petty they could get in the face of a simple delay.

As I walked down the aisle, I noticed splashes of white powder on the floor. Puzzled, I knelt down and followed what seemed to be a trail of powder along the length of the plane. At the end of the trail, crouched behind a seat with huge grins on their faces, were the answers to the mystery.

'Oh no! The bloody Plastercasters,' I laughed, pulling the girls to their feet. 'Caught up with us at last have you, ladies?'

I had better explain about the Plastercasters before you meet them; I've said a little about the lengths that groupies would go to in getting close to their band of choice, but the Plastercasters were something else entirely. I'd heard a lot about those girls from my friend and colleagues in the music industry.

It was a little shy girl called Cynthia who had started it. Too quiet to approach band members through the traditional means of persist-ence, she had started The Plastercasters with a friend and turned it into a kind of hobby. They collected plaster casts of famous British and American pop stars; more specifically plaster casts of their genitals.

I had met and spoken to many men who'd been their 'subjects' – the girls were said to have a vast collection. But The Plastercasters hadn't caught up with The Animals, until now . . .

'Good morning, boys,' they shouted down the plane to The Animals, waving their bags of white plaster powder in the air. 'Which one of you wants to be first?'

The lads laughed, all irritation at the flight delay forgotten as they thought about what was to come.

'Over here, girls,' shouted Eric, 'I'll go first. I've got a great specimen for your collection, but I doubt you'll have enough powder left in those bags for the rest of them when you get done here.'

The girls ran down the aisle to Eric. One got on her knees in front of him, unbuttoned his fly and applied herself to the business of getting his cock erect while the other mixed up the plaster. As soon as Eric's cock was hard, the plaster was slapped on over his genitals. As they waited for it to dry, they whispered lewd comments into his ear, making sure that his erection stayed in place. Talk about in-flight entertainment! We hadn't even left the ground yet.

Once the mould was dry, they removed it and filled it up, finally producing a perfect replica of Eric Burdon's, admittedly enviable, cock. When his mould was ready, Eric held it up in triumph.

'I'd like to see you lot beat that!'

The Animals drew lots and Hilton was next for the star treatment. Unfortunately for Hilton, he got an attack of the giggles. Whether it was the ridiculous situation, a few too many drugs smoked beforehand, or a combination of the two, he couldn't manage to get a hard-on. No matter what the girl between his legs did for him, nothing was happening.

Now, another thing I'd heard about the Plastercasters was that they were never that interested in what their subject thought of the end result, and they proved true to their legend. After some time trying to help Hilton out, the girl with the plaster lost patience and slapped on the plaster anyway. When Hilton saw the measly mould this produced, he begged and pleaded with them for another try. But, as the girls explained, time and plaster were precious to them and they had to have some rules to their trade. If Hilton couldn't get an erection, it was his problem, not theirs.

In the end, we invited our stowaways to join us on the flight to Chicago and gave them free tickets to the gig that night. The only one not delighted by this was Hilton, who sat at the back of the plane sulking and casting black looks at his own little contribution to the Plastercasters' collection.

So The Animals were back on the road again and I was back with them. Could it be that the laughs would finally manage to outweigh the arguments, and that one of the greatest bands that the Sixties ever saw could patch up their differences and carry on to even bigger and better things?

CHAPTER 6

Bitter Ends and Sweet Beginnings: The End of The Animals

John and Anne

Any of you who know anything about the history of The Animals will know where this chapter is heading, but let's start with a happy beginning for one of the band members – John Steel.

John was the drummer. He was a fabulous musician and a good man. That sums him up really – 'a good man'. Whilst so many artists of the Sixties were finding themselves sucked deeper and deeper into the indulgences of the age, whether that be drugs, booze or women, John kept his feet firmly on the ground. As the road manager of The Animals, John was the one I could always rely on and the one I never had to worry about.

The one thing that John Steel loved above all else was his childhood sweetheart Anne, to whom he had remained faithful since they had first got together back in Newcastle. He consistently resisted the offers from groupies who threw themselves at his feet. Puzzled by his attitude, we'd often tease him about being 'under the thumb' and even go so far as smuggling a beautiful girl into his bed at the end of a long and lonely day on tour. John never gave in, though; he'd politely ask the girl to leave and then phone Anne to tell her about his day. Eventually we admitted defeat. We all liked Anne, she was a lovely girl; I think that we were just trying to justify our own behaviour by attempting to get John to take part.

But Anne won through. John took every chance he could to get back to Newcastle to visit her, even if it was just for a couple of hours and, in the end, he moved her down to London, so that they could spend more time together.

It shouldn't have been a surprise, therefore, when John turned up to a gig one Saturday night in 1965 and introduced Anne as his wife. He'd told none of us about his plans. He and Anne just turned up at the London Register Office and grabbed two people working outside (a bricklayer and a road sweeper) to be their witnesses; they hadn't even realised that he was a member of The Animals.

Anne smiled round at us all as her new husband explained what had happened. She looked very happy and very beautiful.

'You could have told me you know, John,' I said, catching his arm as the lads gathered round to kiss the bride. 'I wouldn't have told anyone, but I would have liked to be there. It must have been strange getting wed without any family or friends to see it?'

John smiled and gave me a hug. 'I couldn't have done it to her, Tappy. You've seen what it's like for The Animals. This wedding had nothing to do with The Animals; it was about me and Anne. I would have loved you and the guys to be there, you're my best mates, but think about what the papers would have done with Eric in the front row. It wouldn't have been our day at all.'

He was right. Maybe it wasn't as bad then as it is today, but the media would still have wanted their piece on a wedding of a member of one of the biggest bands on the planet. Watching John standing there with his wife I realised that maybe it was the rest of us who should feel envious. Sure, we could fill our beds with any groupie we chose, but John had found something special. The Animals was a job for him and, proper Newcastle lad that he was, he could do his day's work and then head home to a wife who loved him; that was a gift of which none of the rest of us could boast.

Japanese if you Please

But despite the thoughts of true love running through my head on that Saturday's gig, The Animals' schedule soon caught us up again. John Steel's 'day's work' took him with us away from his new bride and the UK, to a brand-new audience in Japan.

Tappy enjoying himself with two Japanese fans in Tokyo in 1965.

Japan in 1965 was an amazing place. The Japanese people seemed almost completely Westernised. They wore Western clothes, listened to our music and played games of baseball, but they still had a lot of traditions of their own, some of which I was happily able to enjoy during our stay there.

The Animals were popular in Japan, not least because 'The House of the Rising Sun' fitted very neatly with their national flag. The single had been at Number 1 for weeks, and the people wanted to meet the band.

At first we stayed at the Tokyo Prince Hotel and contented ourselves with several TV appearances. One show in particular, a kind of Japanese version of *Top of the Pops*, caused us a few problems. The benefits of being in a hugely successful pop band went far beyond wine, women and song. Alan Price had been given the latest version of the Dual Manual Vox Organ by Vox, to try it out and to drum up some publicity for the instrument before it was marketed. On the day of the TV show, however, it appeared to have broken down. Alan was panicking, the show was only hours away and he hadn't even had a chance to play on the new Vox. Two Japanese technicians came to the rescue; they said they could take it away and repair it before that evening's performance. And they lived up to their promise, the organ arrived and it sounded great.

We toured Japan for ten days before heading back to London. By the time we left we heard that an organ company in Japan had released a new organ. Yes, you've guessed it, those Japanese engineers had not only fixed Alan's organ, they had made a replica of it. The Japanese copy even beat Vox to the marketplace; there was nothing they could do. How those guys managed to make and distribute a replica in ten days is beyond me, but we kept our heads down and no one seemed to suspect our involvement.

Now I've said that John Steel was the one member of The Animals never to cause me worry, but during that Japanese tour he had me in a state of pure terror. He had stomach pains and, although he said that everything was fine, the promoter panicked. If I had a dollar for every panicking promoter that I've had to calm down over the years . . . Anyway, there was no calming this one; he insisted on an ambulance to take John to the hospital. It was sweet of him really, to be so concerned for John's health, but he was a melodramatic little man. Every time John said 'I'm OK', the promoter would start screaming again, 'No, no, you go hospital now!'

Eventually, John and I ended up in the back of an ambulance, dashing through the city with sirens blazing. On our arrival at the hospital he was rushed to the emergency room and I went to the waiting room. Despite John's reassurances that there was nothing wrong, I began to feel anxious sitting there. John was always the quiet one of The Animals; what if there was something seriously wrong and I had failed to notice because I was too busy messing about with girls and partying with the other lads? Anne would never forgive me. The Japanese promoter came to join me in the waiting room and my guilt swelled at the worried look on his face. Did this man know something I didn't?

After 20 minutes, though, John emerged from the emergency room. I got to my feet.

'Well, Johnny, what's up?'

John laughed. 'Doctor agreed with me. All I needed was a good crap.'

And there was no way that Anne could blame me for *that*.

Now, I say I was messing about with girls and I know that after John's wedding I'd had a moment of doubt about the worth of the hedonistic lifestyle that we'd been living when it came to women. But Japan was different to any other tour experience I'd had. Japanese girls are characteristically polite and demure. This was a bit of a shock, coming after the excesses we had all enjoyed in the UK and the States. But thankfully there was one Japanese tradition that more than compensated: Geisha girls.

We were on tour and Alan convinced me to accompany him to a Geisha house, ostensibly as moral support, but this was one duty of friendship that I really didn't mind fulfilling. When we arrived at the house it became clear that the host knew who we were, and was keen to make us feel very welcome. We were given two girls each and I was soon forgetting all about true love and concentrating on their hands sliding over my body.

Now, contrary to popular belief, Geisha girls are not prostitutes. They do not have sex with you; they bath and wash you, then massage you with oil. They just use some very special techniques in going about it.

I was there, laid flat on my back, delighted with the careful washings and dryings that I'd just received from my two naked Geisha girls. One girl picked up a huge bucket of green soapy water and a brush, which looked like a large shaving brush. I thought I was in for a third soaking and settled back, closing my eyes. Nothing happened. When I opened my eyes she was lathering herself with the suds from the bucket. I enjoyed the view, but was a little confused at the turn of events. Where did I come into this? Then the girl leant and slid her naked body over mine: she was washing me with her body! I lay there, trying desperately to control myself as the girl snaked on top of me. Alan's voice reached me across the room:

'Please, God, don't let me ever leave this place.'

But we had to. We all loved Japan and swore to return as we took off for England once more. (Though, unfortunately, it took us until 1983 to keep that particular promise.)

As for Alan's cry of 'don't let me ever leave', that was a request that he obviously forgot all about in the preparations for The Animals' next tour in Europe.

Swedish Surprises

Why is it always the case that it's just when you think things are getting better that they suddenly get so much worse? I'm not going to try and claim that The Animals were all reformed characters; the old tensions and the old rows were still there. But I remember thinking, as I was packing up the equipment for a trip to Sweden with the band, how much I liked them all and how remarkable it was that, against all odds, despite all the difficulties, we were still here, still doing what we loved.

I got into the van that day filled with a kind of crazy hope that things could just continue getting better; Chas, Eric and Alan could patch up their differences, The Animals would continue to get better and better, there could be more Number 1s, more tours, more success to come. I drove towards the airport, picking up the boys along the way. Alan lived furthest from my flat, so he was the last on the list to collect. I jumped out of the van to ring his doorbell and waited for the familiar shouts and delays as he gathered his stuff to leave. Nothing. I rang again. Silence. No one was home.

'Where's Alan?' Chas asked, as I climbed back into the van alone.

'I don't know, I was hoping you could tell me. You didn't see who he was with last night, did you?'

None of them had seen him. I left the boys to watch Alan's door and ran down the road to the nearest phone box to call round a couple of his friends, trying to trace him. Still, there was no clue as to his whereabouts.

Admitting defeat I returned to the rest of The Animals. 'No sign. We're going to miss the flight if we wait any longer. He's probably already at the airport. Dirty stop-out, probably just picked up some bird and didn't come home. Let's get going or he'll be the only Animal in Sweden tonight.'

But Alan was not at the airport. In the end, we had to catch the flight without him and it wasn't until we reached Sweden that Mike Jeffery informed us that Alan Price had officially left The Animals.

To say that the rest of the boys were furious would have been an understatement, but I think that it was shock rather than fury that first greeted the news that Alan had left. There had been no real warning; Alan hadn't mentioned his decision to any other member of the band. He just left. And that was that.

There have been a lot of rumours over the years about the possible reasons behind Alan's departure from The Animals. Among them are his tempestuous relationship with Eric Burdon, his claim on the rights of 'The House of the Rising Sun' and a fear of flying. Now, Alan was scared of flying, but before he abandoned us on the morning of the flight to Sweden, he had always managed to cope with it. But I do remember one occasion, when The Animals were flying to the South of France, when Alan's fear got the better of him, and nearly the better of me!

However, we all knew in the band that Alan did not want to share the royalties from one of the biggest-selling records of all times.

You have to remember that international flights were not nearly as common back in the mid-Sixties as they are today, and we often had to rely on small chartered flights to get us to various destinations on tour. On this occasion, the small plane that we were using in France was fighting against some strong headwind as we came in to land. I was sitting between Hilton and an increasingly nervous Alan, when the plane suddenly tipped. We were so close to the ground at this point that the wing was scraping against the runway, sending a shower of bright sparks up behind us. The pilot panicked and thrust the plane back into the sky; we roared straight up like a rocket, leaving the ground far behind us. We were all terrified, Hilton and Alan both grabbed at my hands and squeezed hard. On one side I had Hilton, a Buddhist, starting up a long mumbling chant and on the other Alan, who made several attempts at the Lord's Prayer, getting the words wrong every time, and finally descending into random swear words. My swollen hands testified to Alan's very real fear of flying, but if he could get back on to a plane after that trip, I don't really see why one routine flight to Sweden should have been his breaking point.

Meanwhile, the Swedish tour was due to start in two days, but the boys had a television performance to attend on the night of their arrival. Mike had talked to a young keyboardist from Newcastle, Micky Gallagher, who said that he'd be willing to step into Alan's shoes for the tour, but what were we meant to do before he arrived? That was how, for one night only, Tappy Wright became Alan Price on Swedish television. Luckily, The Animals were only miming, because I wouldn't have fancied my chances if I'd actually had to play!

The ridiculous thing was that nobody noticed. After the show, walking down the street with the boys, girls even pointed and shouted across at me, 'Hey, you're Alan Price! I saw you on TV. Could I have your autograph?' If Alan's abrupt departure from The Animals had been done under the assumption that he was more famous than the rest of them, I would have liked to see his face when his road manager was signing his name for adoring fans who had no idea what he looked like!

Still, with Micky Gallagher now with us, the Swedish tour continued and, despite the shock of Alan's absence, things seemed to be going well. Micky certainly enjoyed the bonuses of working with one of the world's greatest rock bands and I had literally to drag the poor boy up in the mornings, after he'd overindulged on the ever-willing groupies.

Micky was a nice lad and I think his presence did something to remind us of the wonderful position that we were holding. It was somewhat with him in mind that I approached a pair of beautiful Swedish women one night on tour. Chas clocked that I was 'catching a fish' and wandered over to join me. True to form, within five minutes he'd caught the most stunning of the pair and soon we were all heading back to The Animals' hotel.

I was sitting up front with my girl, chatting away as I drove, when I felt a tap on my shoulder. I twisted round in my seat to see Chas, with the biggest grin I've ever seen spread across his face, and the gorgeous Swedish girl between his legs only visible as a mass of long blonde hair, bobbing up and down. That was Lotta, stunning, wisecracking Lotta, a girl full of life and fun, the woman who, within a couple of months, would be Chas's wife and whose eventual impact on music history could never have been guessed at.

Rocky Replacement

So, even without Alan Price, The Animals continued. We said goodbye to Micky Gallagher after the Swedish tour and Mike Jeffery found a permanent replacement for Alan in Dave Rowberry. Alan was probably the member of The Animals that I'd had been least close to over the years and, after he left, I must admit that I was hoping for a bit more peace and quiet from the band. Maybe with Alan gone the rows would be defused? And maybe a fresh face would make them appreciate what they'd got? But after the dust had settled and Dave Rowberry had bedded in, I began to miss Alan.

The Animals had always been that group of lads who I'd known for years and the sudden introduction of anyone new would have been difficult, but Dave Rowberry was a man I just couldn't get on with. The members of The Animals had always treated me as an equal; we had all come from the same place and shared the same history. I honestly believe that it would have been unthinkable to any of them (Alan Price included) to look down on me, just because I wasn't a member of the band. I was, and always had been, the sixth Animal to them and they respected the work I did for them. Maybe I'd taken my position for granted, but Dave Rowberry's attitude to me when he joined The Animals came as a far greater shock than Alan's departure.

Dave had been in a band called The Mike Cotton Sound; they hadn't even had one hit. You would have thought that he'd have appreciated the great opportunity that playing with The Animals gave him. Well, if he did, I saw no evidence of it. He treated me like some kind of personal slave, throwing orders at me day and night. I may have had my problems with Alan, but I always respected the man, both for his attitude towards me and for his superior talent on the keyboards. Now I had some jumped-up little nobody, with less talent than Alan had in his little finger, treating me like dirt. I loved The Animals, but I didn't see how long this could last.

From Poland with Love

Looking back on it now, I'm glad that I stayed, because we had a tour in Poland to attend and it was there, in that most cold and depressing place, deep behind the Iron Curtain, that Lady Fate had decided I would play the part of the boy in a fairytale and finally find my princess waiting for me.

The Animals were the first British pop group to tour Poland. Life behind the Iron Curtain in 1965 was a grim mystery to the West and the decision to tour was mostly influenced by the desire in all of us to witness what was really happening first-hand.

It was late November when we arrived and we all dressed up for the bitter climate, arriving in huge imitation fur hats and coats, our feet smothered in fur boots. We looked like a pack of bears trooping out of the airport but, with temperatures of -20°C, at least we were warm.

The Polish people received us with open arms; they only managed to listen to pop music through the pirate station, Radio Luxembourg. All Western music was banned on the State radio. The performances by The Animals were to be used as a test by the State; if the Polish youth could control themselves during their gigs then other bands may be allowed to perform.

And, at our first concert in Warsaw, we saw just what the Polish State meant by 'control'. None of the audience members were allowed to stand and were only allowed to applaud at the end of each song. The Animals were forced to perform to an impassive seated audience the like of which they had never seen. Where were the screaming girls? The banners? The heckled calls for 'more', for favourite songs? It was an eerie event, and although we knew that the audience were strictly controlled and had no choice but to behave in the way they did (in fact, our continuing presence in Poland relied on it), I think The Animals were relieved when the gig was finally over.

With the lads safely in their dressing room, I went on stage to check the equipment was all switched off. It was then, out of the corner of my eye, that I saw her. Lady Fate. She was standing by the barrier, right in front of the stage, waving to me. I stood stock still for a moment trying to place her – a sweep of blonde hair, bright blue eyes shining under the lights, a slight, delicate face. She was beautiful. I walked over to her.

'My God, it's you. You used to live above me, didn't you? You were my neighbour.'

She smiled at me; I realised I'd missed that smile.

'That's right, in London. I remembered you worked with The

97

Animals and thought that I might . . .' she stopped there, looking embarrassed. 'Well, I thought I might see you. I didn't think you'd recognise me.'

It was the pretty girl from the stairs in Earl's Court. My Lady Fate. The girl whose morning smile and wave had haunted me. The one girl, out of all those hundreds, all those thousands of different girls, that I remembered as just a sweet smile, a sweet feeling; and here she was, a year later, in Poland!

'But, what are you doing here?' I asked, still stunned by meeting her again.

'I live here. Listen, I have to go,' she glanced over her shoulder and I saw two men hovering in the background. 'My chaperones,' she explained, with another smile. 'It was nice to see you again.'

I caught her arm; her sleeve was warm under my cold fingers. 'Don't go.' I don't know what made me say it, but I think that I knew then, maybe I'd always known, that this girl was special.

'I have to, they're waiting for me.'

'Well then, meet me tomorrow. We could have lunch? I'll tell you about what's been happening in London and you tell me about Poland.' My hand was still on her arm; she took it in her hands and then laid it carefully on the barrier between us.

'OK,' she said finally, her eyes lowered, but the smile still in place. 'Tomorrow.'

I was on cloud nine. I had a date with Lady Fate and I didn't even know her name.

The next day we met at The Crocodile, Poland's most famous restaurant, where I did my best to impress her. Her name, she told me, was Malgozata Slesinska, but after a couple of garbled attempts at pronouncing it in my Geordie accent, she let me call her Margaret. Margaret was beautiful, she had a kind of effortless elegance and grace. I found myself, even there on that first date, just sitting and watching her move. She told me of her studies in the UK, where she had trained to be a doctor and we talked a little of London and music.

'I miss it,' she said, hooking a curl of her blonde hair between her fingers. 'I was sad to leave. But my father only sent me there for school and as soon as that was over I had to return. It's difficult, for my family in particular, to leave Poland.'

I was watching the blonde hair between her pale fingers and

thinking how lovely she was. I shook my head and took a forkful of food. 'What do they do then? Your family, I mean.'

She looked embarrassed. 'My father is Prince Puzyha. I thought you knew.'

The fork never reached my mouth. I was having lunch with a Polish princess! So much for impressing her with stories of The Animals! I caught a movement to my left and realised that we were being watched by two heavy-set men on a neighbouring table. Margaret caught my glance.

'That's why they're here. I'm always chaperoned. Anyway,' she picked up her glass and smiled at me, 'you Animals have a reputation, you know.'

We talked on and gradually I relaxed enough to almost forget our observers and even Margaret's royalty. She was a lovely girl and when she invited me out to cocktails that night with the British Ambassador, I agreed immediately.

Margaret had a way of putting me at my ease in any situation, and even when I realised that I hadn't packed a suit and had to turn up for cocktails in my casual clothes, she didn't bat an eyelid. When the princess is happy, who else can complain? The British Ambassador was very polite and welcoming, praising The Animals and myself for our work in Poland. Though I did catch him glancing over my attire when Margaret was out of earshot, when he took the chance to remind me that we 'were Ambassadors for *England* out here'.

Darker States

The day after the Ambassador's party, The Animals set out on their Polish tour. We travelled off through Gdansk, Katowice and Krakow, and I kept in touch with Margaret constantly. I just wasn't interested in any other women. I don't know what the rest of the boys must have thought of me, but I caught John Steel looking at me now and then, with a knowing smile on his face. I booked a couple of days off at the end of the tour, so that I could spend some more time with her, and passed through the gigs automatically, thinking of the things that we could do together. So it was with new love blossoming in my heart that I visited the most horrific place on earth.

During the tour we had been invited to visit the Auschwitz museum. All of The Animals and I had been brought up with stories of the Second World War; we'd seen some of the documentary and news footage of the concentration camps, but nothing could compare to the experience of walking through the actual gas chambers that had been the death of so many thousands of innocent souls. Everything had been left as it was at the time of the camp's liberation in January 1945. Here we were, 20 years later, standing in rooms full of the personal belongings stolen from the walking dead, before they entered the gas chamber. There were tobacco pouches made from breasts and testicles, lampshades of the stretched fabric of human skin and piles of children's toys on the floor. These people had been reduced to little more than animals, degraded and abused in every way possible. It's hard to describe the range of emotions that the walk through the Auschwitz museum provoked: anger, grief, revulsion and pure terror at what one man can be driven to do against another.

After that trip to Auschwitz and the general deprivation that we witnessed in Poland, it was a far more sombre Animals that left Poland than the group of laughing lads dressed up in furs that had arrived only a few weeks before. I'd had my two days with Margaret and knew now that it was serious; this was not a woman I would forget.

As we left, we collected together all of the monies that we had been paid for the tour. We had been paid in the Polish currency, zlotys, which were worthless outside of Poland. We'd also discovered that two of the fold-out wooden chairs, which the audience had used for our first gig in Warsaw, had been broken. The Polish authorities had used this 'riotous behaviour' as an excuse to ban Western pop acts from performing in Poland for a further three years.

My last memory of that first visit to Poland was standing in the airport, the image of Margaret swimming in my mind, and watching the crowds of fans, standing silently in front of us and waving goodbye. Then seeing the change in their faces as The Animals took that moment to throw all their Polish monies out into the crowd. It was their last gesture to the Polish people and, I think, rather a beautiful one.

Happily Ever After?

I kept in contact with Margaret when I got back to London. I'd call her as often as I could, but it surprised me just how much I missed her. We'd known each other's names for under a month, but I couldn't get that girl out of my head. Our telephone conversations started to follow the same pattern every time:

'Come to London . . . just get on a plane and I'll meet you at the airport.'

'You know that I can't, Tappy. I was only able to be there with my student visa. They wouldn't let me leave, Tappy. They just won't let me.'

I felt terrible for pleading with her; the Polish authorities kept a tight rein on their royalty and I knew that my princess was trapped. But the time without her was unbearable. I gave up all my old girl-friends; The Animals had to catch their own fish. Margaret was all I could think about.

After a month I realised that I had to come to a decision. The Animals were off to the Bahamas, I booked some more time off and caught a flight to Poland, arranging to meet the boys later after I'd seen Margaret and put a certain question to her.

It all happened so fast. I asked Margaret to marry me; she accepted and we spent a couple of blissful days together before our marriage. But the chaperones were still in tow and I soon discovered that Poland without The Animals was a very different place.

When we'd travelled there before, for the Polish tour, we had always known that we were being followed and observed by agents of the Polish authorities, but this was as much for our protection as anything else. The Animals were a massive rock band and Poland had been aware that the world would be watching their treatment inside the Iron Curtain. But this time round I knew that our escorts (through the streets, at restaurants and bars, anywhere I travelled with Margaret) were not the minders that I'd been used to. These men were watching their princess and I was just another strange Westerner to be kept an eye on.

It did start to get to me. Once, as Margaret and I walked down the street in Warsaw, the man following us took so little care to remain unseen that I doubled back to meet him.

'We're going for a coffee at my hotel', I told the startled man. 'We'll turn left at the end of the road and then take a right. Just so you know.'

As The Animals' road manager, I'd been given a list of contact numbers at the Polish Foreign Ministry and, after a few days of heavy tailing, I thought that I'd give some of them a call and see if they could do anything to cool off the attentions of the Polish Secret Service. Not one of the telephone numbers was recognised; they had all been wiped from the databases since our last trip to Poland. I was in the middle of a society steeped in secret information and the darkness of the Cold War. But Margaret was worth it. If marrying her would mean a lifetime of shadows in the street and tapped phone calls, at that time I believed that I could cope with it, as long as I had my princess by my side.

We were married on 18 January 1966. There was 2ft of snow on the ground outside the register office and cameras from Russian and Polish television companies inside. The Animals' road manager marrying a Polish princess was big news. Margaret wore a dress

"TAPPY" WRIGHT pictured with his wife, Margaret Slesinska, daughter of a Polish prince.

POP GROUP MAN WEDS PRINCE'S DAUGHTER

JAMES "Tappy" Wright, road manager of The Animals, the Newcastle pop group, has married the 21-year-old daughter of a Polish prince.

"Tappy" met his wife, Margaret Slesinska, in London a year ago. The couple were married in Poland after the group toured and filmed there recently.

Studying

Margaret's father, Prince Puzyna, is a writer and her mother, a famous sculptor and architect, has designed buildings and bridges all over the world.

Whitley Bay-born "Tappy" said: "We will be living in London as I will continue to work as road manager to the group.

My wife is studying music and plans to take up teaching.

He added: "We hope to return someday to the North-East and make a home there."

Note for pop fans — The Animals will visit Newcastle on Friday, February 25, when they perform at the university.

Tappy on one of the happiest days of his life – marrying his Polish princess.

of white-and-brown lace, and she had a tattered bouquet of what looked little more than twigs in her hands (the only flowers to be found in the cold Polish winter). She had never looked more beautiful. We took our vows and I felt like the luckiest man in the world. We took our honeymoon at the Grand Hotel in Sopot, a seaside resort in Poland next to Gdansk, where they made us produce our wedding certificate before giving us a room. And it was only then that I could take my virgin princess, my wife, to bed.

Too soon, the time came for me to leave my new wife and set out for the Bahamas, to meet The Animals. Margaret remained in Poland, to pursue her application for a British visa whilst I was away working. Our brief honeymoon was over, but we had a lifetime to look forward to. But now I had a wife to look after and it was time to get back to work.

Shark Bait

If you're going to miss your wife, then the Bahamas is the place to do it. The Animals had been there before, for a short tour back in 1965. On that occasion the band had even managed to make their first movie appearance. Our yacht is clearly visible in scenes from *Thunderball*. The James Bond movie was shot on the gorgeous shoreline that we were lucky enough to overlook and we were able to watch Sean Connery and the stunning Claudine Auger as Domino, working through their scenes on the beach. Thanks to the fabulous scenery and with a little help from 007, the Bahamas had made a great impression on us all. So, when it came to finding a location for a month's break so that The Animals could start work on a new album, *Animalism*, it was the Bahamas they chose.

The location was also convenient for Mike Jeffery. Always elusive, The Animals' manager appeared again with a new plan. It was during this trip to the Bahamas that Mike first proposed the now infamous tax scam that he had told us would secure The Animals' fortune. He'd created an offshore company, Yamita, with help from some of his numerous contacts and was set to convince the boys that his idea was a good one.

I flew straight out from Warsaw to meet The Animals before Mike's arrival, full of the good news about my wedding, but it only took me a few minutes aboard the yacht to realise that all was not well in paradise. We'd got the boys back on the yacht to allow them some privacy. We were all sick of hotel rooms and The Animals had become virtual prisoners in the hotels we visited with the scores of fans, always one step ahead of our schedule, waiting outside. A yacht in the Bahamas had seemed like the perfect place for The Animals to work, relax and spend some quality time together. But quality time was the last thing they needed.

Chas was in a foul mood. As soon as I climbed aboard he started to berate me about a bag that he'd lost in New Orleans.

'It had my passport in it, Tappy. Do you even realise the trouble I've had getting here? What the hell are we paying you for?'

'Jesus, Chas. I've just got here; I don't see how I'm to blame for a bag you left in your hotel room.'

But Chas was unshakable. He was obviously frustrated and wanted to pick a fight; I was in the right place at the wrong time. I'd not even unpacked my bag before Chas's harsh words turned into blows and, before I knew it, we were fighting on deck. What was going on? I'd stepped aboard a happy, newly married man, looking forward to seeing my friends again, and now, less than an hour later, I was staggering below deck nursing a blooming black eye and listening to Chas's shouts above my head as the other boys struggled to calm him down. I'd done nothing wrong. Chas had lost his own bag and decided to take it out on me. I did a lot for The Animals; I'd left my new wife, days after our wedding, to be with them, but this time I was not going to put up with it. It was about time for a little revenge.

I went to bed early that night. The next morning Chas seemed to have forgotten all about our fight and greeted me with a bright 'good morning', completely ignoring my bruised face. 'I'm just off for a swim before breakfast, Tappy. Fancy joining me?'

'No, you're all right. I'll get on with the cooking.'

Think you'll get away with it that easily do you, Chas Chandler? Well, I'll show you just what you'll get for trying to bully Tappy Wright! I walked through to the kitchen where huge pieces of steak had been laid out for our breakfast. Now I mentioned that the last time we'd been in the Bahamas had been during the shoot of *Thunderball*; I don't know if you remember the film, but one of the most famous scenes involves Sean Connery's Bond coming face-to-face with a tank full of sharks. I decided to find out just how heroic Chas Chandler could be with a little 007 treatment.

I picked up a chunk of raw steak and a knife in the kitchen; then headed up on deck, where I stood overlooking the spot which Chas had chosen for his swim.

'One for Chas and one for the sharks,' I chanted, as I cut off slivers of meat and tossed them overboard towards the floating Chas. 'C'mon, sharks, breakfast time! Reckon you could fight them do you, Chas?'

I was screaming over the side of the boat, banging my hands against the handrail. I'd totally lost it. All that time spent dragging The Animals out of their beds, getting them girls and then seeing them off when the boys had had enough of them; all that hard work seemed to culminate in that moment. I didn't even know if there were sharks in the water, but just then I hoped so.

As for Chas, well he'd definitely seen *Thunderball*. As he realised that he was surrounded by floating shreds of red meat, he seemed to break all Olympic records in his swim back to the boat. As I watched him haul himself aboard and lay panting on the deck, I think I began to realise just what I'd done. The rest of the band, who must have been attracted by the sound of my screams, started to file out on deck; I pushed past them and hurried back downstairs to the kitchen. I put my hands on the work surface and breathed deeply, waiting to see what would happen next.

Chas gave a bellow of rage from the deck; he'd obviously recovered enough to realise what I'd tried to do to him. I stood where I was, staring straight ahead. I could hear Chas coming down the stairs to find me and I turned as he entered the kitchen. His face was white with fury.

'Just fuck off, Chas,' I said.

He didn't even open his mouth; there was a pause of little more than a second, where we just stood there looking at each other. Then, with one mighty punch, he knocked me out cold.

Goodbye to The Animals

It was only a few months after that incident with Chas and the sharks, late spring of 1966, that I decided that my time with The Animals had come to an end. Chas and I had made up our differences within a couple of days and we were all friends again when we left the Bahamas, but that moment on the deck, screaming for Chas's death, had made me realise just how much the internal pressures of the band were getting to me.

Dave Rowberry was still a problem and, to be honest, The Animals just didn't feel like the band it had been. The rows and bickering hadn't stopped and I was still breaking up fights and cooling arguments every day. I still loved each of those boys individually, but together they were unbearable.

And I was a married man now; I had Margaret to consider. She was living with me in London. We had our first home together, a small flat on the Edgware Road, and we were happy. I'd changed as much as the boys in The Animals. As a new husband, all the antics with groupies and girls went out of the window; I was loyal to my wife.

The question was, now that I knew the time had come to leave The Animals, where was I going to go next?

CHAPTER 7

All Change: Peter Noone, Herman's Hermits and at Home with the King

Finding Herman

I was back in the States with The Animals in the summer of 1966, when Bob Levine called me up and invited me out for dinner. He must have sensed something of my state of mind, because he came prepared with just the offer I'd been waiting for.

'Peter Noone contacted me, Tappy. You remember our trip to Hawaii, don't you?'

'Sure. Meeting Elvis Presley isn't something I'm likely to forget.'

But Elvis aside, in 1966, you would have been hard pressed to find anyone who didn't know the name Peter Noone. Herman's Hermits were massive; in 1965 they had outsold The Beatles, The Rolling Stones and The Animals and were voted the number one vocal group in the US by *Cashbox*, a prestigious American music magazine. They were also one of Micky Most's bands and worked through Bob's agency, Premier Talent, for their US tours. I'd spent some time with Peter on that trip to Hawaii and I'd run in to him several times since, at Premier Talent's New York office.

We'd always got on well; he was a nice kid. It seemed that I'd made a good impression on him, too.

'Peter likes you, Tappy,' Bob continued, carving up his steak and throwing me an appraising glance. 'He likes you and he likes the way you work. I know that you'll always be loyal to The Animals, but you did such a good job with The Hollies and we had a great time in Hawaii and, well . . . I'm talking round in circles here, but Peter needs a personal road manager for the new tour and you're the man that he wants for the job. What do you think?'

Bob's timing was perfect. I'd been talking to Chas on the flight over to America and he'd confided in me that the tour that we were about to start would be his last with The Animals. John Steel had already gone. Much as I loved and respected Hilton and Eric, the band as I knew it was over. A tour with Herman's Hermits was just the chance I was looking for. A chance to move on.

So I accepted Peter and Bob's offer and started work. The Animals understood my decision and it all worked out amicably. My original impressions of Peter proved correct; he was a lovely guy. At only 19, I always think of Peter as the start of that pretty-boy band look, which is so prevalent today. But even though he was just a teenager, Peter was in charge.

Life in a band without the constant struggles for control made working with Herman's Hermits a refreshing change. Also, as I worked for Peter and not the band as a whole, disputes and rows would not be my problem even if they did arise. My job was immediately easier and less stressful. Why hadn't I done this years ago?

Unfortunately, my easy escape from The Animals was short lived. The first tour that I went on with Peter was in the US and was therefore organised by Premier Talent. The Animals were set to share the billing with Herman's Hermits and the two bands toured together. So that meant the first tour in my new job was spent with my old band. This lasted two months! Far from making me nostalgic, the tour just confirmed that I'd made the right decision in shifting my loyalties to Peter and Herman's Hermits. It was sad to see those same old rows still going on. I was glad when it was finally over.

Playing with Peter

One of the main things that secured my friendship with Peter Noone was his sense of humour. I mentioned some of the silliness that Bob and I got up to on tour, and Peter was more than happy to join us in some of our practical jokes. So happy, in fact, that he was not above getting me into trouble if it meant a laugh along the way.

We were taking an inter-State flight to Seattle on Braniff airlines. Braniff had become very popular thanks to the skimpy uniforms that the airhostesses wore. They were very short dresses in a variety of colours and the girls would change several times throughout the flight. This was back in the days when air travel was still relatively new and exciting and the airhostesses were as glamorous as Hugh Hefner's Bunny Girls. But like Bunny Girls, there were rules to your behaviour in their company: you could look, but you didn't touch.

We were all sitting in first class; I was alongside Peter, who had a window seat, and across the aisle were Bob Levine and his girlfriend Cathy. As the airhostess served Bob and Cathy their drinks, she bent over and revealed a pair of very sexy white lace knickers. I grinned at Peter and was sitting back to admire the view when Peter leant across me and planted a kiss on her exposed buttocks. Before she could turn round, he was back in his seat and staring out of the window as if nothing had happened.

'What the . . . ?' the airhostess span round, took one look at my grinning face and gave me a sharp slap on the cheek.

I was trying to protest my innocence when Peter cut in. 'I'm so sorry, miss. Please, Tappy, control yourself. He's got an obsession with women's bottoms you see, we never know what he's going to do next.'

The girl took one look at Peter's angelic face and her fierce expression melted into a smile (though she managed to summon up one last filthy glance at me before she moved off down the aircraft).

'Pervert in row eight,' she warned her colleagues, her voice clearly audible from behind the hostess screen at the back of the plane.

Peter burst out laughing as Bob and Cathy shook their heads in disgust. I hadn't done a thing, but it was no good arguing with Peter's big blue eyes. I spent the rest of the flight being completely ignored by all the airhostesses, while they lovingly catered for Peter's every whim.

My job with Peter may have been new, but the routine of touring soon made it all very familiar. And now I was married, I didn't even have the distraction of groupies to entertain me. Practical jokes were the only safe distraction. Not that my wedding ring discouraged some familiar faces along the road.

On one night in Atlantic City, Peter and Bob even managed to save me from temptation by introducing me to a new game. I'd arrived back to my hotel room to find a beautiful busty blonde stretched out in my bed, completely naked. I recognised Denise immediately; I'd met her before and we'd had some fun together when I'd passed through the area with The Animals. I was trying to be faithful to my poor Margaret back in England, but it had been over a month since I last saw her, I was feeling lonely and this girl was naked!

I don't know if anything would have actually happened, but I was approaching a rather compromising position with Denise when there was a loud knocking on my door. Not sure whether to be pleased or annoyed at being interrupted, I peeled myself free of Denise and went to answer it. Bob Levine shoved me to one side and ran into the room.

He was soaking wet and dressed only in a pair of very baggy Y-fronts and his socks, which left a trail of soggy footprints behind him as he paced the room.

'Nice underwear, very sexy,' Denise commented from the bed, pulling a sheet round her. Did nothing faze American girls?

Bob glared at her. The usually carefully arranged scraps of hair he still possessed were standing in wet fronds around his face and starting up a steady pit-a-patter of drops on to the carpet.

'Anyone out there, Tappy?' he said, turning to me.

I was still standing at the door, staring at him, but I glanced quickly up and down the corridor.

'No one. What the hell happened to you, Bob? What happened to your clothes?'

'Had to get rid of them. Incriminating evidence has to be disposed of, Tap.' He grinned.

I got Bob a robe and he explained. The boredom of a tour does funny things to people; it makes them come up with funny things to entertain themselves with. It was under the burden of boredom that 'Wash Out' was born.

Bob and Peter had filled up an ice bucket with freezing cold water and then laid in wait at the elevator doors on their floor of the hotel. As soon as the doors opened, they hurled the bucket in at the occupants, totally soaking everyone inside. Unfortunately for Bob and Peter, 'Wash Out' also soaked their trousers as well. He'd managed to run off before anyone recognised him, dump his wet trousers and then . . . well, gatecrash my evening.

'It's fantastic, Tappy!' Bob said, really laughing now. 'You've got to try it, man. We could do another one right now; it's the last thing they'd expect.'

'But where's Peter? Tell me he didn't get caught!'

'Shit, Peter! I forgot all about him! I'll go find him, hang on here.'

Bob left the room, his robe flapping behind him, and I was left alone with Denise once again. She was not looking impressed.

'I mean, how immature!' she said. 'A man of his age . . .'

The girl was beautiful and usually it would be against all my principles to disagree with a chest like that, but when Bob fell back through my hotel room door with a soggy Peter in tow, I realised that 'immaturity' was probably the best way out of an awkward situation. Soon it was me crouched alongside my small bald friend and one of the greatest pop stars of the age, ice bucket in hand, just waiting for the elevator doors to open and 'Wash Out'!

The Plastercasters #2

But the lovely Denise was not the only familiar face along the road and, running into groupies, it was not long before, once again, I met the best in the business: the Plastercasters.

Herman's Hermits were booked to play a gig in Los Angeles. I saw Peter to his room and left him to get some rest before the performance that night. Meanwhile, I strolled downstairs to get a drink and grab a couple of minutes to myself. There were two girls sitting propped up on barstools at the end of the bar; they caught my eye and grinned.

'Tappy!' the Plastercasters shouted. 'Long time no see. We hear you're a married man now, can that be true?'

'That's right. I finally found the girl of my dreams. Well, you girls wouldn't have me and I couldn't wait around for ever.'

'Oh, that's not fair, you never asked. We also heard that you're working with Peter Noone now. Don't suppose there's any chance that you could get us up to meet him? It's for the collection you understand.'

The Plastercasters were great fun, but I wasn't sure what Peter's reaction would be. The groupies for Herman's Hermits were generally very different from those I'd encountered with The Animals. They were much more respectable; either very young girls or middle-aged housewives. Peter and the band's relationship with the fans was relatively innocent; a few kisses on the cheek and signed autographs and that was that.

Peter and the band were all very young themselves and their behaviour was positively saintly compared to the antics I'd got up to on tour with The Animals. This suited my marital status, but I must admit that I was a little worried about introducing Peter to a pair of girls that specialised in plaster-casting genitals!

But we went upstairs. I woke Peter and told him about the girls. He looked shocked, but he was a sweet kid and wanted to be polite, so he got up and went through to greet them. At first Peter seemed reluctant to join the Plastercasters' collection; that was until the suggestion of casting his face came up.

'If you cast my face, then I'll let you do . . . well, the other thing. But I'd like a cast of my face. It'd be great, wouldn't it, Tappy?'

'Sure, Peter, whatever you want. But I don't know if the girls could do it.'

The Plastercasters looked at each other, then shrugged. 'We've never done a face before, but I don't see why not . . .'

Peter looked thrilled and was convinced to drop his trousers for the first cast, before they moved on to his face. It didn't start well. Even with a girl on her knees for him, Peter was obviously finding the whole situation strange and not at all exciting. After witnessing the tiny mould that Hilton had been forced to contribute to the Plastercasters' collection after he failed to rise to the occasion, I thought that I had to do something to help Peter out. I nudged the girl that was busy mixing up the plaster and whispered in her ear.

'Do him a favour and remind him about the other cast.'

She smiled and leant down to Peter's ear, where I could hear her telling him just how beautiful that face-cast was going to look. Soon enough her words had the desired effect and the Plastercasters added a very respectable mould of Peter Noone to their collection.

'Now my face!' Peter shouted, pulling up his trousers. 'You promised. Please let's do it now.'

Laughing, the girls laid him down and mixed up some more plaster. We placed a straw in his mouth, so that he'd be able to breathe; I even tried to fit a couple more straws up his nostrils, but it was too painful for Peter and we had to remove them. The plaster was spread on and everything seemed to be going to plan, that is until the plaster started to set and, therefore, to swell.

This was the first face-cast that the Plastercasters had attempted and, in their usual line of business, there was no need for breathing holes, but as the plaster set and swelled it squeezed the straw in Peter's mouth and cut off his air supply. Peter thrashed about, banging his hands against the floor.

'He can't breathe!' I yelled to the girls. 'Quickly, we've got to get this thing off him!'

We tugged and pulled at the plaster mask, but it was stuck firm. The Plastercasters were hysterical and screamed at me to do something. What could I do? Here was the man that I was personally responsible for, suffocating on a hotel room floor in front of me, because of two girls that I'd introduced him to. I looked around the room, desperately searching for something I could use to free Peter from the mask. In the end I grabbed a beer bottle from the side table and smashed it against the plaster. I didn't really think about what I was doing; I just knew that I had to do something or Peter was going to die.

Thankfully, it worked. The plaster cracked and we were able to free Peter's mouth and nose. Peter gasped for air, chunks of white plaster still clinging to the rest of his face.

'Christ, thank you,' he panted. 'I thought I was a gonna there.'

So the plaster cast of Peter's face was never completed. After the girls left, he had to soak for ages in a hot bath before the remains of his plaster mask eventually dissolved. The red marks, where the plaster had gripped his skin, still showed on his face at that night's performance. I made sure that Peter was out of the way when tales of the Plastercasters came up. He may have made a proud contribution to their collection, but not many artists had nearly died in their company. It wasn't a situation that he or I really wanted to be reminded of.

Married to the Princess and her Mother

While Peter was recovering from his close encounter with the Plastercasters, I was still dealing with the more enthusiastic of his fans. I had remained faithful to my wife since our wedding six months before, but the nature of my job as a road manager kept me away from home the majority of the time. Despite most of Herman's Hermits' fans being a far gentler crowd, there were still beautiful girls willing to do anything to meet their heroes. And, when I was back home, things were not as easy as they could be.

I loved my wife and I loved spending time with her. Whenever I got some time off, I caught the first flight to London, drove straight back to our little flat on Edgware Road and later to our beautiful new apartment in Devonshire Close, which was just round the corner from Margaret's offices in Harley Street. It was wonderful to fall into Margaret's waiting arms. We had some beautiful times together, but our happiness was always clouded by her worries for her family back in Poland.

Margaret's mother was Alina Slesinska, one of the world's leading sculptors. It was only a matter of months after our wedding that she was able to join her daughter and me in London. The requirements for her political asylum in England required her to prove that she would be an asset to the UK and her artistic talent more than fulfilled that proviso. After a couple of gruelling meetings at the Home Office, we organised her flights and she came to stay with us.

Alina was a fantastic woman and we always got on well, but with my brief visits to London being the only time that I got to spend with Margaret, having my mother-in-law under the same roof did start to cut into our love-life. Margaret didn't believe in having sex at night. 'Night-time is for sleeping, Tappy', she'd tell me. We'd always managed to entertain ourselves well enough with passionate afternoon sessions, but with Alina in the next room, it was hard to keep that romantic mood alive . . . at least for us.

Alina, on the other hand, was having a great time. As her husband was the Prince of Poland, there was obviously no way that he would be allowed to join her in England. But Alina was a beautiful and

Tappy (middle row, second from the right), in 1956, wearing a naughty nude tie, posing in his school photograph at the Park Secondary Modern School Whitley Bay. He was later reprimanded by the headmaster.

In 1956, kneeling in front of his school band (front, centre) at the Park Secondary Modern, Tappy is playing the guitar of his teacher, Mr Glegg.

(Left) Loving music and playing guitar, Tappy is showing off his first professional guitar in 1958.

(Below) Wild days began when Tappy played guitar with The Wildcats. From left to right: Harry Dixon, Tappy, Hilton Valentine and Ronnie McKenzie.

(Right) Tappy Wright was the man with the van. Seen here, in 1963, sitting on the roof of The Animals' Commer Van with Harry Dixon (beside him) and Ronnie McKenzie of The Wildcats. Without it the bands would not have made it to the gigs.

(Above) First sign of success for the Animals on their US tour, as they headline on The Paramount Theatre's marquee, in New York in 1964.

(Right) The Animals: (back row) Chas Chandler, Eric Burdon and John Steel, (front row) Alan Price and Hilton Valentine.

(Left) Tappy looking very dapper and charming for an interview about Jimi with local press in Whitley Bay in 1970.

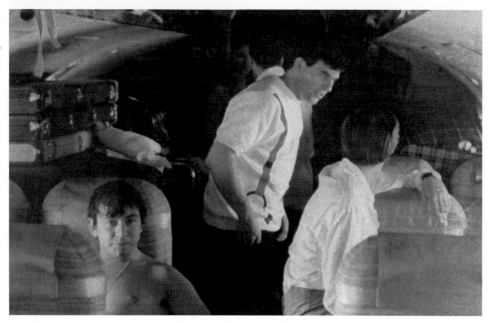

The Animals enjoying their private plane, a DC6, going from gig to gig during their 1966 US tour. Eric Burdon is in the foreground with Tappy behind talking to Johnny Steel.

Hilton Valentine grinding up for his special brew on the plane.

(Right) Taking some time off for a little sight-seeing, here is Johnny Steel and Tappy in New York in 1964 outside the City Squire Hotel.

(Left) Mike Jeffrey, rock manager extraordinaire, was always wheeling and dealing on the telephone in his New York office.

(Right) Brian Jones (guitarist with the Rolling Stones) was to introduce Jimi Hendrix at the Monterey Festival in 1967.

Tappy playing Jimi Hendrix's guitar – a Fender Mustang – in 2009.

34 Montagu Square was rented to Jimi Hendrix by Ringo Starr. Jimi wrote 'The Wind Cries Mary' here, before his eviction for rowdy behaviour.

The Hendrix management team's reunion at Gerry Stickles' in Venice Beach Hotel in 2007. Sitting front left, is Tappy, next to Gerry who is sitting in the middle.

Tappy and Ike Turner reminiscing at Ike's home in California just before Ike passed away in December 2007.

Reunion of old friends and colleagues in Orlando, Florida, in 2007. From the left: Tappy, Eric Burdon (centre) and Bob Levene.

vibrant woman and she was never short of offers during her time with us in London. Lord Bertrand Russell was her most frequent visitor and, with their dinner dates often not ending until breakfast, it soon became obvious that they were *very* 'good friends'. At least someone's love-life was working out!

What with my long absences and these pressures at home, resisting the ever-willing groupies became harder and harder. Margaret always kept well away from my working life; she'd met some of my better friends in the business, but I think that she wanted to keep our married life separate. This made it even easier to stray and, much as I still loved my wife, eventually I did.

Pleasing Peter

It was the summer of 1966, I had been married for about six months and I can't really explain how it first happened. One too many drinks and one too many lonely nights and, before I knew it, I was sleeping with groupies again. As my wife had always insisted on the separation between our personal and professional lives, I think that I truly thought of my life in the States with Peter as something different. The girls were nothing to do with Margaret, nothing to do with love or married life. I was still young and I thought that I was just having fun.

For Peter Noone, however, the man who could literally have had any girl he chose, sex was off the agenda. He was young, but to be honest he was about the same age as I had been when The Animals first came to America. You would have thought that, with all those teenage hormones racing around his body, he would have grabbed anything in a skirt, but Peter wasn't like The Animals and me. He'd been a child star back in the UK; screaming girls were nothing new to him and, despite his different background and upbringing, I think that he wanted to save himself for something special. Maybe even for his beautiful French wife, Mireille Strasser, whom he would meet and marry in November 1968 and remain with to this day.

But in 1966, Peter's attitude was a puzzle to me and the other members of Herman's Hermits. However, I soon discovered that it wasn't that he was disinterested in sex (he was a healthy young boy, after all) it's just that he didn't really want to be directly involved. I was his personal road manager and if I could give the boy a little education and a little performance, it wasn't harming anyone and I was happy to help.

One night Karl Green (the bassist in Herman's Hermits) and I picked up a mother and daughter and brought them back to my hotel room. Peter hated to be alone, so when we were on tour I always made sure that we had a suite with adjoining rooms and a connecting door, so that I would be on hand if he needed me. This meant that when Karl and I got the girls back, I was able to introduce them to Peter, who was lying in the living room area watching TV. After a couple of minutes of polite conversation Karl and I moved the girls into my room and left Peter to his TV programme.

I could hear the TV blaring through the wall and I felt sorry for poor Peter, through there on his own. As I went to close the door, I paused. Well, this was bound to be better to watch than some lame cable show! I left the door ajar and returned to Karl and the girls. Karl and I had already agreed who was with whom: me with the daughter and him with the mother. They were both lovely, but age before beauty, and the mother and Karl took the bed and the daughter and I settled down on the floor. Determined to give Peter something good to watch, I set about giving the performance of a lifetime. I kept twisting my poor girl round so that she'd be clearly visible through the gap in the door. This would certainly give Peter something to think about on those long nights alone.

Once we were done and the girls had settled down for the night, I crept back into the living room of our hotel suite. I wanted to know how Peter had rated my performance. But there was Peter just as we'd left him a few hours before, curled up fast asleep on the sofa, with a teddy bear under one arm.

He'd missed the whole thing!

Glorious Graceland

Despite my failed attempts to corrupt Peter's innocence, he continued in the same way. One of the most desired men in the world, who only wanted his right hand for company.

We continued on our tour and I liked Peter more and more. We worked hard, played the occasional pranks and, although I was still a young man and the age difference between Peter and me was less than a decade, I was protective of him. I knew that Peter needed looking after and I was the man to do it. Of course, my major memory of trying to protect Peter was the day that I had hung up on Elvis Presley after accusing him of being a prank caller, back in 1965 before I'd even started officially working for him. Although Elvis had been very gracious about my mistake, it still played on my mind, and when Herman's Hermits passed through Memphis, I couldn't help remembering Elvis Presley's invitation to his Graceland home.

I spoke to Peter about it, but he was too busy to take a day out.

'You should go though, Tappy. He invited you at the same time.'

'He wouldn't even remember me; it was you he wanted to see.'

'Don't be like that. You've met Elvis, he's a lovely guy. I'm sure he'd be happy to see you. Anyway, he's not likely to forget the man who put the phone down on him!'

So that day, after giving Elvis's people some warning of my visit, I set off for the white towers of Graceland. Elvis was there to greet me, just as handsome and polite as he had been a year ago.

'It's great to see you again, please come in and make yourself at home. Me and the guys are just hanging out.'

Graceland was stunning. I'd been in America long enough to spend time at some of the most incredibly glamorous houses and hotels, but Graceland was something else. The first thing that struck me, and I know that this will sound stupid, was the sofa. It was a huge thing, beautifully white and long enough to seat at least ten people. The whole place was like a palace; everything on a scale five times larger than normal.

'Like it?' Elvis said, walking up behind where I stood, frozen in awe at the splendour surrounding me.

'It's beautiful.'

Elvis grinned. 'Thanks. It's home, you know?'

We walked through and sat down on the sofa. There were groups of people hanging around the place, sitting at the white grand piano and curled up laughing on the floor. They were mostly men and the few women present were obviously wives and girlfriends of the other guests. Elvis Presley was a man's man and he enjoyed, as he put it, 'just hanging out with the guys. No pressure.' This was no groupie party, just friends over for drinks. Maybe Elvis and Peter Noone had more in common than they realised?

Again, I was struck by Elvis's shyness. One of his friends brought over a pitcher of lemonade and it was Elvis who served out the drinks. He was the most famous man in the world and yet there was not an ounce of egotism in him. Another friend, dressed casually like the others in jeans and a cowboy shirt, sat down next to me and we got to talking about England. Elvis cut in, interested to hear what I had to say. He seemed to find it easier to talk when he wasn't the centre of the conversation.

'I'd love to go there, man,' he said, talking about England. 'I'd love to meet some of my British fans in their own country. But it's difficult, you know. I have a duty to my American fans after all.'

He trailed off and I got the feeling that we were touching on a sensitive area. It was only afterwards that I learnt that Elvis's ability to travel was limited by his manager, The Colonel. The Dutch Colonel Tom Parker's immigration status was always in dispute and he obviously did not want to risk being refused entry back into the US for the sake of a foreign tour.

Along with the beautiful piano, the living room in Graceland was also home to an enviable collection of guitars; just glancing around I caught sight of a number of Gibson guitars propped up in a corner. One of Elvis's friends picked up one of the instruments and started plucking out an old blues tune, which Elvis immediately recognised.

'Man, I love that tune!' He sat back with a smile, drumming out the beat on the sofa cushions. 'Without black music like that, none of us would be here now. Wow, that beat is something else.'

I seized the chance to steer our conversation on to music and mentioned that I used to work with The Animals. There was a barely perceptible change on Elvis's handsome face as I mentioned the British band, but I realised I'd put my foot in it again.

'Well, sir, I can't say I know that much about those Animals guys. I keep my stable as The House of the Rising Sun.' He laughed and told me about the new golden Palomino he'd just purchased, called Rising Sun. But he soon switched back to his gracious self. 'It was a great track, "The House of the Rising Sun", and that man Eric Burdon has a fantastic voice. I didn't want to offend you, Mr Wright.'

Here he was offering me his company and incredible hospitality, and he was worried about offending me! I assured him that nothing could be further from the truth.

After a couple more pleasurable hours with Elvis and his friends, the time came for me to leave and get back to Peter. He sent me on my way with best wishes to my wife and Peter Noone. 'I'd love to come see him play tonight, but it all gets so crazy. It's a shame, sometimes it would be great to just get out and hear some of the live acts around at the moment. But I can't complain; I'm a lucky man.'

It was with a strange kind of sadness that I drove away from Graceland that day. Elvis was a wonderful man and Graceland was his palace, but it was also his prison. He was a lucky man, but as I went off with Peter to the gig that night, I did pity him the restrictions of his success.

Little did I know that after spending some time with the King of Rock 'n' Roll, I was just a few months away from meeting the future contender for the Crown.

CHAPTER 8

Destiny Calls: Old Friends and New Adventures

Down the Boardwalk

After my incredible encounter with Elvis Presley at his home in Graceland, I honestly believed that there was nothing left in the trappings of musical success to surprise me. That was until, after following Herman's Hermits out of Memphis, we arrived in Atlantic City and took a trip down the Boardwalk. And in all my years as a road manager, it proved to be the most original drive I ever remember taking.

Herman's Hermits were due to finish their tour with a performance at the end of the pier, but the promoters were struggling to find a way to get us to the venue. Thousands of fans were packed into the world-famous walkway, desperate to catch a glimpse of Peter and the boys. The fans had been there all day and, in their panic, the promoters had been driven to desperate measures; they'd hired us an armoured truck!

'It's the only way that we can get you guys through safely,' the promoter explained when we arrived. 'It took some getting, but those girls are going crazy out there. We had to do something.'

A huge, grey-plated truck pulled up and with some trepidation we climbed in. The windows were blacked out in the back of the van and, with all of us squashed in together, it was very claustrophobic. But it seemed that the armoured truck was our only option, so we set off down the Boardwalk to the pier.

But we were only halfway there when the fans realised exactly who was hiding inside the truck. They went totally wild. We could hear them clambering up on to the sides of the truck; their heels clattering as they fought to find a foothold on the steel-clad exterior. The truck started to sway and rock and soon the chaos outside was mirrored inside. The driver wasn't able to hear us over the noise of the crowd and we started to worry that the truck could tip over into the water. The stale air in the back of the truck seemed to be running out; we were locked in and, frankly, terrified.

By the time that we finally reached our venue, Peter was justifiably furious. We stood there drinking in the fresh air and freedom as he screamed at the promoter.

After Herman's Hermits had finished the gig, there was no way that we were getting back into that truck. I don't think that any of us could have coped with a repeat of that nightmare journey. So we took our chances and made a run for it. *Hard Day's Night* eat your heart out! I wouldn't have thought that our journey back to the hotel could have been any more hair-raising than our arrival at the gig, but running down that pier with what felt like the entire audience at our heels was a truly fitting, if terrifying, end to my time with Herman's Hermits.

In fact, even after we got back to the safety of our hotel rooms, the police had to be called to disperse the crowds. Not content with nearly tearing an armoured truck apart, these girls were willing to pull down the hotel brick by brick if it meant getting close to Peter and the band.

Bliss with Billie-Jo

With the tour finished, we headed for New York as there was still work to be done in the Teen Mail offices of Bob Levine. I was sitting sifting through the fan mail and attempting to compose some answers on behalf of the acts that we represented, when Bob Levine's wife Cathy came into the office, bringing with her Billie-Jo, a friend of Allan Clarke of the Hollies.

I'd met Billie-Jo before, but she looked different. It was a hot and sultry mid-morning in New York and it's always amazed me how much sexier women become in the heat. I don't think that I've ever been as grateful for humidity as I was sitting there at my desk and watching the beads of perspiration creeping down into Billie-Jo's cleavage.

'Is Bob about?' Cathy asked, glancing around the office.

'Right here, baby!' Bob answered, grabbing his wife and nuzzling her neck. 'Oh, you're hot. Just the way I like you!'

'Well, I aim to please.'

What was all this about? Someone must have put something in the water if even the old married couples were rubbing up against each other in public. They didn't show any sign of slowing down and, when a red-faced Bob Levine finally announced a coffee break, I thought that it would be best to leave them alone.

'You fancy joining me for a milkshake?' I asked Billie-Jo. She looked over at Cathy and Bob, who were wrapped in each other's arms and nodded. We left the office with the sound of Cathy's laughter echoing after us down the hall.

We grabbed the first booth that we could find in the milkshake place and made ourselves comfortable.

'I guess that we should take our time,' Billie-Jo said with a laugh, as she picked up a straw.

I took a moment to study her, as she sat there opposite me, busy with her milkshake. She was a lovely girl and she had a one of those bubbly personalities that lit up her face and made her even more attractive. Her light-brown hair was hanging loose around her shoulders. The heat had gathered it into tendrils, which pointed down to those small pert breasts. I swallowed hard as I noticed the firm nipples pushing out against the fabric of her sleeveless vest and the dark sweat patches that gathered under each breast, causing the material to cling closer to her beautiful body. I could imagine those nipples in my mouth; licking the sweat from her chest . . .

'Tappy?' Billie-Jo must have been talking to me, but as I looked up she laughed. 'Like what you see?'

'Definitely,' I said closing my mouth and giving her a wink.

'I'm my own person, Tappy. I'm free to do what I want with whomever I want to do it with.' She sipped at her milkshake and then lifted her glass up, resting its cool surface against her cheek. She shifted in her chair so that her leg was pressed against mine. 'I've got an idea. It's far too hot to think about working. Do you think that I could use your apartment? I could do with a long cold shower.' She glanced down at the massive bulge in my trousers. 'And it looks like you could do with one, too.'

I laughed. 'I think that it's heat of a different kind that's doing this to me,' I said, gesturing at my trousers. 'But a shower sounds too good to miss. Fuck it, let's do it! I'm sure Bob won't even notice I'm gone. But it will have to be my hotel rather that my apartment. Gerry, the guy I share the place with, has his girl in town for the weekend, so I'm in a hotel.'

'Even better,' Billie-Jo said, grabbing my hand. 'We won't have any interruptions.'

We ran out of the milkshake place, giggling like teenagers. I hailed a cab and soon we were standing in my room at the City Squire Hotel. Billie-Jo turned to me with a smile and peeled off her damp clothes, flinging them to the floor.

'Phew! That's better. I hate being so hot and sticky.' She ran a hand over her breasts, wiping the sweat into a shine. 'Now where's the shower?'

I stood and watched as she crossed the room and disappeared into the shower. As I heard the water start, my imagination ran wild.

'Are you coming or not?' Billie-Jo shouted.

I didn't need to be asked twice. I quickly pulled off my clothes and climbed into the shower after her. The cold water made me gasp as it struck my body, but as soon as I'd become accustomed to the temperature I could direct my attention to more important things. The sight of Billie-Jo with the cool water running over her naked body was hypnotising. Her nipples stood out, rigid against the cold stream, and I couldn't resist a moment longer. I pulled her towards me, but she wriggled free and giggled.

'You behave yourself, Tappy,' she said sternly and then handed me a bar of soap. 'I need someone to wash my back.'

I groaned, but did as I was told. With long, slow movements I massaged the soap into her skin, lingering over her buttocks. This was doing nothing to help me cool down. Billie-Jo started to lean back into my caresses and then she leaned forward so that the water was beating down directly onto her back. The white soap suds ran down her buttocks. Her legs slid apart and I grabbed her tightly and rammed my cock deep inside her.

'Yes! Yes!' Billie-Jo shouted. 'Do it harder, you bastard.'

Always happy to oblige, I banged away, desperate to ease the ache in my groin. She spun round to face me and I picked her up off her feet, so her legs were wrapped tightly around my waist. With the water still pouring over us we worked our way to orgasm. I seemed to be making a habit out of only sleeping with women for the first time when they were soaking wet! Not that I was complaining.

Billie-Jo and I remained in the shower for over an hour, examining and exploring one another's bodies. That was the start of a marathon sex session which lasted from that Friday afternoon, straight through to Monday morning. We shut ourselves off from the outside world. I took the phone off the hook and put the 'Do Not Disturb' sign on the door. When we needed to eat, we did it in bed; drinking champagne and munching fruit, before our desire for one another took us over again.

But with Monday morning, reality dawned. We stood and laughed at how we had wrecked my hotel room: tables were knocked over; towels, sheets and clothes lay knotted together on the floor, along with trays of discarded room service food. The worst damage was to the headboard. It had managed to remain intact through all of our activity, but I had to wrench it free of the wall behind, leaving a huge dent. It was as good as a metal plate on the wall, to commemorate a wonderful weekend.

I walked Billie-Jo to the elevator and we said our goodbyes. We knew that it would never happen again. For all her talk of being a free agent, I knew that, when it came down to it, she was devoted to one man. But, despite the fact the weekend had obviously just been about sex, I was very fond of her and I was sad to see her go. With one last lingering kiss, Billie-Jo left and I walked over to the stairs. I'd go down the slow way and get some breakfast in the hotel coffee bar. Maybe I could find some friendly faces there to lighten my mood?

Shocking the Neighbours

I was pleased to see Peter Noone sitting downstairs drinking coffee. I knew that he was staying in the City Squire Hotel over the weekend and was hoping that I'd manage to catch up with him. I sat down with him and we caught up on the latest gossip. I didn't tell him all about Billie-Jo, but I did say that I'd had a hectic weekend and I thought that he guessed what that meant.

We were just finishing our coffee when Peter's manager, Harvey Lisberg, came charging over. He looked furious. 'Tappy! Maybe you can help me, because no other fucker seems to want to,' Harvey gestured over towards the reception desk. 'Do you know whose staying in 301?'

Oh, shit. That was my room number. But there was no way that I was going to mention that to Harvey when he was in this mood. 'Why? What's the problem?' I asked, trying to look innocent.

'The problem is that my mother is staying in 302 and she hasn't had a wink of sleep all weekend. I left her here because I thought it was a respectable joint and she had to put up with some fucking pervert holed up in the room next door with a broad. They've been swearing, screaming and slapping one another all weekend. My mother's hysterical. She was too embarrassed to even ask to swap rooms. She's a nice Jewish wife; she's not used to all this kind of crap. I'm gonna kill the bastard when I get my hands on him!'

Peter must have seen my horrified face and put two and two together, because as I caught his eye he coughed and spluttered into his coffee and Harvey had to bang him on the back.

'Take it easy, Peter!' Harvey said, mistaking his reaction for disgust. 'Here's my mother now. I need something in this hotel to make a good impression on her.'

Harvey's mother came through the tables towards us. She really did look distraught; I couldn't believe that I'd subjected this little old lady to an audio version of my sexual antics with Billie-Jo, but at least her arrival gave Peter time to recover himself from his fit of laughter.

'It's terrible, just terrible,' she was muttering, a handkerchief pressed to her eyes. 'You have to get me out of here, Harvey; I can't bear it any longer. What is the world coming to?'

Harvey sat his mother down at our table and introduced us. I could feel my face burning as she burst into the story of her weekend once again. Peter was obviously struggling to keep a straight face as I squirmed in my chair.

'Don't worry, Mrs Lisberg,' I said finally, giving her hand a reassuring pat. 'It sounds to me like those people next door were just watching movies and got carried away. These modern movies can make very loud sounds, you know? Now I better get going.'

I left the hotel quickly, Peter giving me a wink and dissolving into laughter as I left, much to the confusion of Harvey Lisberg and his mother. I did feel guilty about Mrs Lisberg's traumatic experience, but even that wasn't enough to dampen the wonderful memories that I had of my time with Billie-Jo.

I got back to my apartment, showered and changed, and then set out for work. But it seemed that Mrs Lisberg wasn't the only person that I'd shocked during my weekend away from reality.

'Where the fuck, have you been?' Bob Levine bellowed as I walked into the office.

'Sorry Bob, I had some . . . urm . . . family business to attend to this weekend.'

'Oh yeah? And Billie-Jo just happens to be a close family friend does she? Pull the other one! Allan's pissed at her and it's just as well that he didn't know that we couldn't find you. As usual, I covered your ass, Tappy. Anyway, now you're back you can get going. You're off to Ohio.'

'Ohio? With who?'

Mr Como and Mr Wright

The answer to that question was Perry Como. I met him at the airport in New York and we flew to the Kentucky Derby together. He insisted that we be seated next to one another so that he could get to know me. I'd obviously heard of Perry before, as a great entertainer, but by the end of that flight I had gained a genuine personal respect for the man. My work at Teen Mail had meant that I was dealing with a lot of new and young artists; it was great to be back working with a true old professional.

We arrived in Kentucky and prepared for the late afternoon show. There was no need for me to arrange a hotel, as Perry liked to fly back home straight after a performance if possible.

I was looking forward to the show and Perry did not disappoint. He sang to a full orchestra and his entire performance was faultless. In order to add a bit of glamour to the proceedings, Perry had a song and dance act supporting him, The Young Americans. They were meant to represent the good, clean-living American ideal. All their costumes were based around the American flag, stars and stripes mounted on soft silky material. It was refreshing to see a good, wholesome family show for a change.

The good feeling created on stage stayed with me as I saw Perry to his limo after the show.

'It's been a pleasure to meet you, Mr Como,' I said, shaking his hand. 'It's not often I get to work with such pleasant people.'

'Thank you, Tappy, that's real nice to hear. You take care of yourself and I hope that I get to work with you again some day.'

I waved until the limousine was out of sight and then turned back into the venue. I felt truly uplifted and content and I wanted to keep the feeling for as long as possible. I thought that I may as well head back inside and see what was happening.

I collapsed into the hotel bed that night, wondering if I was getting too old for this. I missed my Polish princess and looked forward to seeing her back in London.

Happy Coincidence for a New Beginning

But before I returned to London for a holiday with my wife, I received a call from Chas Chandler. Chas had left The Animals shortly after me; the tour they'd done with Herman's Hermits had been his last. It was great to speak to him again. I was feeling pretty sorry for myself, to be honest. I'd let what could have been the job of a lifetime with The Animals pass me by; I'd have to leave my wife hundreds of miles behind me again and I couldn't think of any way to change my situation.

Chas, however, had great plans for his own career. After his experiences with The Animals, he was in no hurry to join another band. Chas was stepping into management and he was viewing a prospective act that very night.

'Could you come along, Tappy? I'd really value your opinion, but I think that I might have found something really special here.'

Keen to spend time doing anything rather than consider my future, and happy with the idea of catching up with Chas again, I put off my flight and set off to the Café Wha? which was (and is) one of the most famous nightclubs in Greenwich Village and had long been associated with profiling new acts. It was September 1966 and the trendy Village area was alive with jazz and blues. Chas had been approached by a girl called Linda Keith. Linda was Keith Richards' ex-girlfriend; she'd seen this new and unsigned act perform and fallen for them. She had tried to interest The Rolling Stones' manager, Andrew Loog Oldham, in taking them on. He'd refused, saying that he 'didn't think they had a future', but Linda hadn't given up. When she heard that Chas Chandler was looking for new artists to start his career in management, she had called him immediately to tip him off about the fantastic band that would be performing at the Café Wha?

It's strange to think of the list of coincidences that go into making musical history and, for us, the list didn't end there. Chas and I got to the Café Wha? and took our seats at the side of a small dancefloor.

'I saw this guy last night,' Chas explained. 'I think he's great, but I could do with a second opinion. This is a big step for me, Tappy.'

'Don't worry about it, Chas. I'm happy to help. Hey, look, they're starting.'

Jimmy James and the Blue Flames took to the stage. They were a good band; they started beating out some soul and rock covers and Café Wha? started heaving. I could see why Chas was interested, but I didn't really see anything truly remarkable about their performance. That was until the guitarist really started getting into the set. This guy was incredible; the tunes just seemed to roll through him. As the tempo picked up he began playing the guitar with his teeth; pulling it up behind his head and tearing out the tunes.

Chas caught my expression and leant over with a grin. 'That Jimmy James is something else, isn't he?' he said, gesturing at the guitarist with a tilt of his glass.

'You're right there!' I watched as Jimmy crawled round the tiny stage, the crowd roaring their approval. 'You know what, Chas; I think I recognise him from somewhere.'

After the set was finished, Jimmy came over to our table and Chas introduced us to each other. 'It's Jimmy Hendrix really,' Jimmy told me in his soft, polite voice. 'That Jimmy James thing is just for the band.'

Jimmy was obviously a lovely guy but, as we settled down with our drinks to talk about his future with Chas, I couldn't shake the idea that we'd met before. In the end I asked him.

'I don't think so, man,' Jimmy said, looking carefully at my face. 'But you do look kinda familiar. You work in the business, right?'

'Yeah, that's right. Tappy's been with me and The Animals since the beginning, but we lost him to Premier earlier in the year.'

'And you just couldn't carry on without me, could you, Chas?'

Chas choked on his drink. 'Oh yeah! Something like that!'

But Jimmy was watching me again. 'Premier as in Premier Talent?'

'That's right.'

Jimmy clicked his fingers and laughed. 'That's how I know you, Tappy. I played the Paramount with Little Richard. Jeez, what a day that was! I was one of the guys that helped you push him into that elevator.'

'*You* were the guitarist in the bear-skin hat!'

'Don't remind me!' Jimmy said, letting his head fall into his hands and groaning with laughter.

'You were great, though; I remember that you were the only one of the band to stop and help me and Bob out.'

'Hey, man. Anyone giving his band a dressing down like that . . . then they are asking for it!'

Between us, we explained to Chas about that night at the Paramount Theater back in April 1965 with Soupy Sales giving Little Richard a lesson in good manners.

'Well, I'm glad that you guys know each other,' said Chas, 'because I want to take Jimmy to England in a couple of days' time. I know you're headed back that way, Tappy; we're going to tour and I'd really like it if you'd be willing to go on the road with Jimmy. What do you think? It'd be just like the old days with The Animals, eh?'

'Just like the old days' was not really what I was looking for. Jimmy was obviously a magnificent talent, but could I face the idea of getting back on the road in the UK with a new act? It was just what I was trying to escape from. I explained my position to Chas and he seemed to understand where I was coming from.

'I'd still like you to be involved, Tappy. I need to keep hold of all the people I can trust, just now. Listen, there will be an office. I know that it'd be a bit of a change for you, but it sounds like that's what you're after. Anyway, I can't think of anyone that knows more about this business than you. What about joining as part of the management team and helping me get Jimmy Hendrix out there in that way?'

It was a fantastic offer and just what I was looking for. This would give me the chance to settle down properly in London with Margaret and give me an exciting and challenging new job. It wasn't quite Hollywood, but it was good enough for me.

The Anim Experience

That short meeting in a smoky club in New York's Greenwich Village was the start of my time with Anim Ltd, the London-based company that Chas and Mike Jeffery created between them. Chas had decided to go 50:50 with Mike, letting him deal with the management side of the business and leaving Chas free to concentrate on record production. I had stepped into a completely different life.

That unknown guitarist from Jimmy James and the Blue Flames had arrived in London with Chas on 24 September 1966. They'd changed his name from Jimmy to Jimi on their flight over. But he was not the only name on our books: we inherited Eric Burdon and the New Animals, the Alan Price Set, and a collection of other names gained through Mike's connections and Chas's ear for new talent (Goldie and the Gingerbreads, The Soft Machine, Eire Apparent, Emperor Roscoe [a BBC DJ] and Madeline Bell, to name a few).

Anim Ltd was situated on 39 Gerard Street, in what is now Chinatown in London. I was proud to walk up to the four-storey red-brick building with its bronze plate on the door, announcing the name, which was an obvious homage to the time that Mike and Chas had spent with The Animals.

A Chinese restaurant and a mysterious dark-fronted building lay on either side of Anim. The unknown building offered us the chance for much speculation but, with the combination of gorgeous-looking girls and guys and shady-looking characters who moved in and out of the place, it was probably a porn movie studio. But we had plenty of space and we shared the building with Terence Donovan, the fashion photographer, so we had plenty of beautiful girls passing our doors on their way to his studio upstairs. Not that I was looking, of course!

I loved the work that the office gave me to do. Our management team was very strong and, with Chas and Mike at the helm, I knew my bosses well and respected them. Chas had already installed Jimi Hendrix at the Hyde Park Towers Hotel on Inverness Terrace in London and had arranged two British musicians to form a band for him: Mitch Mitchell, a fabulous drummer who'd worked with Georgie Fame, and Noel Redding on bass, whom Chas had discovered when he came to audition for Eric Burdon and the New Animals. The Jimi Hendrix Experience was born.

Hey Joe

In October, Jimi and the Experience went on a four-day tour to France, supporting Johnny Hallyday. But it wasn't long before Chas got Jimi and the band into the studio. Chas was excited about the results and asked me to come and see what they were producing. I headed down to the De Lane Lea Studios on Kingsway in London, to see what Jimi and the boys were up to.

I had no idea that I was walking in on musical history; this was just another day at work. I wandered in as the Jimi Hendrix Experience was taking a short break from recording. Jimi seemed relaxed and wandered over to say hello, but Chas could barely contain himself and grabbed my arm as soon as I entered the room.

'We've got a single here, Tappy. There's no doubt about it, this one is going to be big!' He lowered his voice. 'Don't tell Jimi I said that, I'm trying to bully some more out of him. Don't want my artists getting complacent, now do I?'

I laughed. 'You're a producer through and through, Chas Chandler!'

Chas grinned. 'That I am and I'm loving it.'

I hung around for about an hour and watched them record.

'It sounds great, Chas. But I know this song, don't I?'

'Should do, it's one of the numbers we heard Jimi perform in Café Wha? "Hey Joe". It was the song that made me sign him.' Chas looked across at Jimi and the band. 'It's going to be the making of him, mark my words.'

I left them to it and headed back home to my wife. In the same way that I'd experienced with The Animals, recording sessions went on through the night. But by 1966, the recording process was much longer. I'd witnessed the recording of 'The House of the Rising Sun'

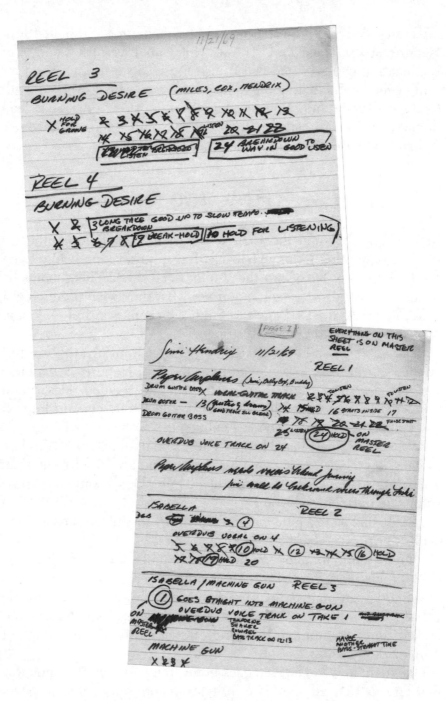

*Jimi Hendrix's studio notes made by the sound recording engineer, just in case
they forgot the music.*

in just four minutes, but 'Hey Joe' was a much longer project. Like 'The House of the Rising Sun', 'Hey Joe' was a cover of an alleged folk song which Jimi had adapted to his own unique style, from the arrangement of composer and folk singer Tim Rose's slow version that Chas had heard performed back in Greenwich Village. He was able to take days getting it right, but the final product proved that it had been time well spent. Now all Chas had to do was find a record label to release it.

This wasn't as easy as it should have been. Chas's vision, when it came to Jimi Hendrix's talent, was not immediately shared by the music industry bosses in the UK. In the end, he had to rely on Mike Jeffery's connections to get 'Hey Joe' released on the French label, Barclay Records. We just had to hope that Jimi's performances in a UK tour could convince the public to pressure a UK record label for a pressing that we could more easily distribute.

Eventually we struck gold with a new independent label that was being formed by The Who's management team. Track Records came along at exactly the right time; just as Chas had before. They signed The Jimi Hendrix Experience and released 'Hey Joe' for distribution through Polydor.

Jimi's reputation was building and UK chart positions were looking hopeful, but I'd rejected the job of trailing round after the Experience when they hit the road in the UK; so they set off and I remained behind. It felt wonderful to be back home. I could, at last, go home to my wife after a day's work at the office. Her mother, Alina, had got financial backing for her own studio by this time, so our home was our own again. My relationship and marriage blossomed. Finally, our life could be relatively normal.

However, before I could settle down properly into a happy home life, I discovered that Chas had different plans for me.

'I'm really sorry about this, Tap. I know that you didn't want to go on the road . . .'

'Chas! I told you! You promised me an office job, son.'

'Yeah, well, it's just this once. I promise you, Tappy, just once. I need a man I can trust. It's an American act, Ike and Tina Turner, and it's their first solo tour in the UK. They need your experience, Tappy. It won't be for long.'

On the Road with Ike and Tina

So I set out into 1967 doing the job that I'd promised myself that I would leave behind. I wasn't happy about it, but Chas had been good to me and I didn't want to cross Mike Jeffery, so I took it on. It was just this once after all . . .

I drove round to Ike and Tina Turner's hotel in Kensington and introduced myself. They were still jet-lagged from their flight over from the States, but were very polite and seemed like a nice couple. Tina mentioned that they'd had to leave the children behind in California. 'It wouldn't be right to drag them round after us,' she told me. But apart from that one insight, she was mostly silent through that first conversation; it was Ike who did the talking.

We arranged to leave for Brighton the next day, for the first stop on their British tour. 'River Deep, Mountain High' had just hit the UK charts and received a much more positive reception than it had in the States, so Ike and Tina were keen to meet their British fans.

The following day we set off. Ike and Tina would drive down to the venue with me, their band following on in a hired van. Ike and Tina chatted to each other as I drove; they talked about their performances, shared anecdotes about the children and their relationship appeared normal. My first impressions of Tina as a quiet woman were confirmed; it was Ike that I heard talking most of the time. He was undoubtedly the boss of the act and the marriage; Tina's soft whispers seemed to fade into the background.

But right from that first performance in Brighton, I realised that Ike and Tina were no ordinary act. I can honestly say that Ike and Tina Turner were the most exciting musical act I ever worked with. It was almost worth giving up a steady life in London to watch them perform each night. I had a little Philips record player that was installed in my car, not very glamorous compared to modern-day systems, but it was top of the range at the time.

Some of the happiest times of my life were spent spinning a 45-rpm disc in the front of a car and singing along at the top of my voice with Ike and Tina. Elvis Presley, The Beatles, old Soul and Blues classics, those two could put their own twist on to anything. I sometimes felt that I'd heard the best performance before we got to the gig. They were great journeys. As Ike and Tina relaxed in my company, our drives together became more and more of a pleasure, full of laughter and song. Tina may have been quietly spoken but, man, that girl could sing!

Of course, writing this now, it's tempting to view those days with Ike and Tina from a perspective coloured by Tina's later revelations of the intimidation and violence which she said that she suffered during her marriage to Ike, but the thing is that I liked Ike Turner.

Don't get me wrong, I liked Tina, too; in fact, it became a ritual between us to travel to Petticoat Lane every Sunday. They both loved London and insisted on being driven back to their hotel in the capital after a performance, however far away the gig had been. I didn't mind; at least I got to sleep in my own bed, even if I didn't get back to it until the early hours of the morning.

During the tour, I drove the three of us from London to Blackpool. When we arrived in Blackpool, I drove straight to the Pier to do a sound check for the show that evening. I wanted to make sure that everything was spot on. This was my first time that I'd ever worked with a full band including a brass section. Once everything had been checked, we decided to find a restaurant and eat before the show rather than after.

We arrived at a Chinese restaurant at 6.00pm. The restaurant had not long been open and only a few tables were occupied. 'Hi. Could I have a table for three please?,' I asked the Chinese-looking guy behind the counter. Suddenly another appeared and came running over to us waving his hands in the air: 'No! No! Sorry but we are all full tonight. There are no tables for you. Please you leave now.'

'Full! What do you mean full?' I asked, indicating to several empty tables. 'Have you got some kind of private party booked?' The guy behind the counter lowered his eyes in embarrassment, as he repeated, 'As I say, we are full! Please go away, shoo.'

'It's OK,' said Tina, quietly pulling on my arm. 'Let's go somewhere else; we're used to this by now.' I looked at her, puzzled and then suddenly it dawned on me what was happening. We were being refused entry to the restaurant because Ike and Tina were black! Furious, I grabbed hold of a table and threw it to the floor. 'This is my country,' I screamed. 'You lot don't belong here, so why don't you go back to China, where you belong!' Just who the hell did this horrible slimy man think he was? Ike and Tina tried to drag me out of the restaurant. As I struggled against them I hurled abuse at the guy. He shouted out something in Chinese and several more of them came running out of the kitchen carrying meat cleavers. 'Come on then, come on,' I shrieked at them, ready to fight, 'What's the matter? Too frightened now are you?' By this time I'd completely lost it and was out of control. With one almighty heave, Ike pushed me out of the restaurant door. The door was quickly locked after us.

When Ike and Tina eventually calmed me down we found a small fish and chip shop and sat outside eating our meal. They laughed at my earlier outburst and explained that it wasn't a big deal to them. They were often met with this kind of treatment. Apparently it happened a lot and the less fuss made the better. After this incident an immediate friendship struck up between us. I had proved to them that their colour did not matter to me, something that they both greatly appreciated.

On weekends, Ike remained back at their hotel and I'd collect Tina and take her to the market on Sunday morning. Sometimes my wife would come with us, but no one could match Tina's passion for the jumble sale of junk that could be found on the market stalls. By the end of their tour she'd collected so much stuff that I had to crate it up for her and ship it back to California; there was no way that they'd have got it all on the plane.

But Ike was the comedian of the pair. He was usually more than willing to share a joke, even if it was at his own expense. But he took his appearance very seriously; particularly his hair. And it was only through that concern that I got a taste of the famous Ike Turner temper.

Ike had a set routine before each performance: before leaving his hotel room he would smother his Afro curls in hair-wax, pulling his hair back until it was smooth and glossy and lying straight against his scalp. To preserve his hairdo he'd then wrap his head up in a turban, that way he could be guaranteed to arrive without a hair out of place. It was my job to inform him when we were around ten minutes from our destination and then he could remove the turban and present the waiting press photographers with a perfect sleek head of hair. This didn't bother me; I knew the pressure that artists were under to look good and I'd worked for far vainer performers in my time. Ike Turner was nothing compared to Little Richard.

One night we were travelling to Stevenage. The weather was horrendous; rain lashed against the windscreen and I had to struggle to keep the car on course as the wind butted against our flank.

'Good old British weather this,' I said, squinting to see the road in front of me, as the windscreen wipers lashed back and forth. 'Ike, if I'm still on the right road, then we should be there in the next five or ten minutes.'

I caught sight of Ike's nod of acknowledgement in my rear-view mirror and he carefully began to unwind his turban. But the bad weather persisted and we were making slow headway. I wasn't even sure we were where I thought we were. Finally a road sign, glowing white in the headlights, sprang up by the side of the road. I pulled up and peered at it, but I couldn't make out a thing with the rain driving against the glass. Without thinking, I rolled down my window and stuck my head out to read it. A huge gust of wind, driving the rain along with it, burst through the open window and struck Ike full in the face. I heard the outraged scream from the back of the car and turned to see what had happened. Ike's perfect hair was blowing out around his head; the Afro curls had sprung up despite the lacquer. He looked a total mess.

'Wind up the fucking window!' Ike screamed, 'Now! Wind up that fucking window, now!'

'Oh, shit! Ike, I'm sorry.' I said, struggling to pull the window up as quickly as I could.

'Wind it up!'

He continued to shout as I wound the window, banging his fist against the back of my headrest. Finally, the window was sealed and there was a moment of eerie silence, punctuated only by Ike's panting. I didn't dare look at Tina; she was silent, tucked up in the far corner of the back seat. I couldn't even hear her breathe.

'Look, Ike, I'm really sorry. I didn't even think,' I said, finally.

'Of course you didn't think, you fucking idiot. Don't even speak to me. If I hear your voice, I'll shoot your fucking brains out, you hear?'

I heard and I kept quiet. I could see Ike spitting on to his hands and desperately trying to flatten down the curls, eventually he gave up and wound his turban back into place.

'Let's go, Tappy. I don't want to be late on top of everything else. You know where we are now at least, I hope?'

'Yes, sir.'

'Then let's drive, idiot. Do something right tonight.'

We finally arrived, after probably the most tension-filled drive of my career. We were half-an-hour late and there were already fans gathered outside, waiting to meet and greet Ike and Tina. I could hear Tina whispering to Ike, trying to calm him down.

'It's OK, baby, you go in and I'll do the signing and stuff. They know you're a busy man and they'll know that you'll have things to do inside. You just run in there, honey, and they'll see you all handsome up on that stage, OK?'

It seemed to work and Ike ran straight to the dressing room, while Tina was left to work the crowd and sign autographs on behalf of them both. Ike didn't quite manage to salvage his hairdo for the performance and, I have to say, after the way he'd spoken to me, I couldn't help but laugh as I watched Ike's normally immaculate hair style bursting up into a flurry of curls during the course of the set.

Ike did eventually forgive me; he even gave a slightly begrudging apology for his own behaviour, but he did make sure that it never happened again. Every time we set out for a gig, he said the same thing: 'Right, Tappy, I want you to check those windows are locked. And I mean *locked*!'

Dodging Jayne

Halfway through their tour, Ike and Tina took a couple of days off to unwind and relax. They'd been working hard and so, therefore, had I. I was looking forward to the time off and being able to remind my wife that we did actually live in the same house. But being back in England, working for Chas and Mike, meant that a lot of old faces from my days with The Animals kept emerging and sometimes at the worst possible time.

I was at home one day, when I got the call from Don Arden. 'Tappy! I heard you were back, son,' Don said. As soon as I heard that broad Manchester accent I knew that I was in trouble. I wasn't wrong. 'I was wondering what you were up to this weekend.'

'I've got the weekend off, Don. I'm spending some time with the wife, it's been a while since I've been able to do that, you know?'

'Yeah, sure. She's a lovely girl; it's just that I need a favour, Tappy. I've got Jayne Mansfield in town. She's due to start her tour this weekend, but I can't get a road crew until Monday. My boy David is in the band travelling with her. I was in a jam and I heard you were in town and I thought "Hey, who would be better?"'

'Jayne Mansfield? The blonde from the movies? What the hell's she got to tour with?'

Don laughed. 'It's a cabaret thing. You know; singing and dancing, the usual thing. People seem to love it. Look, Tappy, I need someone who knows what he's doing; can you help me out?'

'Don, I've promised my wife . . .' I whispered into the phone, cupping the receiver in my hands and turning my back on the kitchen door, where Margaret was making our breakfast.

'Come on, Tappy. She'll understand.'

I groaned.

This conversation took place after the infamous Robert Stigwood incident of 1966. Don and a group of his 'minders' had hung the impresario out of a window when he approached The Small Faces, one of Don Arden's bands, with a change of management. Don was certainly a man that I wanted to stay on the right side of. I was back in that world of dangerous men and it was best to keep your friends close.

'All right then, Don. But you owe me one.'

It wasn't the easiest conversation I've ever had with Margaret. The time off was cancelled, I was leaving again and I was going to be spending all my time with Jayne Mansfield! She wasn't happy but, as Don had said she would, she did understand why I had to go.

Don had told me that Jayne was doubling up her shows at the start of the tour. This was why he needed me; Jayne would perform on 31 March 1967, an early show at the Latino Club in South Shields and then we'd have to set out immediately for Newcastle to arrive in time for a late performance at the La Dolce Vita Club. Don had also warned me to hire a station wagon; 'You won't believe the amount of luggage this girl needs!'

So, I hired the station wagon and drove up to Jayne's London hotel to pick up her luggage for the drive to Geordie Land. Don had warned me about the luggage, but nothing could have prepared me for the stack of pink suitcases that were piled up outside the hotel entrance. The uniformed bellboy came over to the car, dragging some of the collection along behind him.

'These would be yours then, would they?' he said, raising his eyebrows.

'I suppose so. We better start loading them in.'

Not long after we'd finally stowed away the last of her bags, Jayne Mansfield came tottering out of the hotel entrance and jumped into a waiting taxi to go to King's Cross Station for the trip to Newcastle. She was all tits and hips; with a bright blonde wig and a full mouth, painted scarlet.

I did eventually get to South Shields after having met Jayne off the train at Newcastle Station and I sighed with relief as the Latino nightclub came into view. But the place already seemed to be packed out and there was a crowd gathered outside. I checked my watch; we were here at the time Jayne had specified. What was going on?

'Oh, don't worry that handsome head of yours,' Jayne said, when I asked her about the crowd. 'I'm always late; it pays to let people wait for what they want. Now, could you be a darling and just pop in and ask the manager for a little help with my bags? I think four men should be enough . . . just make sure they're good and strong.'

I did as I was told, relieved to be out of her clutches. The manager quickly assigned four doormen to carry her pink luggage through the waiting fans. Jayne walked between them, smiling and blowing kisses to the crowd. It was only when we got inside to her dressing room that I found out that all but one of the bags was empty. All that effort and a specially hired car just to let her make an entrance!

I only watched a couple of minutes of the show. After watching Ike and Tina Turner perform, this lame Marilyn Monroe act made me cringe. Not that I told her that on the drive to Newcastle after the show.

Finally, after the show she planted herself in the passenger seat. A fug of musk perfume filled the car and I almost choked.

'Bye, bye, sweeties,' she squeaked, waving and blowing kisses at her gentlemen friends, as I wound down my window and tried to find some fresh air. 'Ohhh, will you look at those two. They look totally exhausted.'

I grunted a reply and started the engine.

'That's the problem with young men today – no staying power.' Jayne gave a twittering little laugh and her hand crept over on to my leg; I felt her red talons grip my thigh. 'So, what's your name then, honey?'

'Erm . . .' The hand was working its way up to my crotch; I shifted in my seat, trying to throw her off. 'I'm Tappy. Tappy Wright.'

'Well, Mr Tappy Wright,' Jayne said, not loosening her grip. 'I have a feeling we're going to have a lot of fun together.'

Fun wasn't really what I was after. I'm not going to claim to have been the best of husbands and I wasn't always faithful, but a weekend away with a female sex siren was not something I wanted to do. The move back to England, the new job, had all happened to give me and Margaret a fresh start. Anyway, to be honest, Jayne Mansfield terrified me.

Even before I'd agreed to this trip, I'd heard all about Jayne Mansfield's reputation as a man-eater. It was said that she could get through three or four men in a night and still be hungry for more. The woman was like a female version of me and I certainly wasn't ready for that! I was used to doing the chasing when it came to women and I wasn't even doing that now that I was living full-time with Margaret again.

'You were great, Jayne. It was a fantastic show; all the men in the audience had their tongues hanging out for more.'

I know that it wasn't honest, but Don Arden had told me to keep her sweet and if a few compliments could keep her hands out of my trousers, then I was more than willing to dish them out. Jayne ate it up.

'Oh, I know. They love me, don't they?' She patted her blonde curls and looked over at me with a smile. 'You're a sweetie, Tappy. We should have a nightcap later, just you and me. If you're a very good boy, you might even get a private performance.'

The hand was back on my leg. Compliments were definitely *not* the answer.

We got to the La Dolce Vita club in Newcastle where Jayne orchestrated a repeat performance of her grand entrance to the South Shields gig. She stalked in, with her pink suitcases held high around her and I headed for the bar, not even attempting to catch any of her act. I was in trouble with this one and I knew it. I didn't want to offend her, but there was no way I was going to bed with that sex-crazed blonde, no matter how famous she thought she was. With a sinking heart I realised that, in all my efforts to keep my eyes on the road while fighting off Jayne's increasingly determined advances, I'd forgotten that we'd be sharing a hotel. The drive there would be terrifying enough!

It seemed like no time at all before we were back in the car together. Jayne laid her head back and stretched out in her seat, letting her skirt ride up and revealing a pair of very tiny pink lace panties. I tried to keep my eyes on the road and my cock under control as she started to run her hand up and down my thigh.

'Oh, Tappy, these shows are so exhausting. I need to wind down, darling, and you know there is only one thing that will really relax me.'

Down boy, down! I chanted in my mind, trying to shift out of the way of her exploring fingers. Why would my cock not obey my mind? I really didn't want anything to do with her. *Think of your wife, Tappy. You're lovely, loving wife, waiting for you at home.* It was no good; I could feel my cock starting to stir under Jayne's fingers. I pressed my foot down on the accelerator; the quicker we got to that hotel, the quicker I could get some breathing space between me and Jayne.

Finally, it came into sight; I don't think I've ever moved faster. I was out of the car and checking us both into our *separate* rooms, before Jayne had made it through the hotel entrance. But I wasn't taking any chances and, after half-pushing Jayne into the elevator, I headed for the bar. I needed a drink; in fact, I needed more than one.

I didn't see how I could go to my hotel room that night, I'd heard and seen enough of Jayne Mansfield to realise that a little delay was not going to put her off. Our rooms were pre-booked and right next to each other. I resigned myself to a sleepless night at the bar.

'I'll have a Jack Daniel's on the rocks,' I said to the bartender. 'You know what; you better make that a double.'

I have never been much of a drinker, but after I'd tipped the double bourbon down my throat, I ordered another. This was an emergency and there was nothing else I could think to do.

'Bad day, mate?' the bartender asked as he passed me my drink. Newcastle is quite close to my home town and it was nice to hear that familiar accent again.

'You a Geordie?'

'That's right. The name's Mick; I'm from North Shields, and you?'

'Whitley Bay.'

'Should be good for you, coming back home. Why are you turning to the hard stuff, son?'

I introduced myself to Mick and explained about the situation with Jayne Mansfield.

'Man-eater, eh?' Mick commented, when I was finished and served me up another drink on the house. 'To be honest with you, Tappy, I don't see the problem. It's sex on a plate and with *Jayne Mansfield*! Jesus, that's most men's idea of a fantasy, not a problem!'

'Well I guess I'm not most guys, at least not any more. I've got a wife, Mick, and I don't want to do anything to hurt her. She's bound to hear about it if I bang bloody Jayne Mansfield. I don't even want to; she scares the life out of me!'

'Hang about,' Mick said, with a glint in his eye. 'What room's she in?'

'Jayne? 58. Why?'

'Well, you don't want any of it and I guess I can see why, but I've got no wife to worry about. What do you reckon about me popping up and seeing if she fancies a glass of champagne?'

I spluttered into my bourbon. 'Champagne! Have you heard anything I've said, Mick? You'd be taking your life in your hands, son!'

'That's what I'm hoping for! Look, my shift finishes in a couple of minutes; you show me where her room is and I'll see if I can work some Geordie charm. Go on, Tappy, it'll mean that you can get some sleep and I get to meet Jayne Mansfield.'

I was sure that Mick would be getting more than an autograph, but he seemed keen and it did mean that I'd be safe for the night. I could even get some sleep! So, I agreed to Mick's plan and, after waiting for him to work out the last of his shift, took him up to Jayne's room.

'That's her room, there,' I told Mick, who was following me along the corridor with a tray holding four bottles of champagne and two glasses. 'I'm next door. You had better keep her entertained, mate; I'm desperate for some sleep.'

'Don't worry about that. I owe you one for this, Tappy.'

I ducked into my doorway and listened as Mick knocked on Jayne's door.

'Yes, who is it?' I heard Jayne call from inside.

'Room service, madam. I have some champagne here, compli-

143

ments of the house; for the most beautiful young lady staying here.' Mick twisted round and shot me a wink. 'Go get some sleep,' he mouthed, giving me a thumbs up.

Gratefully, I stepped into my room and closed the door behind me. I could hear Jayne cooing at Mick, as she let him in.

'Oh, how lovely. I do *love* champagne. You're such a sweetie to bring it up to me; I'll need a big strong handsome man like you to pop the corks.' She gave her twittering little laugh and the door closed.

I got myself ready for bed. I could hear the murmur of Mick's compliments, mingled with the pop of champagne corks and Jayne's delighted laugher, drifting through the wall.

'You keep that Geordie charm working, Mick,' I muttered to myself, as I finally drifted off to sleep.

Unfortunately for me, the cunning plan to get me a quiet night's sleep was not fool-proof. Within half-an-hour I was shocked out of my sleep by the sound of screams and moans and squeaking bedsprings from next door. The Geordie charm had certainly worked, but there was no way that I could sleep through this racket.

'Oh, you naughty boy! Where ever did you learn to do that? No, don't stop! More! That's it, more!'

I buried my head in the pillow, as the headboard drummed against the dividing wall. This woman was insatiable! Not only was I not getting any sleep, but I was lying there alone listening to the longest sex session in history! Mick was obviously the man to match Jayne's stamina; they never seemed to stop!

After a couple of hours, wrestling around in my bed and trying to sleep with my fingers in my ears, I gave up and decided to take a walk round the hotel. To be honest, I was feeling lonely. It was too late to call Margaret, but the band who were working with Jayne had followed us down to the same hotel; they must have arrived by now and my misery was definitely in need of company.

I pulled on some clothes and, with one last furious glance towards the continuing barrage of squeals coming from Jayne's room, I left my room. David Arden, Don's son, was playing in Jayne's band and I knew vaguely where the band was housed in the hotel. I reached the right corridor and wandered along until I came to an open door. There on the bed was a naked girl, crouched on all fours with her beautiful smooth behind pointed right at me.

She must have sensed me standing in the doorway. 'Is that you, darling? Come in, quickly,' she purred, not turning round but spreading her legs wider and raising her arse into the air.

What was with this place? There seemed to be rampant women waiting behind every door. I can't say that I'm particularly proud of what happened next, but when a beautiful woman appears, ready and waiting, it was too tempting, despite having earlier disregarded Jayne Mansfield's advances, and hard to remember the wife at home. Without waiting to be asked twice I climbed on to the bed and unzipped my trousers.

'Oh God, yes! That's just what I was waiting for,' the girl moaned as I entered her. 'Oh, David, please don't stop.'

'David?'

The girl twisted round and looked into my face. 'Jesus, who are you? You're great!'

We both laughed and carried on.

Just as we'd finished, I heard a cough from the doorway. 'Having fun are you?' It was David Arden. 'Jesus, Tappy, I leave a girl for five minutes to visit the bathroom and you're in there!'

I struggled back into my trousers, muttering apologies, but David was already laughing.

'Tappy Wright, ladies and gentlemen . . .' he announced to the room at large. 'Only you could get away with that one!'

I left them and headed back to my room. *So much for staying faithful*, I cursed myself on the walk back. I reached my door just in time to meet Mick staggering out of Jayne's room.

'Christ, Tappy, you look terrible!' he said, looking at my face. 'I thought you were going to get some sleep?'

'Fat chance of that with you two next door. I thought you were meant to be keeping her *quiet*.'

Mick grinned and rubbed his eyes. 'Sorry, mate, but that Jayne Mansfield is one hell of a girl. She's just never had enough. Thanks a lot for fixing me up.'

I grunted and headed back into my room. Maybe there was just enough time to catch half-an-hour's shut-eye before I had to start work? But just as I'd laid my weary bones down on the mattress, there was a knock at the door.

'Good morning, sweetie. You ready to go?' That voice again. Bloody Jayne Mansfield, didn't she need sleep?

I pulled myself up and opened the door. 'No, love, I'm not ready. Wait for me downstairs in the morning, eh?'

'Now, now, darling,' Jayne twittered, wagging her finger at me. 'Don't be like that. I'm sorry about last night, but it's not very often a girl gets to have some fun with a big handsome stranger like my guest. Don't be jealous, Tappy, I'll make it up to you,' she strained her head and looked over my shoulder at the bed. 'Why don't we just have a quick one right now?'

I'd had enough. I know that I could hardly claim to have been on my best behaviour during my stay at the hotel, but I wasn't about to add fuel to the fire by bedding her.

'No, Jayne, let's not do that. I'll see you in the morning.'

I slammed the door in her face and then immediately phoned Don Arden.

'I'm sorry, Don, but I've had as much of Jayne Mansfield as I can take. This was just why I didn't want to be back on the road again. Ike and Tina are married and that's easier, but this woman . . .'

'Calm down, Tappy. Look, it's just for one more day.'

'No, Don. You'll have to find a replacement. I'm out of here.'

Not even Don Arden's reputation could have kept me in Jayne Mansfield's company for another moment. (In fact, Don himself had enough of her lateness and prima donna antics, and he sacked her after that weekend). I packed my bags and left as quickly as I could, without so much as a goodbye. It was time to get back to the life I'd chosen and not the one that chose me.

It was time to get back to Margaret.

Within a few months of my episode with Jayne, unfortunately, she was killed in a car crash on 28 June 1967.

Keeping Up with the Turners

But, before I could return to my wife, I had my commitments to Ike and Tina Turner to fulfil. I wasn't sad to see them again; after a day with Jayne Mansfield, meeting Ike and Tina on Monday morning was like greeting a pair of long-lost friends. Working with them may have meant being back on the road again, but at least they were a married couple. I was sure that, travelling with them, I could avoid all the old temptations and tensions thrown up by my time with Jayne. Well, that was what I thought . . .

After I said hello to them both, I wasted little time filling them in on my disastrous weekend (leaving out my encounter with poor David Arden's girl). Tina was very sympathetic; she actually seemed stunned that a performer could behave like that. Ike had been uncharacteristically quiet, but when Tina moved into the bedroom to change her clothes, he immediately leant forward with questions about Jayne Mansfield.

'I've already told you what happened, Ike. There isn't anything else to say.'

'Come on, Tappy, tell me again,' he nodded towards the closed door, behind which Tina was changing. 'Now it's just us; you don't need to leave anything out. I want to know more about what this girl Jayne Mansfield would do.'

I sighed and told my story once again, but I still wasn't going to tell Ike about my brief encounter with the girl in David's hotel room. But Ike wanted to know about Jayne, the idea of the sex-crazed star seemed to excite him as much as it had my barman friend, Mick. I just couldn't tell him enough.

'Look, Ike,' I said, finally. 'I spent my time trying *not* to do anything with her and nothing really happened. She was bloody frightening. I'm not going to sit here and make up stories for you. If you want some then you'd better go get yourself a blonde bimbo of your own, there's plenty about.'

'I might just do that,' Ike replied, with a grin and then quickly changed the subject as Tina came back into the room.

We set off for their next gig in Manchester and I forgot all about my conversation with Ike. My Philips record player was playing again and we sang and laughed our way through the long drive up North.

I was excited by the prospect of seeing them perform again, especially after the warm-up session in the car. As soon as we arrived I took my place backstage to ensure that I'd have a good view when Ike and Tina took to the stage. I started talking to the band's sax player about the Ikettes, Ike and Tina's backing singers.

'Their harmonies are amazing, don't you think?' I asked him. 'It must be great to have such a group of talented people to work with.'

The sax player raised his eyebrows and then looked over his shoulder to check that we couldn't be overheard. 'Only two of those girls can sing, Tappy, haven't you noticed? Watch the girl in the middle tonight; she'll make all the right moves, but she can't sing a note.'

'Are you serious? How did she get the gig then?'

'Come on, Tappy, don't be so naïve,' the sax player said, lowering his voice still further. 'She's Ike's bit on the side. I thought you knew; it's pretty much common knowledge. Don't say anything to Tina, but I think even she has some idea what's going on.'

I whistled in amazement. I know that I'd spent the morning with Ike trying to drag sexual details out of me, but I'd taken that for a bit of voyeuristic curiosity from a married man. Meanwhile, the dirty old sod was travelling with his own personal mistress. I did feel sorry for Tina, but I was in no position to be giving lectures about fidelity. It just made me sad to think that even here, with a couple I both liked and respected, I was still not free from the cheating and lies so prevalent in the music industry.

I tried to forget about what the sax player had told me. Ike and Tina's performance that night was fantastic; it was at least great to remember how good some acts could be. The Manchester crowd were perhaps a little rowdier than those Ike and Tina had been used to, but Tina worked them well. She shook her stuff and roared out the tunes, drawing the applause up to new levels. I always enjoyed their gigs, but they pulled out all the stops that night. They really were a remarkable pair of artists.

Now, although I'd heard the rumours of Ike's affair with his backing singer, I knew that he was always protective of his wife. But in the throes of a show, it was necessary for Ike to ease up on Tina. Their performances were each unique, but they were very professional when it came to giving the crowd what they were after; plus a little more. They had a very American sense of showmanship and were always willing to lay on the glamour and keep the audience on their toes.

I can honestly say that I probably saw Tina as much naked as I saw her clothed, over the months that I worked with the Turners. She would fit in a change of clothes after every three songs, leaving Ike to perform a song alone as her personal valet stripped her backstage and prepared her for a whole new entrance. She even had specially designed wigs, with other wigs sewn inside, meaning that she could change her hairstyle as well as her clothes periodically through the show.

One of her outfits did get her into trouble, though. It was during that performance in Manchester, my first night back with Ike and Tina. Tina had just completed her first change and she charged back on stage in a tiny mini-dress to perform 'River Deep, Mountain High'. I've said that the crowd were a little wild that night, but the response to the sight of Tina's famous legs combined with the first notes of Ike and Tina's massive UK hit was enough to lift the roof off the venue. Tina seemed to be enjoying it. She moved right up to the front of the stage and the crowd roared their appreciation. But as she curled over to push the final notes of the chorus out of her lungs, a man in the audience jumped forward and made a grab for Tina. He managed to get close to her, before a couple of stage hands and I leapt up to drag him off the stage. The band had ignored the incident and continued to play and Tina simply carried on with the song, flashing me and the stage hands a smile of thanks as we manhandled the over eager fan backstage. Ike, although he was obviously still visibly furious, continued playing as the 'show must go on.' *Pure professionalism*, I thought. *Only Ike and Tina could have dealt with that so smoothly.*

But back in the car after the show, things were far from smooth.

'What the fuck were you doing dancing at the edge of the stage anyway?' Ike screamed at Tina. 'Just waiting to give every fucking asshole in the place an eyeful!'

Tina began to sob. Off stage, she was back to her demure, quiet self and, anyway, she knew better than to answer Ike back when he was in a mood like this one. She just sat there weeping as Ike raved at her, but he showed no sign of letting up. 'I've told and told you something like this was going to happen. But would you listen? No. You're such a stupid bitch; you never fucking listen! Well, I'm telling you now, I will not have any fucking perverts touching my wife. You listening to me? I said, ARE YOU LISTENING TO ME?'

'Yes, Ike,' Tina muttered through her tears. 'I'm sorry, Ike.'

'I should hope you are. It would have to happen during that fucking song, wouldn't it?'

I didn't understand that comment at the time, but later I discovered that their hit song, 'River Deep, Mountain High', was rather a sore spot for Ike Turner. It had been produced by Phil Spector and not Ike himself; in fact, Spector hadn't even allowed Ike in the studio during its recording and only Tina's vocals appeared on the final record. Ike was obviously terrified by the idea that Tina could achieve stardom without him.

I think that the horrible car journey after that Manchester gig was probably more triggered by Ike's feeling that he was losing his control of Tina's talent. It was the only time in the months that I spent with them that I witnessed any sign of Ike's temper being directed at Tina and it seems like a sad note on which to end the story of my time with them. I've always thought it a shame that Ike Turner should only be remembered as a man who beat his wife and not as one of the founding fathers of rock 'n' roll, which he undoubtedly was.

It was horrible to have to say goodbye to Ike and Tina when the tour did finally come to an end. Despite those few occasions when Ike's temper had got the better of him, I felt that there was a genuine bond of friendship between the three of us. Their UK tour had been a resounding success, but Ike and Tina were looking forward to getting back to their children in California. They had another tour planned in the US and both of them pressed me to join them for it, but I knew my home was in England with my wife.

Tina hugged me and wept openly as I saw them off at Heathrow Airport. I wished them both well and waved as they walked off through the departure gate but, emotional as our goodbyes were, I was excited about getting back to the office and seeing what new adventures my job at Anim would give me.

I kept in touch with Ike over the years and one night, back in 2004, he rang me up and asked if I could come to his San Marcus home, near San Diego. He wanted to show me costumes that Tina and her backup group, the Ikettes, had worn on stage. Ike was aware that I would buy pop memorabilia for my clients. I agreed to go since I figured I had nothing to lose, and if I was not interested in the costumes, maybe I would get a good story or two out of Ike.

The costumes were in perfect condition even though Ike showed me how he and Tina would tear the hemline of the dresses so that Tina and the girls would look much sexier as they showed off their fantastic figures and legs. He also showed me several guitars he wanted to sell; I took some photographs of the merchandise to help sell it for him. After a while we reminisced about his life in the Fifties and Sixties. Many rock historians believe that Ike Wister Turner was the godfather of soul music and that the recording of 'Rocket 88' by Jackie Brenston and the Delta Cats, which Turner wrote, was the first 'rock 'n' roll' song ever recorded. I was a good audience for his stories and he continued on to wax nostalgic.

Ike considered the British Invasion of America in the early Sixties to be the best thing that ever happened to him and many of the black blues artists at the time, because the British bands such as The Beatles, The Rolling Stones and The Animals introduced many young American kids to their music. After a while I grew brave enough to change the subject and ask Ike about the stories relating to his constant abuse of Tina and the fact that I knew he openly cheated on her. In fact, everybody in the band knew that Ike was having sex with one of the Ikettes when I worked with them in the Sixties, but nobody said anything as we were all scared of Ike and his famous temper.

I mentioned to Ike that Tina had written in her autobiography that as early as 1968 she had considered suicide because of his constant physical and emotional violence and abuse. He said it was all 'bullshit' and I could see that he was getting more and more annoyed with me. Maybe he didn't want to remember certain facts as I had.

I remembered when I used to take Tina to Petticoat Lane. One day I had noticed what looked like bruises round her eye but I could not see properly as Tina always wore huge sunglasses. I didn't ask her then, and she never let on to me, but that day she was not her usual bubbly self and she looked like she was in pain. I mentioned that to Ike, but he just snarled at me and with his fists clenched told me that he had slapped and punched the 'bitch', but that he didn't classify it as beating her up like it showed in the 'fucking movie'. He was clearly annoyed. 'You would think I was the only star who slapped his wife,' he growled. 'There were lots of bigger stars than me that beat their wives up.'

I don't know. Something about his tone caused me not to believe him. Tina was a beautiful person and his temper and rages were common knowledge. I'll never know how she put up with him and the violence he inflicted on her, his tantrums and his obvious cheating on her. Although at the time of our conversation, Ike was in his seventies and was a lot quieter than he was back in the Sixties, he still had the look that scared you. I came away from Ike's house and that conversation feeling like he still had the power to hurt.

CHAPTER 9

It was an Experience:
Jimi Hendrix and Anim Ltd

Getting Hendrix in a Haze

'Hey Joe' had eventually reached Number 4 in the UK charts after its release through Track Records, but the follow-up single, 'Purple Haze', released on 17 March 1967 beat it by one chart position, reaching Number 3. I'd arrived back at the Anim offices just in time; Jimi was booked to perform on *Top of the Pops* alongside the Alan Price Set. Both acts were represented by Anim, so I headed down to the BBC to ensure that everything ran smoothly.

Alan and his band would be performing their hit single 'Simon Smith and the Amazing Dancing Bear'; it was a Randy Newman song that I'd recommended to Alan and I was proud to be there representing two artists that I'd had such a lot to do with.

It was nice to be back in my position as a member of a management team. I had an overall responsibility, but was free from the niggling concerns of the roadie. But as it turned out, it seems that *Top of the Pops* could have done with a helping hand when it came to checking the details of each performance.

The Jimi Hendrix Experience was the first to hit the stage. Although the bands were all present, it was customary on *Top of the Pops* for a backing track to be played. This at least avoided any embarrassments for band members in the live show, those whose instruments were out of tune or who couldn't remember their notes. This was never likely to happen with Mitch Mitchell or Noel Redding, but the Experience boys played along. Jimi was never the most confident man when it came to his vocal abilities, but he was the only member of the Experience who would actually be performing live. Nevertheless, he jumped up to the microphone, ready to give it his best, only to be met by the backing track of 'Simon Smith and the Amazing Dancing Bear'!

'Whoa there, man!' Jimi laughed into the mike, 'I don't think I know the words to this one.'

The camera quickly spun back to the *Top of the Pops* host, Jimmy Savile. 'Now then, we seem to have a little problem there. Just a little mistake ladies and gentlemen, that Mr Jimi Hendrix has spotted for us. Thank you, Jimi.'

The stupid bastards had mixed up the tapes that came from Anim. I was on my feet, desperately searching for someone to shout at, when I realised that the incident had actually served to put Jimi at his ease. The BBC teams had quickly found the correct tape and Jimi performed fantastically, better than any of us had ever hoped that he would. When Jimmy Savile came up to us at the end of the show to apologise for the mix-up and congratulate Jimi on the way he'd handled it, Jimi laughed it off. 'Sometimes, mistakes are the best thing that can happen, man.'

Cruising Carnaby, Hendrix Style

Jimi Hendrix had broken the UK, but the US was flagging far behind. The chart positions for 'Hey Joe' and 'Purple Haze' had been negligible on their release in the States, especially considering the quality of the tunes. The USA had to be woken up and made to realise just what a home-grown talent they were ignoring. Chas and Mike were planning a US tour for the Experience and, as part of the preparations, I took Jimi shopping. And what better place could there be to kit out the newest star of swinging London than its most fashionable street: Carnaby Street.

Although Jimi was well on his way to becoming a household name, he had little money of his own. If he needed anything he came into the Anim office and Mike handed over whatever he asked for. But he could be a little unreliable when it came to producing receipts and, having seen one too many stars veer off the rails into serious drink and drug habits, Mike and Chas wanted to make sure that Jimi was spending the money on what he claimed it for. Hence I was sent out to hold Jimi's bags and collect the receipts. But even on swinging Carnaby Street, the ever-theatrical Jimi Hendrix was able to make a simple shopping trip a day to remember.

Carnaby Street was *the* place to shop in 1967 and, thanks to the influence of the likes of Brian Jones of The Rolling Stones and other flamboyant contemporaries, even the male tailors to be found there were prepared to create the most unusual and colourful of suits. Jimi and I stopped outside a woman's boutique, Lady Jane, and I asked Jimi where he wanted to start.

'What about here?' he said, nodding up at Lady Jane.

'This is a *girl's* shop, son. There's a tailor's just down there.'

'Nah, this is the place.' He craned his head to look at the window display. 'Suits aren't really my thing. I've been in here before; they've got great colours, man.'

I followed him into Lady Jane and glanced around me. 'Where's the men's section?'

Jimi looked puzzled. 'What do you mean? There's no men's section, Tappy, this is all women's stuff. I always wear women's clothes, man. The colours are much better.'

I watched him as he wandered through the rails and pulled out a collection of women's blouses, holding them up against himself in a mirror to check that the colours suited him. The sales girls didn't seem to know what to do with themselves as he moved over to a display of silky neck and head scarves.

'Check these out, Tappy,' Jimi called across the shop holding out a fistful of silks. 'They all match up. How cool is that?'

'Sure,' I muttered, shuffling over to join him.

But, to be honest, it was hard to maintain any embarrassment in the face of Jimi's unselfconscious enthusiasm. He knew exactly who he was and no one was going to convince him that he should be ashamed of that for a moment. The sales girls got over their initial shock and started to get into the spirit of things, particularly when Jimi bared his chest in the middle of the shop to try on some of his selections. They brought over some other blouses and advised him on co-ordination and accessories. Jimi was revelling in the attention, prancing around and flirting with the girls as they strapped scarves around his head and arms.

But whether due to the female attention that Jimi was receiving or just the sight of a man in women's clothing, there were two occupants of the shop who obviously wanted to make sure that Jimi Hendrix knew exactly what they thought of him.

'All right there, are you, love? Why don't you try and find some wee panties to match your blouse?'

'I think the brassières are over there. You may as well get yourself the whole outfit, eh?'

The heckling came from a pair of large Scottish lads, who were waiting outside the changing rooms for their girlfriends. Jimi ignored them, but their comments and their laughter got louder and I could feel my temper rising. Who the hell did they think they were to be mocking Jimi Hendrix? They must have known who he was. If Jimi wanted to wear women's clothes, this pair of little nobodies had no right to tell him any different. I walked over to Jimi and touched his arm.

'We've got a right pair of prats over there,' I growled. 'You want me to go sort them out; believe me, it'd be a pleasure.'

Jimi was checking the effect of his latest outfit in the store's mirror; he grinned at my red and furious face, sitting over his shoulder in the reflection. 'Chill, Tappy! You're clashing with my colour scheme here.' He turned round, looked at me and then lowered his voice. 'Don't let them bother you, man. Listen, I've travelled through the Deep South and these assholes have nothing compared to the stuff I heard there. This kind of stuff happens all the time; you just can't let it get to you. They'll give up.'

Jimi carried on with his shopping and I did my best to swallow my anger. The sales girls were rewarded for their efforts and, by the time we left, both Jimi and I were piled high with bags. We looked in on a couple more shops and then decided to stop for a drink. Jimi wanted to phone his girlfriend, Kathy Etchingham, to tell her about what he'd bought and to make sure that she ordered his favourite Indian curry as a take-out for that evening.

They'd moved in together shortly after Jimi had reached the UK and were very happy together. I often wish they had stayed together; Jimi might still be alive today. I got us a booth in the main bar as he made the call and then groaned as I saw the two men who were entering the bar. It was our two Scottish friends from Lady Jane.

'Oh, check it out, Bill,' one of them shouted, as Jimi crossed the bar to join me. 'There's that pretty boy from earlier. Get all the petticoats you needed did you, flower?'

'Backs to the wall, lads,' the other commented to the room at large, before turning to the barman. 'I didn't know you served fairies in here, chief.'

Luckily the barman was not amused. He said a couple of quiet words to the pair of them and I saw one raise his hands in defeat. They still muttered to each other and laughed as they passed Jimi and me and headed for a booth behind me, but at least they'd calmed it down. But when I turned back to look at Jimi there was no disguising the tension in his face.

'You all right?' I asked.

'Sure,' Jimi said, giving me a grimace which I think was meant to pass as a smile. 'Just some people don't know when to stop, that's all.' He laughed. 'Ah, don't worry about me, Tappy.'

We carried on with our drinks and Jimi seemed to get back to his old self, although I did notice him looking over my shoulder towards the booth where the Scottish lads were sitting. But it was Jimi who had talked me down back in Lady Jane, so I didn't really consider the fact that he could be looking for revenge.

We had just about finished and I was gathering together Jimi's bags when he stopped me. 'Actually, I'll just use the bathroom here before we go; won't be long.'

I sat back down to wait for him and finished my drink. Jimi was taking his time and I went up to the bar to order another round. A man passed me on his way to the toilets; I watched as he opened the door and then turned swiftly on his heel and came back to the bar.

'Let's go somewhere else,' I heard him whisper to his wife, who'd been waiting for him. 'There's a fight going on in the gents.'

They got up to leave, but I caught the man's arm. 'Sorry, but I couldn't help overhearing; what's all this about a fight?'

The man shook his head. 'Don't ask me, looked like it was all over by the time I got there. I wouldn't have thought that skinny black kid could have done such damage.'

I thanked him and ran over to the gents toilets.

'Jimi! What the hell's happened here?'

He was stood at the wash basin, quietly washing his hands. The two smart-mouthed Scottish guys were lying on the floor, one with a bloody nose and the other face-down and groaning.

'Some people, eh,' Jimi said, his soft polite voice seeming grossly out of place. 'You hope they'll give up, but they just don't know when to quit.' He turned to me and smiled. 'I think it's about time we got out of here, Tappy.'

I nodded mutely, still stunned at the scene in front of me. 'I'll get the bags.'

'Yeah, thanks, Tappy. Might be best to leave a tip, too, we don't want to get into any trouble for the damage. You guys enjoy the rest of your day, won't you?' he called to the two prone figures on the bathroom floor.

Jimi Hendrix may have worn women's clothes, but he was no one's 'flower'. His army career may not have been the most distinguished but, as an ex-paratrooper, he'd learnt a trick or two when it came to dealing with mindless bullies and I doubt that the two Scottish loudmouths would forget the lesson dished out by that 'fairy boy' in a hurry.

Office Pranks for a Done Deal

Sadly, my job at Anim was not just shopping trips with the rich and famous. Not that I minded too much, they were a nice group of guys to work with. Along with Chas, Mike and myself, there was Henry Henroid and Tony Garland. I'd known Henry for years; he had longstanding connections with Don Arden and Micky Most and had been about when The Animals were first getting started. He was a great guy, an ex-boxer with the nose to prove it and a large cackling laugh that would burst out of his flexible face and increase his resemblance to the actor, Sid James. Henry was responsible for a well-established DJ called Emperor Roscoe, who worked for the BBC as a radio DJ, appearing occasionally on television. He also worked for a band, Soft Machine, who had taken their name from the William Burroughs novel and who would join Jimi Hendrix for his American tour.

I worked at one end of the large front office on 39 Gerard Street and Henry worked at the other. Tony, meanwhile, was in charge of Public Relations and was another old friend to keep me company.

So we all knew one another and were happy to spend time in each other's company, but I soon found that despite leaving my life on the road behind me my ways of entertaining myself during the working day still very much played a part. In fact, practical jokes in an office environment gave me a whole new challenge and the other boys in the office were more than willing to step up with some killer comebacks. None of us were used to the daily grind of working behind a desk and a few practical jokes helped to lighten the mood and remind us of our wilder days on the road.

But Chas Chandler seemed to take to his new role like a duck to water. As I'd said to him, back during the recording of 'Hey Joe', he was 'a producer through and through' and he obviously loved every minute of it. But occasionally he did get close to taking it all a little *too* seriously. Maybe the time was right to give my old friend Chas a bit of a shake up?

With Tony and Henry acting as lookouts, I snuck into Chas's office and prepared one of my favourite pranks for him: the exploding cigarette. To make sure of it working, I even gave the cigarette that I pulled from the pack a double dose of explosive. Chas certainly had a temper on him, but he could take a joke. I just hoped he could take this one.

Chas got back and, giggling like guilty schoolboys, we waited in the outer office to hear that tell-tale 'bang'. But nothing happened. Then Chas appeared at the doorway, holding his briefcase.

'What are you lot looking at?' he asked, looking at us suspiciously.

'Nothing,' we all replied, trying to look busy.

'Where are you off to, Chas?' Henry asked, shifting some paperwork off his desk and attempting to sound unconcerned.

'I've got a meeting at Buddah Records. Hopefully we're in line for a world deal on that new band Eire Apparent, that is if I can convince them that they like what they see. Now where are my tabs?' He walked back into his office and came back with the cigarette pack that I'd doctored held up in his hand. 'Got them. Anyway, wish me luck lads. I have a feeling I'm going to need it.'

'So do I,' Tony muttered, as Chas left the office, 'especially if he decides to light up one particular cigarette during that meeting.'

'Oh shit!' I cried, banging my head down on to my desk. 'What the hell have I done? Chas'll kill me!'

Looking back on it, I should have just run after Chas and admitted what I'd done, but I honestly didn't even think of it. Henry, Tony and I just sat and stared at each other, horrified by the possible conse-quences of a simple joke. What if it ruined the deal? Chas would never forgive me.

'It's just one cigarette,' Henry pointed out, after a long silence. 'Chances are he won't even smoke it.'

'Yeah, well, fingers crossed.'

We got on with our work as best we could, each of us glancing nervously at the door every couple of minutes, expecting a furious Chas to charge in at any moment. Eventually he came back. He slammed the door after him and looked at each one of us in turn, stony-faced.

'You lot, in my office. Now.'

We followed him silently into his office and stood in front of his desk as he dropped his briefcase and removed his jacket.

'Right, I want some answers.' Chas sat down at his desk and laid his palms flat. I felt like I was standing in front of a Mafia don, about to be asked to take a walk. 'Which one of you stupid bastards was it that put a fucking explosive in my cigarette?'

I wasn't going to let the other two get into trouble because of me. 'I did it, Chas,' I muttered, staring at my feet. 'I'm sorry; I didn't realise you were going out, let alone going to a meeting. But it was my fault; you can leave the other two out of it.'

I looked up at Chas, bracing myself for the bollocking of a lifetime, but he just burst out laughing.

"Tappy Wright, you are undoubtedly the luckiest bastard I have ever met!' He moved round the desk and shook me by the hand. 'You just got me the best deal I've ever made. Thanks a lot, mate.'

I didn't know what to say. I glanced over at Tony and Henry, but they looked as astonished as I felt. Chas just continued laughing and explained what had happened. 'Well, it was a tough meeting. I was desperately trying to get the Buddah boss on side, but he was having none of it. Then, I offered him a cigarette . . .'

'Oh, God!' I shouted, burying my head in my hands.

'No, Tappy, that was the thing. I handed him the cigarette and he lit it up and it blew up in his face.' I groaned, but Chas grabbed hold of my arm. 'Not only that, but the noise gave him such a shock that he dropped the fucking tab and burnt a massive hole in his expensive shirt. I'm not going to lie to you, Tap, I was fucking livid. I knew that it'd be one of you idiots mucking about, so there I was mopping up the flames on this shirt and trying to explain that my co-workers were a bunch of bastards.

'Thing was, he didn't believe me. He just kept saying, "Yeah, sure. There's no need to lie to me, Mr Chandler." I was practically begging when I realised that he was laughing. Seems that he thought I was being original; said he'd never actually had someone come in a try and blow him up to get a deal before. Anyway, it broke the ice and after that I had the deal on a plate. So to be honest, my old son, I think I owe you a drink!'

We congratulated Chas and then left the office for a local bar to celebrate. Who would have thought that a stupid prank could have backfired to create one of the best deals Anim ever pulled off? And that Chas would be buying me drinks for acting the fool?

Unfortunately, my relief at the exploding cigarette's success meant that I was soon tempted to use it again. After all, the worst had happened when we'd tried it out on Chas and the only repercussion had been a pat on the back. At least I *thought* that the worst had happened, until I tried it out on poor Tony Garland.

Again I planted the exploding cigarette in his pack in the office and again he managed to avoid it the whole time we were in the office together and *again* I was left wondering when the damn thing was going to go off in his face. Unfortunately, there was no record deal at the end of this story. Tony had lit up whilst shifting through his briefcase in the back of a black cab. When the cigarette had exploded, the cab had screeched to a halt, sending Tony's briefcase flying into the back of the driver's head. The poor guy had ended up with a black eye from the cab driver, who'd thrown him out into the street and accused him of 'IRA tactics'.

After Tony had got over the shock, he gave me a call. 'It's me, Tappy. I'm in a mess. I'm guessing it was you that put the exploding cigarette in my pack? Well, I think you must have overdone the dose. I'm in the eye hospital; it looks like they are going to have to operate to see if they can save my eye. Why did you have to do it, Tappy?'

He rang off and I grabbed my coat and car keys. Bloody hell! It was only meant to be a joke and I'd managed to blow my friend's eye out.

I drove to the eye hospital, dreading what could be awaiting me. What if Tony was blind? I'd never forgive myself. Tony Garland was waiting for me outside the hospital. He looked dishevelled and had a huge black eye, but otherwise he seemed fine. In fact, he was laughing. 'Thought I'd teach you a lesson,' he said, as he got into the passenger seat next to me. 'And get myself a ride home. You owe me that at least.'

So Tony got the last laugh, but even without a serious injury it took a lot of grovelling to get him finally to forgive me. It did convince me that it was probably best to consign the exploding cigarette trick to the back of the drawer. But smoking *is* very bad for you and maybe I at least managed to do my bit to get the guys to cut down!

Joining Jimi for Monterey

On Sunday, 11 June 1967, I got the chance to escape the office in style and flew across in advance for the weekend of The Monterey International Music Festival, to meet Jimi and the Experience before they made their US début. Monterey was to be one of *the* musical events of the Sixties. I'd been in London as it started to swing and now I was in California, where the hippies were threading their hair with flowers and breathing life into a whole new American scene that would dominate the late Sixties in music and fashion and outlook. *Sgt. Pepper's Lonely Hearts Club Band* had been released two weeks before; the world was readying itself for the 'Summer of Love', but it was still looking for some fresh soundtracks.

Artists performed for free at Monterey (with the exception of Ravi Shankar, who was alone in his demand of $3,000), but there was no doubt what an opportunity it was for new artists. It may have been the Experience's first major performance in the States, but Jimi's reputation had preceded him across the Atlantic to his homeland. His performances in the UK had ensured a firm support base from the famous British groups that were present (it was Paul McCartney's insistence, as a Monterey Festival board member, that Jimi had been booked to play and my old friend Eric Burdon had stayed on after his performance with The New Animals on the Friday to see the show) and the mood seemed to be infectious.

The Who, also now signed to Track Records along with the Experience, were also making their début in America, but they seemed more excited about playing alongside Jimi. There was a little confusion about who was to headline the event, as both The Who and The Jimi Hendrix Experience shared top billing. There have been stories about the bands flipping a coin backstage but, as I remember it, The Who offered to go on stage first.

'We just couldn't follow you, Jimi,' Pete Townshend said, as The Who prepared their set.

Jimi was obviously flattered, that is until he saw their performance. After what was admittedly a wonderful show, Townshend wasted little time burying his guitar in an amplifier and then smashing it to pieces on the stage. Now, I know that The Who were famous for the wreckage they could generate on stage, but it was a showpiece that Jimi and they shared. So much for not wanting to follow the great Jimi Hendrix, they'd made sure that if he smashed anything he'd look like a poor copy of The Who, chasing glory by mimicking their antics.

I turned to Jimi, aghast. 'Jesus, what are you going to do, mate?'

'Don't sweat it, man,' Jimi replied, returning Pete's grin as he left the stage with the remnants of his guitar trailing after him. He threw a pink feather boa around his shoulders and laughed. 'They want to play it that way; then that's fine by me. I'll show those bastards how to put on a show, I just need you to do me one favour, Tappy . . .'

The Experience took to the stage as the headline act, but I wasn't there to cheer with the rest of the crowd, I just caught Brian Jones, of The Rolling Stones, giving his personal introduction to the band: 'Ladies and Gentlemen, please welcome the most exciting performer I've ever heard . . .'

I then ran off, on an errand that would go down in musical history and teach Pete Townshend never to attempt to upstage Jimi Hendrix. They were reaching the end of their set when I finally reached the edge of the stage. 'Jimi! Here you go, son!' I passed him a small metal canister of lighter fuel that Tony Garland had purchased and stepped back to see the effects.

After pouring the lighter fuel over it, Jimi Hendrix set light to his Fender Stratocaster guitar, the crowd and the backstage crew went wild and Jimi wrote himself into American history to the resounding notes of 'Wild Thing'. As I watched him kneeling there in his frilly shirt and headband, holding his hands aloft as he watched his guitar dissolve into smoke and flame, I realised that Jimi Hendrix had broken America. Stage crew, on the orders of the promoters, ran on stage to help extinguish the burning Strat.

He had become the psychedelic rock god of the Sixties; the sound-track of the 'Summer of Love'. Things would never be the same again.

The Name's Wright, Tappy Wright

The trip to Monterey had also offered the chance to escape my home-life with Margaret. I was still very much in love with my wife, but my hopes for a happy and peaceful home in London were shattered soon after my return to England. I was made to realise what Margaret had lived with whilst I'd been off on the road in the States. It seems that the Poles were still unhappy about their Princess leaving her home country. And shipping her famous mother, Alina Slesinska, out to join us had just added fuel to the fire. We were under constant suspicion. Our telephones were tapped, we were followed everywhere and I had little doubt that meetings, however innocent, were being reported back to the Polish authorities.

At first I thought that I could live with it. We had a lovely home, a gorgeous Tudor Mews house in Devonshire Close and Margaret worked on Harley Street, which was only a few streets away, but over time the pressure did start to get to us. I really do believe that we could have been happy, if they would have only left us to get on with our lives. But there was little chance of that happening; I just had to accept that a constant surveillance was the price I had to pay for my beautiful Polish wife. But there was one night when I was forced to realise just how serious these guys could be when it came to monitoring international relations.

It was a humid Friday night, soon after I'd returned from America, and I was left home alone. I may have given up the crazy hours of a life on the road, but my wife was a doctor and her patients had a habit of needing her just when I did. Feeling hot and sticky and a little lonely, I decided to take a walk down to our local pub, The Devonshire Arms, to indulge in a gin and tonic and catch up on the local gossip.

But when I arrived, the place was quiet. It was still early, so I decided to get myself a drink and wait for the regulars to arrive. But as soon as I found myself a table, a man came over and asked to join me. There were plenty of other tables going spare, but the guy was tall and well dressed, he certainly didn't strike me as crazy or a groupie on the hunt for a contact in the business, so I nodded my head and he sat down.

'I'm Michael, by the way,' he told me, offering me his hand. The evening heat had obviously got to him; beads of sweat were gathering on the sides of his clean-shaven jaw and his hand was warm and spongy to the touch.

'Pleased to meet you, Michael. I'm Tappy.'

'Yes, Mr Wright, I know who you are,' he said with a smile, pulling a crisp white handkerchief from his breast pocket and wiping his face. 'My card . . .'

I looked down at the business card that he placed on the table between us. The Home Office? Bloody hell, surely I'd filed Margaret's papers correctly? They would have told us months ago if there had been any problems, wouldn't they?

I took a sip from my drink and eyed Michael suspiciously. 'Is there a problem?'

'No, no, there's no problem. I have a proposition for you Mr Wright. Could you give me, well let's say . . .' He glanced at his wristwatch. 'Twenty minutes of your time and I can explain?'

I was still wary (it's not every day that a stranger comes up to you in your local and tells you your last name), but I was also curious to find out what this was all about, so I agreed to hear Michael out.

'I want to offer you the chance to serve your country and also make yourself some extra money. In fact,' he lowered his voice to a whisper, 'rather a lot of money. You may be aware that we have been watching you for some time, Mr Wright, and we like what we see. We feel that you are in an ideal position to help us, that is, to help your country in tackling some necessary investigations abroad.'

'You want me to *spy*? Like James Bond?' Of all the job offers I'd received over the years, this had to be the most bizarre.

'Well, I don't know that I would have put it quite like that, but to all intents and purposes . . . yes.'

'This is a wind up! Did one of the guys at the office put you up to this?'

'I assure you this is completely serious. You are in a prime position to help us, Mr Wright. Your job means that you are able to travel into areas beyond the Iron Curtain without suspicion and we know that you visit your wife's relatives in Poland . . .'

'How the hell do you know all this?'

Michael held up a hand. 'Please, Mr Wright, don't be alarmed. Britain is at war, albeit a cold one; it pays for us to keep an eye on the movements of our citizens. We're on the same side here; we're just asking for your help.'

'What do you mean "help"? I don't understand how *I* can be of any help to the Home Office.'

Michael went to the bar and brought us back another round of drinks and then filled me in on exactly what the Home Office had in mind for me. They wanted me to take photographs of air and naval bases in the Communist countries I visited. We may have been on the same side, but the knowledge that Michael displayed of my movements and relationships was frankly terrifying. He listed family and friends that I had in the north-east of England as well as in Poland. There didn't seem to be anything this man didn't know about my life.

'. . . All cameras, films and special equipment would, of course, be supplied by the Secret Service,' Michael concluded, laying his hands flat on the table and looking up at me appraisingly. 'All that's left to ask is would you be willing to help?'

I'm a massive James Bond fan and the prospect of becoming a 007 did sound exciting, but hearing that list of names had made me realise just what I'd be risking. Besides it would never work.

'The thing is,' I explained to Michael. 'I just couldn't do it. It's not just the undercover business – which I don't think I'd be that great at – it's that I'm a marked man. Me and my wife have been tailed and recorded and goodness knows what else. The situation is bad enough as it is, but if I go trying anything . . . you've got to see what I'm saying here. I'd be caught before I'd taken a single picture.'

Michael seemed reluctant to let it go, but eventually I persuaded him that his proposition would be impossible. He drained the last of his drink and stood up to leave.

'Well, it was nice meeting you, Mr Wright. I must say that I am disappointed we couldn't come to an arrangement. Speaking purely personally, I was looking forward to working with you; I was very impressed with the application you placed for the political asylum of your wife's mother.' He held out his hand for me to shake. 'I hope that you understand that this meeting never happened.'

I nodded and he left. I sat there looking at the door. Had that really just happened? I gave it a couple of minutes and then left my drink half-finished and headed home. I couldn't stop looking over my shoulder the whole way home and, when I finally got back, I ran from room to room, pulling all the curtains closed. It was horrible to think that I was being watched, not only by Polish authorities but also by the British. When Margaret got home, she found me curled up on the sofa.

'Aren't you hot?' she complained, leaning over me to open the window. 'Let's get some fresh air in here. It's boiling!'

'Leave it!' I shouted.

She stopped and looked down at me. 'What's wrong?'

I couldn't tell her. The attention that we received from the Polish Government was already making her nervous and I knew that any further intrusion into our lives could tip her over the edge, let alone the knowledge that her husband had just been offered a job as a secret agent.

'Nothing's wrong, love,' I told her, reaching an arm out and encircling her waist. 'I just thought we could do with some privacy.'

She kissed me softy and lay down beside me on the sofa. I felt terrible, keeping things from her. I sincerely thought that I was protecting her but, looking back, I was just creating another layer in the deception and secrets that would eventually drive us apart.

I Said You'd Call Dr Robertson

But, meanwhile, Jimi had found worldwide success and with success comes groupies and with groupies, inevitably, comes the clap. Jimi was still involved with Kathy Etchingham; she was a lovely girl and I truly believe that she was the love of his life, but the trappings of success soon turn a man's head. If only he'd realised what he had right there with Kathy maybe all the traumas that were to come could have been avoided? But for now I think that he was justifying the odd fling with a groupie in the same way that I did – just a bit of fun, which the women we loved need never find out about.

But this was the Sixties and condoms were not really in use and a dose of the clap would be hard to explain. Jimi certainly didn't want to infect Kathy, so I was enlisted as a secret chauffeur for The Jimi Hendrix Experience when they got back to London; ferrying them back and forth to Dr Robertson's Harley Street medical practice for their doses of penicillin. Dr Robertson was well known in the business and always guaranteed discretion when dealing with famous faces. After six visits, the doctor and I were on first name terms.

'John, can I ask you a question? It's not for me, you understand, I'm a married man . . .'

'Sure, Tappy, question for a "friend" is it? What did you want to know?'

'Well, it's just that I'm sick of shipping these lads out to see you all the time and you know after a while you start to worry about yourself.'

'You mean, you start to worry about becoming one of my patients?'

I shuffled my feet. He'd seen through me right away. 'Yes.'

'Right,' John Robertson sat down on the edge of his desk and seemed to consider the situation. 'First and foremost there's smell. If you are 'entertaining' a young lady, things start to progress and you're concerned about possible infection, then it's best to dip your fingers inside her. If your fingers have a strong or unusual smell, then it would be best to end the evening before intercourse has taken place. But, of course, that is not a foolproof method and passions often get in the way. To be honest with you, Tappy, abstinence is always the safest course of action.'

'You're telling me that I should give up sex!'

'Not *you*, Tappy, we're talking about your friend here, aren't we?'

'Oh yes, of course. My friend,' I muttered.

'Well, if your *friend* is not willing to abstain from sexual intercourse then there is a little home remedy that I have heard can be very effective.'

'Home remedy?'

The doctor laughed. 'Yes, well it's not something that I'd put on prescription, but it is meant to work. You make sure that you always carry a small bottle of Scotch whisky on you. After sex, you excuse yourself and visit the bathroom. There, fill a glass with whisky and place your penis in the glass. It will sting a little, but the alcohol should kill off any diseases that you may have picked up during intercourse. Well, what do you think? Could that advice help your friend at all?'

'I think so,' I said with a grin. 'Thanks, John.'

I got up to leave, seeing Jimi walk out of the consulting room rubbing his behind.

'Let's face it, Tappy,' John called after me, with a nod at Jimi, 'it's a damn sight better than having a nurse shove a needle up your arse once a month.'

Abstinence Makes the Heart Grow Fonder

There may have been problems in my marriage, but I was really trying to make it work. As a part of that I was attempting to stay faithful. I may have had the odd indiscretions with groupies (David Arden's girl on the Jayne Mansfield tour, for one), but I had decided to take Dr John Robertson's advice: avoid the sex; avoid the whisky; avoid the girls. But there was one incident that really pushed the borders of my new determination.

I was in the Anim offices when I received a phone call from the live-in girlfriend of one of The ex-Animals. She was utterly hysterical. He had told her that he was in Manchester on business, but she had found a receipt in his pocket for a hotel room booked under the names 'Mr and Mrs Smith'. It was obvious that I wasn't the only one guilty of playing away from home. I grabbed my keys and drove round to their apartment to calm her down. She wept and screamed at me for a time, but after a few cups of strong sweet tea and a couple of stronger brandies, she seemed to have got herself under control and agreed to phone him and let him explain. I left her and went back home to my wife.

The next day, after work, I popped round to check on her. I knew that he would be back late that night and, although we'd had our problems in the past, he was an old friend and I didn't want him getting into too much trouble. I had prepared myself for some renewed hysteria; I was pretty sure that his imminent arrival would have got his girlfriend all worked up again. I certainly wasn't expecting the greeting I got.

She met me at the door, dressed in a silky négligé, a glass of white wine in her hand. 'Hi Tappy,' she said, sweeping her black hair back from her throat and holding the door wide for me to enter. 'It's good to see you.'

'Hi, did you manage to get through to him?'

'No,' she shrugged and poured me out a glass of wine. 'But he'll be back later; I can talk to him then.'

'Well, you seem better.'

She sat back on the sofa and stretched her toes into the carpet pile. 'I'm great, Tappy. Just great.'

She drained her glass and leant over to pour herself another. I wondered how much she'd had.

'You sure you're OK?'

'You mean the drinking? Oh come on, Tappy, I've had two glasses!'

'OK. OK. I was just . . .'

'Worrying about me, yeah, I know. You're sweet.' She put her hand on my arm and left it there. 'I've heard a lot about you, Tappy. Fancy showing me if any of it's true?'

'Look,' I said easing my arm out of her grasp and shifting away from her. 'You're a great girl and you really are very sexy. It kills me to say this, but this is a bad idea; I'm a married man and he is my mate. I think I'd better go.'

I got up to leave, but she stopped me. She laughed. 'Come off it, Tappy. I'm not going to eat you alive. Stay and finish your drink; I could do with the company.'

I sat back down, but with the wine flowing and a beautiful woman laying half-naked beside me it was hard to keep my mind off sex. She seemed to be having the same problem, but I was keeping my hands to myself. I was determined to try and stay faithful to Margaret, whatever the temptation. Then she came up with an idea: she said that we could have sex without actually touching each other, or ourselves.

'I know that he's been a scumbag to me,' she admitted. 'But I have no intention of lowering myself to his level. But if we want to have some fun, I don't see what should stop us. As long as we don't touch, then there's no cheating, is there?'

'I suppose not,' I answered. 'But I don't see how we can have sex without any touching!'

She grinned and jumped off the sofa. 'Well then, it looks like *I'm* the one who's going to be teaching *you*, Tappy Wright! Come here and I'll show you.'

She was a gorgeous girl and as she knelt down on the living-room floor and let her négligé slip from her shoulders, I wondered whether I was really going to be able to keep my resolution to be faithful. She told me to undress and then directed me to kneel opposite her. My erection was already straining at the sight of her and as she pushed her knees apart to give me a full view, I began to see just how easy it would be for me to finish before anything had actually begun.

She arched her back, pushing her small breasts forward. I groaned and made an involuntary move towards her.

'Stay where you are, Tappy,' she purred. 'This is going to be all about our imaginations. I want you to imagine that you are entering me. Imagine what it would feel like to be inside me right now.'

My cock throbbed and I had to claw my hands into the carpet to prevent myself from reaching towards her or reaching down to touch myself. It was an incredible experience. She started to rock and roll her hips as if I was inside her, first slowly and then with gathering speed. As I watched her, the sensations seemed to spread through my body; it was as if she was right there, sitting astride me, without the three feet of carpet between us. She started to pant and moan and I could feel my orgasm building along with hers. With a jolt and a shudder of muscles we both came hard. It was unbelievably erotic; I'd never experienced anything like it.

After we'd both collapsed on the carpet and recovered ourselves, I got dressed and left her with a polite peck on the cheek. No touching, no cheating, but I'd had one of the nights of my life. He was a lucky man; God knows why he needed to seek satisfaction elsewhere, but maybe he was just the same as me: unable to resist a new excitement.

Never Mess with Mike

I may have left her flat with a relatively clear conscience, but I knew that temptation was never going to leave me completely alone in this business. Even though I'd given up the life on the road, there were still regular trips abroad and across country to deal with the various needs of Anim's clients. I began to look forward to escaping from the pressures that were imposed on my marriage by the constant attention from the Polish authorities and Margaret and I seemed to be spending less and less time together.

My next foreign trip circa 1968 was not on behalf of a band, however; it was at the request of my boss, Mike Jeffery. Despite his management position at Anim, Mike had been spending most of his time in Majorca in Spain. By this time he owned a nightclub in Palma, called Sergeant Pepper's, and was in the process of setting up his second club called Doctor Zhivago. He wanted to continue the 'Summer of Love' vibe by getting Chas to send Jimi Hendrix out to open it. Although I wasn't personally needed for the big opening, Mike called me because, much as he was enjoying the Spanish sunshine, he was missing his beautiful racing-green Morgan sports car and he needed someone to drive it over for him.

That car was Mike's pride and joy; after I'd delivered it to him safely in Majorca, he asked me to hang around for a couple of days and help him out with the preparations for his club's grand opening. I was happy to take a holiday from the complications back in England and readily agreed. Little did I know that I was about to get a taste of exactly how ruthless Mike Jeffery could be when it came to dealing with complications of his own.

The American Navy's 6th Fleet were on manoeuvres in the Mediterranean Sea; they'd already caused a mass panic among the locals in Palma by managing to lose one of their weapons overboard, but they didn't seem to have any mind to ease their relationship with the community when they came ashore. Sailors on shore-leave have always had a reputation and these boys fitted the stereotype exactly. They were regularly seen drunk and disorderly in the bars and clubs that lined the shore and had enraged most of the local fathers and brothers with their lewd and suggestive behaviour towards the modest Catholic girls. Mike had already had to deal with them at Sergeant Pepper's and he'd started to worry about the disruption that they could cause when Doctor Zhivago opened. He didn't want anything to ruin his opening night.

I have always said that Mike Jeffery was not a man that you wanted to upset. Even without the rumours of his mob connections and dubious business dealings, the man in dark glasses had an air of personal menace that had made me ensure that I always remained on his good side. The truth was that Mike was ex-Secret Service and he hadn't forgotten his training. One night, whilst I was staying with him, he donned a wetsuit and blacked his face. He was going to get his revenge on the drunken sailors that were threatening his businesses.

Mike swam out close to the American ship under cover of darkness and began to line up a series of explosives, running along a short distance from the starboard bow. They wouldn't cause any damage to the ship itself, but they'd be enough to shake up the US Navy and give the disgruntled locals a show. He programmed the trigger explosive to detonate at noon the following day, the time when he knew that the beach would be at its busiest.

The next day he invited me to join him down on the sands. I had some idea that Mike had a revenge plot brewing, but I can honestly say that I hadn't expected anything on the scale of what he'd prepared. It was as if the ocean was bursting into flames. People screamed and ran from the sea, gazing out as the explosives detonated one after another and sent geysers of water shooting into the air. But, above it all, came the shrill wail of the American ship's sirens. I turned to Mike and realised that he was laughing.

'Did you have anything to do with this?' I asked him.

He shrugged. 'That'll teach those bloody Yanks to mess up my bar, eh?'

That night we sat with our drinks in front of Sergeant Pepper's and waved goodbye to the American 6th Fleet, who had received orders to leave the Mediterranean shortly after Mike's little revenge plan had exploded over their bows.

'*Adiós!*' Mike shouted after the departing ship, 'And don't fuckin' well come back!'

He explained to me what had happened that night and then we got to talking about his days in the Secret Service.

'You get used to it, you know,' Mike told me. 'Combat gets to be almost fun when you're good at it.' He set his glass down and brought his hands together to imitate a pistol. 'Just firing them off. Pop. Pop. Pop. And they all fall down. It's like an arcade or something; like shooting at those little plastic ducks you get at funfairs, do you know what I mean?'

I nodded warily. It didn't sound much like fun to me.

Mike laughed and refilled our glasses. 'You forget that they're people, Tappy. When they're coming over a ridge at you, they're just targets. The only time that it gets difficult is when you have to go up close. There were times when I was in North Africa when I had to creep right into the tents. I had to creep right up to their beds and knife them where they lay sleeping. You could hear the bayonet scrap against their ribs as the blade was pushed in. They would squeal like pigs and both of us would be rolling in the blood. I tried to hold their mouths shut, you know, grip their lips together, but there was always that squeal and that grind of the knife against the bone.'

Mike had stopped laughing. He was staring into his glass, but I doubted that he was seeing anything but those violent memories of his past life in the Special Forces . . . and then he smiled. Mike Jeffery was definitely not a man you wanted to get on the wrong side of.

A Little Eye-Opener for Alan Price

I left Majorca with Mike Jeffery's glory stories running through my mind; London certainly looked like the better bet. Mike was due to return to England after the Doctor Zhivago club was up and running, but I was ready to leave and I was needed back in the Anim office with Chas and the guys.

Alan Price was having some discomfort in his right eye. Fresh off the plane from Spain, I was dispatched to make sure that he saw a doctor. At least it would give me a chance to pay a visit to Dr John Robertson with a patient who wasn't complaining of VD.

I met Alan at his apartment, giving his girlfriend a friendly wave as she came out to kiss him goodbye. Apart from his eye, Alan was happy and chatty in the car.

'Hello, John,' I greeted the doctor, as we entered the clinic. 'I've got a bit of a novelty for you today; a genuine illness, would you believe? And I don't even think he'll need an injection in the arse!'

John Robertson laughed and escorted us both into his consulting room. I sat down in a spare chair as Alan climbed on to the examination table and let the doctor take a look at his eye.

'Right, I think I can see the problem,' John said. 'It shouldn't take too long to sort out; I'll just have to give you a local anaesthetic and then we can get cracking.'

I'm not particularly squeamish and I sat and watched as the doctor gave Alan his injection. I could tell that Alan was nervous about what could happen and I wanted to be on hand to crack a few jokes and lighten the mood if I was needed. But it was only after the anaesthetic had taken effect that Dr Robertson was able to begin his treatment in earnest. I got a glimpse of what kind of horrors I could have inflicted on Tony Garland if that exploding cigarette gag had gone badly wrong. It would have put Mike Jeffery's anecdotes to shame.

'I see you had some damage here in the past,' Dr Robertson commented.

Alan gurgled a response as the doctor eased his eye completely out of its socket. Alan's eyeball hung loosely from its array of tendons and nerves and rested against his cheek. The doctor cleaned the area behind it and I fought back the bile that was rising in my throat and managed to ask Alan if he was OK.

'Yeah, I'm all right,' he replied. 'There's one thing, though.' Alan's forehead crinkled. The commonplace gesture of confusion looked horrifying sitting over that gaping empty eye-socket. 'I know that I'm looking at your face, but I can see your feet at the same time. I must have some kind of double-vision or something; you better sort that out, Doc.'

'Don't worry, Alan, I'm on it,' the doctor replied, carrying on with his procedure.

'Urm . . . I've just got to go sort something out,' I muttered, making for the door. 'I'll not be a minute.'

I ran out of the consulting room and into the bathroom. After several minutes retching over a toilet bowl, I finally managed to compose myself enough to return to Alan and the doctor.

I entered the room just as Dr Robertson was carefully pushing Alan's eye back into its socket. He stood back to admire his handiwork.

'You'll have to wait for the anaesthetic to wear off completely to really feel the difference there, but how's that for now, Alan. Is your vision OK?'

Alan sat up on the examination table and looked over at me. 'Oh, yeah, that's much better. I'm just seeing your face now, Tappy. You OK, son? You're looking a little bit pale over there.'

'Yeah, Alan. I'm fine,' I replied. 'I'm just glad that you're all in one piece.'

CHAPTER 10

End of an Era: The Last Years of Jimi Hendrix

Losing Jimi to the Ladies

While I was busy with the Anim clients still based in the UK, The Jimi Hendrix Experience were exploiting the attention that Monterey had granted them. They had a wonderful road manager, Gerry Stickles, who had taken up with the Experience when I'd rejected the job. He was a great guy from Kent, in the South of England, and was as dedicated and loyal a roadie as they could have wished for. (In fact, in future years he would go on to prove his credentials as the manager of the world-famous rock band, Queen.) Chas had organised a combined tour of the US, billing other Anim acts alongside Jimi and the boys, and it had been an undisputed success. Jimi Hendrix's popularity just grew and grew.

But, as I have said before, with success comes temptation. Jimi was plunged into a world where girls, drugs and booze were all there for the taking. Jimi had been playing his guitar for years on the circuit and, from his position in the band, he must have seen what could happen to artists after fame struck. But now *he* was the centre of attention and lessons learnt from the wings went out of the window when the world was in love with your every move. Jimi was just a young man caught in the dazzle of his own success. I don't think that he was ready for the road that fame was to take him down, one leading to drink, drugs, sex and his own untimely death.

He'd separated from his girlfriend, Kathy, the woman who had done so well at keeping his feet on the ground. He would speak to me about her now and then and, at times like that, I was able to catch a glimpse of the real Jimi once again, that sweet boy I'd met at Café Wha? with Chas Chandler, who just wanted to be able to play his music the way he wanted. I knew that she still loved him dearly, but understandably she just couldn't put up with his antics on the road. Without Kathy, Jimi Hendrix had abandoned himself to the spirals of fame and now he was at its mercy.

But, to be honest with you, when it came to choosing temptations, Jimi didn't start out too badly. I remember earlier in late spring of 1967, The Jimi Hendrix Experience were back in the UK and booked to appear again on *Top of the Pops*. I'd just got in to the Anim office and was handing Tony Garland his morning coffee (I usually picked us both up a cup from the coffee shop opposite the office on my way in) when I got a call from Gerry Stickles.

'Hi there, Tappy. Have you seen Jimi at all?'

'No, he's meant to be with you, isn't he?'

'Yeah, *meant to be*. The stupid bastard hasn't showed up. I'm at the BBC now with the rest of the boys; the producer is starting to lose his rag. He wants to do a sound check and we can't find Jimi!'

'All right, Gerry, you try and calm him down and we'll see if we can track him down.'

I rang off and explained the situation to Tony. 'I reckon if I use my phone to try and get hold of Jimi and we'll keep your line open if he tries to ring us.'

'Good plan, Tappy,' Tony agreed. 'What the hell is he up to?'

I shook my head and reached for my phone book, determined to find out. I started to call round all the friends and friends of friends that I could think of. Someone must know where Jimi Hendrix was. I was pretty sure that he'd turn up in one of his friend's houses, nursing a hangover and having no idea what time it was. But no one had seen him. I was just starting to panic, when Tony's phone rang.

'It's him,' Tony said, holding the receiver out to me.

'Where the fuck are you, Jimi?' I yelled down the phone. 'Gerry's going spare; you were meant to be at *Top of the Pops* an hour ago.'

'Hey, Tappy, calm down, man,' Jimi replied. 'I'm at the Royal Garden Hotel in Kensington. Look, I'm sorry about the show and all that, but I can't talk now. Could one of you come and pick me up?'

'He's in some fucking hotel!' I told Tony, who was sitting listening

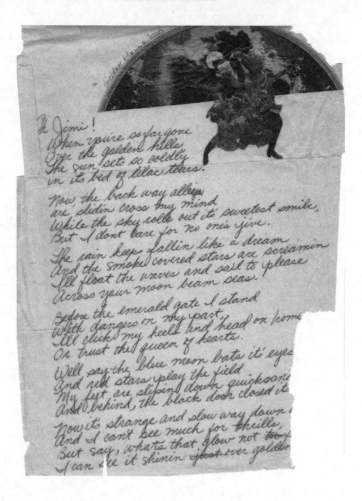

Jimi received a huge amount of fan letters from girls, this one is longer than usual.

to my conversation. 'He's slept in, poor lamb, and now he wants one of us to go and collect him.'

Tony rolled his eyes. 'Tell him to get a cab. Fucking pop stars, eh? Who needs them?'

I was inclined to agree with him, but I could still hear Jimi's pleas for help carrying on in a tinny whine from the telephone receiver. 'Please, Tappy. I need your help, man. Are you still there?'

'I'm here. Why can't you get a cab? If you want to be late, son, you need to learn how to get yourself out of it.'

Jimi sighed and lowered his voice. 'I don't really want to draw

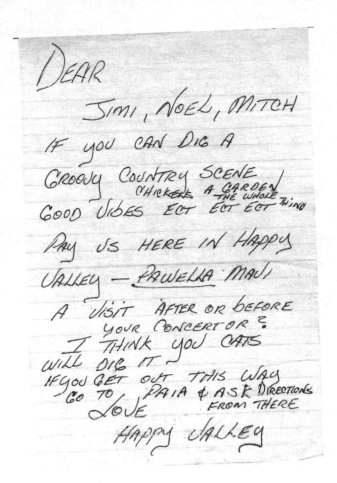

DEAR
  JIMI, NOEL, MITCH
IF YOU CAN DIG A
GROOVY COUNTRY SCENE
    CHICKENS A GARDEN
            THE WHOLE THING
GOOD VIBES ECT ECT ECT
PAY US HERE IN HAPPY
VALLEY — PAWELLA MAUI
A VISIT AFTER OR BEFORE
    YOUR CONCERT OR ?
  I THINK YOU CATS
WILL DIG IT
IF YOU GET OUT THIS WAY
  GO TO, PAIA & ASK DIRECTIONS
    LOVE   FROM THERE
      HAPPY VALLEY

The Experience were sent endless invitations by fans too.

attention to myself. I'm in Room 501. I'm in *Brigitte Bardot's* room, Tappy.'

'Bridgette Bardot!' I exclaimed. Tony sat up in his chair and stared at me. 'I'll be right there.'

'And I'm coming with you!' Tony said, grabbing his keys. 'Let's take my car.'

With those two little words – Brigitte Bardot – Jimi had gone from having no lift at all, to two grown men racing to get to the car first. That lucky bastard! Just a glimpse of that gorgeous French actress up close would be enough for me or Tony, but Jimi was in her hotel room! How the hell had he swung that one?

Fan mail was often embellished by the young writers.

But, unfortunately for us, when we arrived at the Royal Garden Hotel Jimi was waiting outside. Alone. He laughed at our crushed expressions, as we desperately searched the crowd for a flock of blonde hair and a pair of bee-stung lips to no avail.

'A lovely girl, a lovely girl,' he said, as he climbed into the car with me and Tony. 'But, not for your eyes, fellas.' He laughed again. 'Now, I think I'm late for the BBC, aren't I?'

So I never got to see Brigitte Bardot, but I certainly got to meet a fair few of the women that entertained him along the way. He often fell into crazy infatuations, believing that every girl who caught his fancy was the new love of his life. I think that he was desperately searching for the stability that he'd lost when he split from Kathy. She had been a rock for him to lean on when the chaos of a life in the limelight had become too much to bear. Jimi was an extravagant and outlandish performer, but as a man he was surprisingly quiet and gentle. He had always struck me as shy, a human being, who loved his music, but was also desperate to form human connections and to fall in love.

There was one occasion, when I was over in Anim's New York

office, when I received a call from Jimi about a girl that he'd met the night before in Texas. The Experience were due to fly out that morning to Hawaii, so I only half-listened as Jimi rambled on about the amazing sex that he'd had after the gig.

'Seriously, Tappy, I've never had a girl give me head like that before. She was incredible and she's so beautiful, man. I can't believe that I've been able to carry on so long without her. She understands me; I think that she can see my soul, man. I'm in love, Tappy. There's no doubt about it. She's the girl I've been waiting for.'

'Yeah, OK, Jimi,' I said a little impatiently. I'd heard all this before. Every time he met a new woman, in fact. 'You better get going. You've got a flight to catch, remember?'

He rang off, leaving me to get on with my paperwork. I forgot all about the latest girl until Jimi called me again the following morning.

'Is everything all right, Jimi?' I was surprised to hear from him; he usually only called after a gig, to let us know how everything had gone.

'No. I want her, Tappy. I want her with me now,' he demanded. He sounded desperate.

'Who are you talking about? That girl from the other night?'

'Yeah, that's right: Julie. I don't care what it costs, Tappy, I need her here. I want you to find her and fly her over to join me in Hawaii. First-class, Tappy. I can't carry on without her.'

There was no dissuading him. All I had to go on was that her name was Julie, she'd been at The Jimi Hendrix Experience gig in Texas and she worked in a department store. It seemed like an impossible task, but I had contacts who knew how to recognise groupies and eventually we managed to track her down.

But it seems that Julie wasn't nearly as impressed with Jimi as he had been with her. For her it had just been a one-night stand. My friends in Texas had to practically get down on their knees to convince her to fly out to Hawaii. In the end, the prospect of a holiday in Hawaii won her over and we were able to get her on to a plane, as Jimi had instructed. Apparently poor Jimi was delighted to see her, but the ecstasy remained very much one-sided.

If You've Got It, Spend It

Although the incident with Julie was nothing new, especially compared to some of the other demands I'd heard of stars making through the years, this demanding streak did highlight a new element of Jimi's personality and one that I was not keen to see more of.-

But Jimi was at the top of his game. The Jimi Hendrix Experience was approaching the position of highest-paid band in the USA. The money was pouring in and Jimi was more than happy to think up new and exciting ways to spend it.

He wanted a car, but not just any car. Jimi Hendrix was the king of psychedelia and he needed a carriage to fit his station. But this was no Little Richard stage show; Jimi bought himself a Corvette Stingray (the first of six Corvettes that he would eventually purchase) and painted it in rainbow colours. The multi-coloured sports car was not just a showpiece and it was the speed more than the design that really interested Jimi. He almost drooled when he learnt that the car could reach speeds of up to 160mph (250kph). This car was his baby, beautiful and fast, and for his use only, despite his terrible eyesight which prevented him from achieving a licence to drive it.

That's why I was surprised when Jimi's road manager, Gerry Stickles, strolled into Mike Jeffery's offices one morning with a key chain jangling noisily from his forefinger.

'Look what I just got from Jimi,' Gerry said, dropping the keys on the desk in front of me and giving me a smug smile. 'My very own set of keys to the Corvette.'

'He's only had it a week,' I protested, trying not to look too envious. 'I didn't think he'd let anyone touch that car.'

'Well, maybe he just trusts me more than anyone else?' Gerry suggested and walked off with his keys.

But any envy I'd felt for Gerry's chance to use the rainbow Corvette soon wore off, especially when I realised exactly what use Gerry was getting. It seemed that Jimi loved having a flash car, but he didn't like the bother of having to find a parking space. So whenever he went out for the evening, to a club, restaurant or a party, he had got into the habit of just stopping the car as close to his destination as possible. The traffic police were not likely to miss a rainbow-coloured Stingray double-parked or simply abandoned in the middle of the street, but Jimi had managed to solve the little inconveniences of having his car constantly impounded by giving Gerry Stickles his own set of keys.

Poor Gerry had to get used to a new routine. Jimi would leave his night's entertainment and, comfortable in the knowledge that his own car would already have been towed away, hail a cab to take him home to bed. The next morning Gerry would have to get to the car compound, pay the fine and then deliver the car back to Jimi at his apartment. Jimi didn't even have to raise his head from the pillow. So much for Gerry's position of trust.

We were also concerned that Jimi was driving without a driving licence, as the office was responsible for Jimi's car to the authorities.

I caught Gerry coming into the New York office a couple of months later. 'Enjoying all those drives in Jimi's car are you, Gerry?' I asked him. 'It must be wonderful to be trusted. It's just that I thought I saw you come in by cab this morning; I thought that you were travelling in style these days?'

'Fuck off, Tappy. You know full well that I've been up for hours, shipping that bloody car back and forth.' He rubbed his eyes and glared at me. 'And don't you go grinning at me like that. How was I to know that Jimi would rather pay a fine than find a parking space?'

The Truth About 'Musical Differences'

But the money was not always spent in innocent ways. Jimi began to use his new-found wealth to fund an alcohol and drugs habit that was beginning to spiral out of control. He started again seeing Kathy 'on and off' and now seemed determined to upset everyone else who was close to him. Personally, I tried to keep in mind that everything I heard from Jimi during that period was filtered through a haze of experimental drugs and too many nights on the booze. I don't think he really realised what he was saying or doing and I wasn't about to get myself upset over incidents or conversations that he probably wouldn't even remember the following day. But there was one event that he couldn't forget, because it managed to change his life, his musical career and find a place in musical history.

It has always amazed me that, in all the talk and rumour surrounding the life and death of Jimi Hendrix, the truth about his separation from Chas Chandler has never been put into print. It was Chas who'd found Jimi and seen his potential; the idea that he would part company with his prodigy over 'musical differences' (which seems to be the standard explanation) is just ridiculous. But the truth never got out – that is, until now. I think it's about time that the truth was not just the privilege of the industry insiders; I think it's time that you all knew why one of the world's greatest musicians and his manager finally decided to go their separate ways and why Chas Chandler would have been driven to pass Hendrix's management over to Mike Jeffery.

It was a bright, frosty winter's morning. It started much like many others at the London Anim office. Jimi had just finished touring and Tony Garland by now had left Anim for another job.

I had walked into work, stopping in at the barber's on Gerard Street for a shave. Henry Cooper, the champion boxer, could often be found in that barber's and I'd be able to sit and share some bawdy jokes with the man who had famously floored Muhammad Ali, whilst Carlos the barber carefully angled his cut-throat razor around Henry's laughing jaw.

I picked up morning coffees on my way to open up the office. Henry Henroid came in shortly after me and we sat down at our desks with the steaming polystyrene cups in front of us. Henry was nursing a cauliflower ear.

'Thought you'd get back into the game, did you, Henry?' I asked the ex-boxer. 'You look like you've been taking a beating from Henry Cooper downstairs.'

'No. I just figured out that PMT and German women don't mix,' Henry said, attempting a smile and wincing as the movement tugged at his swollen and purple ear.

Henry may have been a tough guy, but his German girlfriend could have seen off the best of them in a few short rounds. This wasn't the first injury that I'd seen Henry suffering at her hands. Every month at the same time he'd turn up with a black eye or some other bruising.

The guy just didn't know when to keep his mouth shut when his Fraulein was in a temper.

I chatted to Henry for a time, but I was restless and, despite the freezing draft that blew through the outer corridor, I propped open the office door, hoping to catch a glimpse of Twiggy or Chrissy Shrimpton as they made their way up to Terence Donovan's photo studio upstairs. But the only thing I got close to catching was a cold; the Sixties supermodels didn't seem to be working that day.

I'd decided to give it a couple of extra minutes, sipping at my cooling coffee and doodling on a pad of paper, when a shadow fell across my desk. I looked up and saw Chas standing in the doorway.

'Jesus, Chas, you gave me a fright. I was looking for a beautiful girl, son, not my boss!'

It wasn't a great joke, but I regretted it almost immediately. There was no way that I was going to get Chas to crack a smile this morning. He stood there staring at me with a face like thunder. I thought that I was going to get the same treatment that Henry Henroid received, joking with his girlfriend at the wrong time of the month. Chas had managed to dress himself for the office, but from his long grey mackintosh to his trademark cowboy boots he looked dishevelled, as if he'd dragged himself into work, rather than been driven. He didn't seem to have even heard me when I spoke to him.

'Get me Mike Jeffery on the phone now,' Chas said, through clenched teeth. I opened my mouth to object. 'And don't go telling me that he's in New York. I said call him and I mean it. I don't care what fucking time it is, you just get him on the phone.'

Chas swept past me and Henry and into his office, slamming the door behind him. Henry stared at me, his mouth open; one hand still cupping his injured ear.

'What the hell is all that about?' Henry mouthed.

I shrugged and got on the phone. I didn't fancy waking Mike up at some ungodly hour, but I hadn't seen Chas this angry since I'd tried to feed him to the sharks! I had just got through to the operator when Chas's door flew open again.

'And you!' he shouted across at Henry. 'You can make yourself useful by getting all this shit boxed up.' Chas reached out and grabbed one of the Hendrix tour posters that were pinned up and lined the office walls. He screwed it up in his fist and threw it to floor, staring at it, white-faced, as if he'd like to grind it into the carpet with his foot. 'I don't want any of that bastard's crap in my office,' he spat, turning on his heel and shutting himself back into his room.

Henry raised his eyebrows at me and pulled a spare cardboard box out from under his desk. I had my own problems to deal with, I'd just got through to Mike Jeffery and he wasn't happy about the wake-up call.

'Do you have any idea what fucking time it is in New York, Tappy?'

'Yeah, I know and I'm sorry, but Chas says that he has to talk to you and he's not taking no for an answer. Something's happened, Mike; he's making us box up all of Jimi's stuff.'

'Well, it had better be something big!'

I patched the call through to Chas's office and started to help Henry load all the Jimi Hendrix posters and discs into boxes. We kept it quiet; straining our ears to eavesdrop on what was being said behind Chas's door. But the mood that Chas was in we didn't have to work hard to hear his side of the conversation.

'I'm finished with that son-of-a-bitch,' Chas was screaming. 'I'm serious, Mike; I want Jimi fucking Hendrix out of my life. I want you on the first flight that you can get to London. Call Tappy and I'll get him to pick you up. I'll call the lawyers. That bastard is your problem now!' We could hear the smash as the phone receiver was slammed down.

What the hell was going on? Chas and Jimi had had their differences over the years; they were both strong personalities and they both had their own ideas when it came to the direction that they wanted to pull The Jimi Hendrix Experience. But it was those differences and disputes that had made the music that they produced so exciting. There had never been any suggestion of Chas giving up on his management.

Henry and I could hear Chas banging about in his office; it sounded like things were being thrown. We caught one another's eyes and got back to looking busy; there was no way that we wanted to draw attention to ourselves when Chas was this furious. Right on cue, Chas appeared at his office door.

'You two, in here now!' he said.

We followed him into his office. Paperwork littered the carpet along with the remains of gold discs and trophies that Chas had acquired during his days with The Animals, which had now been ripped from their display space on the office shelves and were rolling about on the floor. Chas had torn the place apart. Henry and I shuffled nervously into the room, eyeing the devastation that surrounded us. Had Chas just called us in because he'd run out of stuff to break?

But Chas moved around to the other side of his large dark wood desk and collapsed into his leather chair. I could see the fury draining out of him. He put his head in his hands and let out a quivering sigh.

'I'll go get you a cup of coffee, boss,' Henry said, excusing himself in the face of Chas's rising emotion.

Once we were left alone, I made my way over to comfort Chas. It was horrifying to see the big man crumble like that. Something truly terrible must have happened and I knew I should find some way of helping him cope with it.

'Look Chas, son. You've got to tell me what's going on. What's happened?'

I was still gently probing him for information when Henry came back into the room with a battered 'I Love New York' mug in his hands. 'There you go, Chas. I'd almost forgotten that little kitchen was there, we've been getting too expensive in our tastes I reckon.' He tried for a smile, but it faded quickly as he looked down at Chas's shaking shoulders. 'Get some of that down you, mate. It's strong and black, just the way you like it.'

Chas took a deep breath and nodded his thanks to Henry. There was a moment of silence in the room as Chas sipped at the hot coffee. He ran a hand over his eyes and looked up at us.

'You ready to talk about it, Chas?' I asked.

He nodded. 'I think I need to. But what I'm about to tell you goes no further than this office, is that understood?'

We both agreed immediately, watching as Chas took some deeper gulps of coffee. He seemed to be bracing himself. But it turns out that caffeine was not what Chas's unstable temper needed at that moment and he suddenly jumped from his chair, hurling the coffee cup against the wall and narrowly missing Henry's swollen ear.

'That dirty fucking son-of-a-bitch, I can't believe what he's done to me!' Chas screamed, pounding his fists against the table. Framed photographs of Chas with The Animals and his smiling wife Lotta joined the litter on the office floor.

Henry ducked down behind the desk; he'd never seen Chas like this before. I have to say, even with my long history with Chas, I couldn't think of an occasion when I had seen him so overwrought. I managed to calm him down; the burst of fury had only been short lived and soon he was weeping again. I couldn't decide which was worse to witness.

Chas's knuckles were bruised and reddening; I suspected that his office desk had not been the first thing to have taken a beating that day. Henry was obviously thinking the same thing. He'd emerged from behind the desk, holding his ear and staring at the coffee that dripped down the wall. He looked like he would rather bolt now, than become the subject of another upsurge of rage from our boss, and I couldn't blame him.

But Chas had quietened down and I didn't think that there was much fight left in him. He held up his hands in defeat and pulled himself together. 'I'm sorry, Henry. But it's been one hell of a morning.' He sighed and wiped the tears from his face. 'Jesus, look at the state of me.'

'Don't worry about that, Chas,' I told him. 'Just tell us what this is all about. Maybe we can help?'

'It's past help, believe me. But I trust you guys and I have to tell someone.' Chas sat back in his chair and clenched his raw fists; then he told us his story. 'It was this morning. I got ready for work and said goodbye to Lotta. I thought that she deserved a lie-in, you know? So I just kissed her goodbye and left. She hardly stirred; I didn't even think that I'd woken her. Jimi certainly hadn't surfaced, but there was no change there.'

I grimaced. I thought that I could see where this story was going, but I didn't want to believe it. Jimi and Kathy had been staying with Chas and Lotta. Chas knew what it was like to be living at the top of your game and Lotta had always been a party girl, so they were sympathetic to his partying and late hours. But surely Jimi wouldn't have done anything so stupid as to risk that?

'I'd decided to walk to the office,' Chas continued. 'But I'd only gone three blocks when I realised I'd left the papers for that meeting this afternoon back in the apartment. I still had time to spare and I knew that you would open up if I ran late, Tappy, so I turned round and headed back to the flat.' Chas swallowed. Telling us this had become an endurance test and I could see the strain on his face. 'I just turned round and headed back. I think that it even crossed my mind to wake Lotta up properly before I went back to work.

'But when I got in, she wasn't in the bedroom. I figured that she'd got up and was having a shower or fixing breakfast and, when I couldn't find the papers, I thought that she might have moved them. You know what she's like. Christ, Tappy, you've known her as long as I have. She just shifts stuff around and then gets pissed when I complain about it.

'Thing was I couldn't find her. Jesus, it seems like a dream looking back on it: there I was, the stupid fucking naïve husband, wandering round his own home looking for his wife. I could hear . . . well, I could hear Jimi in his room.' Chas bit his lip and screwed up his face in pain. I thought that he might break down again, but after a pause he continued. 'I was thinking, "Lucky bastard; that's the kind of work I'd like to be doing". Little did I know that it was work I *should* have been doing. The fucking bastard! She's my fucking wife! He was screwing my fucking wife right there in my house!'

I heard Henry whistle in sympathy and surprise. We both stood there looking at Chas as he started to beat on the table again, tears rolling down his face.

'Chas,' I whispered, easing his hands off the desk. 'Jesus, Chas, I'm so sorry, but what did you do? Is Jimi OK? You haven't done anything stupid, have you, son?'

Chas glared at me. 'I haven't done nearly enough! You'll be pleased to hear that, as far as I know, your precious little Jimi Hendrix is fine and fucking dandy! After I'd kicked the bedroom door in and found my wife in bed with the scrawny little shit and after I'd dragged my loving wife out of that bed by that long blonde hair, which I pay so much to keep shiny and gorgeous. After I'd flung the lying, cheating bitch out on the street, Jimi was long gone.'

'It wasn't him I was worrying about Chas,' I tried to explain. 'But, if you'd done anything stupid, I'd need to know about it; I'd need to sort it out.'

But Chas was barely listening to me any more. The man seemed utterly destroyed. 'I chased up and down Upper Berkeley Street for a while, but I couldn't find him.' He looked up at me now with nothing but pain in his eyes. 'I can't believe it, Tappy. I invited Jimi into my home and this is how he repays me. I don't even know how long it had been going on. How could Lotta do it to me?

'I looked at her lying there naked – my wife, the woman I loved – and all I saw was a dirty little slag. She disgusts me, Tappy, she just disgusts me. She was begging for another chance and I threw her clothes at her and then dumped her in the street. She's garbage. I don't even want to look at her.'

I didn't know what to say to Chas. What can you say to a man whose world has just fallen apart? I couldn't believe that beautiful lively Lotta, whom I'd met and had introduced to Chas on that Swedish tour after Alan Price had left The Animals, and Jimi, whom Chas had spent so much time and energy in producing and coaching into the great star that he was born to be, had reduced Chas to this and all for the sake of a stupid affair.

Chas never spoke to Lotta again, although he did keep in contact with his son, Stefan (who would eventually go on to follow in his father's footsteps and became the successful manager of several top DJs). Chas could never forgive Lotta and he could never forgive Jimi Hendrix.

The ridiculous thing was that, although many people in the business were aware of the reasons behind the split between Chas and Jimi, it was hushed up and never brought into the open.

It wasn't until the following morning that Mike Jeffery arrived in London. As promised, I was there to meet him at the airport in my own cherry-red Mini Cooper. Neither of us spoke very much on our way to the Anim office; personally I was nervous about seeing Chas again. I was worried that he would regret having confided in me and possibly be embarrassed about exposing his emotions to myself and Henry. Mike didn't ask me what had happened and I certainly wasn't going to offer any information, but as we pulled up outside Anim, 'Hey Joe' came on the radio.

When we got into the offices, Chas seemed much more contained. His eyes were red raw, but he just seemed to want to get the business settled. It was that day, behind the closed door of his office, that Chas Chandler sold Mike Jeffery his interest in Jimi Hendrix. From that point on Mike would have full control of Jimi's management for the bargain price of an alleged sum in the region of £100,000.

A hundred grand was a lot of money in 1969, but compared to the amount of money that the rights to Jimi Hendrix would eventually be worth, it was peanuts.

So there you have it: the truth. I may have sworn never to tell another soul what Chas shared with me that day in his office, but now that Chas is dead and gone I feel that the time is right to set the record straight. Chas Chandler can be accused of many things, but he was a great manager and it was only under the extreme circumstances that I've outlined here that he would ever have given over the control of Hendrix's career to Mike Jeffery. He can take no responsibility for the catastrophic events that were to follow.

Singing in the Rain at Woodstock

That was how I arrived for the Woodstock Music and Arts Festival in the August of 1969 with Mike Jeffery. Woodstock was held in the tiny town of Bethel in upstate New York and the crowds were due to fill a dairy farmer's field owned by Max Yasgur. Mike and I arrived a couple of days early, so that Mike could meet with Albert Grossman, Bob Dylan's manager, and make sure that everything would be ready for Jimi's headlining performance.

Management had not been the only change for Jimi Hendrix; he was ready to début a whole new band: Gypsy Sun and Rainbows. Noel Redding, The Jimi Hendrix Experience's bassist, had become increasingly frustrated by the fact that he could not play his favoured instrument, the guitar, whilst with the Experience and some of the hysteria surrounding the band's performances had started to worry him. He'd decided to leave and start his own band, Fat Mattress, and Jimi took the chance to design a whole new line-up to help him express the new sounds that he was working on. An old friend of Jimi's, Billy Cox, would take Noel's place on bass in Gypsy Sun and Rainbows along with Mitch Mitchell on drums; there was also Larry Lee to play rhythm guitar and Juma Sultan and Jerry Velez on percussion. Out of Chas's control, it looked like Woodstock could prove an exciting new start for Jimi and his band.

But 17 August, the day that Hendrix was due to perform, proved to be a day of disasters. It was pouring with rain; Mike and Albert got their jeep stuck in the mud and had to be towed out. Shortly after that the stage itself collapsed. No one had expected the crowds that actually turned up. This may have been naïve with acts like Janis Joplin, The Who, Sly and the Family Stone, Credence Clearwater Revival, Jefferson Airplane and, of course, Gypsy Sun and Rainbows on offer, but 300,000 people sliding about in the rain had taken its toll on the cow field. On top of that the itinerary of the event wasn't running to plan, with the band changeovers taking far too long. When Jimi finally arrived we realised that he was not to be spared from the problems that seemed to have affected the entire day. He was coughing, sneezing and looked horribly pale.

'Jesus, Jimi, you look awful!' I exclaimed when I saw him.

'Cheers, Tappy, it's good to see you too! I'm all right really. It's just a cold.'

'It looks a bit worse than that,' I said as he gave another almighty sneeze. 'Are you going to be able to play?'

'I'll be fine, man. Don't worry about that. I could do with a glass of water, though.'

I couldn't even get the poor guy that. Some unknown person had spiked the entire water supply backstage at Woodstock with LSD or acid. Jimi looked ill enough; I didn't want to add to his troubles by pumping him full of hallucinogenic drugs. Luckily, Mike was able to have a word with the promoter and, after he had seen the state that Jimi was in, he agreed to put off Jimi's performance until the following morning and effectively extend the festival just for him.

This gave Jimi a good night's sleep in which to recover and early next morning he did look a little better. I think that Mike was more nervous than Hendrix about the performance; it would be the first major gig that Jimi had played with Mike Jeffery as his sole manager.

As Woodstock had officially ended the night before, the crowd had dwindled down to around 25,000, but the atmosphere that truly wrote the Woodstock Festival's name into the history books was still in place. These people had waited on through the rain just to see Jimi Hendrix perform and we hoped that Gypsy Sun and Rainbows could pull it together and impress them.

But when they took to the stage at 7.30am the following morning,

I quickly realised that this was not going to be another Monterey. Gypsy Sun and Rainbows were painfully under-rehearsed making the majority of their set embarrassingly shambolic to witness. Mike was furious. It wasn't Jimi's 'flu that was letting them down, just a lack of preparation and Mike paced back and forth backstage, cursing Jimi's name and the reassurances that Jimi had fed him about the new band. The only highlight of that show, in my opinion, was Jimi's version of 'Star Spangled Banner'. It was amazing, but not enough to make Mike Jeffery happy.

Jimi did little to lighten his mood by messing up the next engagement as well. He was booked to appear on the *The Dick Cavett Show*, a hugely successful TV talk-show going out on ABC from New York. Jimi had been asked to appear in order to talk about the Woodstock experience. It was a high-profile show and, with a new band to promote, it was a great chance for Jimi to get his message across.

But this wasn't the super-keen young Jimi Hendrix that I'd met in Café Wha? three years before; Jimi was becoming more arrogant and unreliable as the days passed. Backstage at the *The Dick Cavett Show*, Jimi managed to lose me and Mike in the crush of people and disappear. When he was called, we couldn't find him. He must have sloped off to some party in New York. Any pity that Mike had for Jimi's attack of the 'flu dissolved as we had to explain that Jimi would not actually be able to appear. Dick Cavett was furious with Jimi for his rudeness, although Jimi did finally do *The Dick Cavett Show* in September 1969.

Under Pressure

Jimi Hendrix wasn't the only one feeling the pressure in 1969. I had said that I'd given up my life on the road, but here I was in the US, thousands of miles away from my wife and home in London.

There were no great changes to my schedule, I was still in a management position and I'd still had to take the occasional trip abroad on business, but before now they had always been taken as quickly as possible and I'd always been longing to return.

The difference now was that Margaret and I were having difficulties; the pressures of the constant surveillance from the Polish authorities and the separation of our working lives from our private one together, had finally started to take their toll on our marriage.

My beautiful princess and I were drifting further and further apart and we couldn't seem to find an answer to the problems. I thought that some space might do us good but, to be honest, it was relief that I felt as soon as I landed on American soil. I was actually happy to be away from my wife. Could it really be that my 'happily ever after' was coming to an end?

But, thankfully, I had little time to think about my personal problems; when I started to realise exactly what was making Mike Jeffery so tense, even my marital difficulties seemed to fade into insignificance. A few days before Woodstock, the IRS had cleared out Mike Jeffery's funds in one swoop; Mike's days of dodging the tax-man had finally caught up with him and now he was in serious financial trouble.

If Jimi had thought that losing Chas Chandler would mean finding a new freedom to experiment with his music, then he was sadly mistaken. Mike didn't just have Jimi's debts to contend with; the IRS investigation had bitten into his own personal funds as well and forced Mike to take some drastic measures. He *had* to start making money fast and Jimi Hendrix was his greatest asset.

After what Mike had witnessed from Gypsy Sun and Rainbows at Woodstock, he had decided that experimentation needed its limits. Mike instructed Jimi to take the band back down to the previously winning formula that Chas had created: a trio. Jimi wasn't happy about being ordered around, but in the end he had to agree with his manager. Band of Gypsies was created, keeping Billy Cox on as the new bassist and, initially at least, starring Buddy Miles on drums. They were sent back out on the road in the States almost immediately and started to generate the much-needed cash flow.

But it still wasn't enough. Electric Lady, the studio that Jimi Hendrix had personally designed in New York, was still under construction and needed constant funding in order to complete. Mike had to find the money from somewhere and he'd fallen back on old connections for a loan. But this was where the trouble really began to start. Mike's old 'friends' were mobsters and the loans that they offered were given at extortionate rates of interest. Tough as Mike Jeffery was in his own right, this was not a group of men that you wanted to upset.

I was in the New York office with Bob Levine when Mike received a visit from one of his debt collectors. The man was huge, with an expensive tailored suit literally straining where the seams met over his bulging frame and a pair of dark sunglasses covering his eyes. Bob and I didn't speak to him; he merely nodded at us and made his way through to Mike's office. The meeting only lasted a couple of minutes, but when I entered Mike's office with a paper for him to sign I found him sitting at his desk with his head in his hands.

'I don't know what I'm going to do, Tappy. He says he wants $30,000 by the end of the day and if I can't find it I'm a dead man! These people mean what they say. I'm a dead man.'

'Surely there must be some way of getting the cash together?'

Mike held out his empty hands, 'I've got nothing. Not a cent to my name. And they know it. Jesus, Tappy, what am I going to do?'

Bob Levine had followed me into the office. He had been working hard for Mike for six years now, and he was about to prove his usefulness to him, with a little suggestion. 'Sorry, Mike,' Bob cut in. 'But I couldn't help overhearing and I might have an idea of how to help you out.'

'Really?' Mike's head jerked up as he allowed himself a little hope. 'Well, what is it? I'll do anything, Bob, you just name it.'

Bob ran a hand up and down his jaw. 'It could be tricky, but I know a guy who might be able to lend me the money. He'd want paying back, though,' he told Mike warningly. 'And he'd probably want some interest for his trouble.'

'How much?'

'Well, let's say $5,000 on top of the original loan, I should be able to get him down to that. Would you be able to come up with the money?'

Mike grabbed a pad and started to work on some sums. 'I should be able to, if he could give me a couple of weeks. There are a couple of guys who owe me and if Jimi keeps earning like he has been, I should be able to make it. That $5,000 would be saving my life after all. Talk to your friend, Bob, and see how quickly he can get us the cash.'

'Shouldn't be any problem there, Mike; I'll get on to it right away.'

Bob and I left the office and returned with a suitcase of the promised bills. I was immediately reminded of that overnight round trip to Newcastle that Mike had sent me on back in my days with The

Animals, again to pick up a suitcase stuffed full of money. How long had this kind of dealing been going on for?

But that afternoon in New York, my main concern was just keeping Mike alive. Bob and I drove to the house in New Jersey where Mike had been instructed to deliver the money.

'You did well getting hold of all that money so quickly,' I commented to Bob. 'I hope that you haven't got yourself into trouble?'

Bob looked over at me with a sly smile. 'Can you keep a secret, Tappy?'

'I would hope that after all the years we've known each other, you wouldn't have to ask me that question.'

'It's just that this isn't something I'd want Mike knowing,' Bob paused. 'That money isn't a friend's . . . it's mine.'

'Yours? Well, why didn't you tell Mike that?'

'What, and guarantee that I'd never see it again? No, it's better if Mike thinks that there's some stranger to be scared of. Anyway, it gave me the chance to get the best interest rate I'm ever likely to on my life savings. I think that it's about time we make a few bucks out of Mike's trouble, don't you?'

The Problem with Monika

I never answered Bob's question; I was just pleased to see Mike alive and well and if that meant that Mike had to pay a little more, then so be it. I returned to London in early 1970 to face my own problems. Margaret's mother, Alina Slesinska, had been forced to return to Poland, despite all of our efforts to keep her in London with us. I stepped back into my house, where the phones were tapped and I was photographed every time I left the door, and realised that I just couldn't cope with it any more. It was never going to be any different. The Polish authorities would follow and watch us until the day we died.

Margaret had put up with it all her life so I guess that she was used to it, but four years was too much for me. We were heading for separation and although I loved my princess, I knew that it was the right decision to part.

Margaret understood.

It was horrible and sad, but I started to move my things back up to Newcastle and into my father's house. I had work to do in London, though, and was still living in Devonshire Close with my wife, but things were coming to an end and I threw myself into my work at Anim to try and escape the painful truths that were waiting for me at the end of each day when I got back home.

It was probably good that I was working so hard, because Anim were getting phone calls almost daily from Jimi Hendrix. His demands for money were growing. This was reasonable enough – he was an artist at the top of his game and he was making a lot of money. But not only was there no real money to be had, the ways he wanted to spend it were highly suspect.

Jimi had met a new girl, Monika Danneman. She was a tall, striking German blonde who worked as an artist and had an apartment in London. She'd become a bit of an obsession for Hendrix and along with her came her cocaine habit.

This was where the money that Jimi requested was going. Unlike Kathy Etchingham, who had loved and cared for Jimi and tried to keep his feet on the ground, Monika revelled in the hedonism of the pop star lifestyle. She had met Jimi when he was famous and she was willing to exploit the situation as much as possible to make sure that she had a good time.

Jimi's excessive drug use was beginning to worry all of us in the office but, under the influence of so many illegal substances, Jimi's personality was changing and he was becoming more and more difficult to talk to.

'Jimi, do you really need more money already?' I asked him one morning when fielding another call, 'Where is all this cash going to, son?'

'You can fuck off and mind your own business, Tappy. Just get me the money today.'

I felt utterly powerless in my attempts to help him. It seemed that Jimi and my marriage were falling apart together and both situations gave me nothing but sadness.

By this time Jimi and the Band of Gypsies (with Mitch Mitchell back in his rightful place behind the drum-kit) had finished their tour across the States and they were working on a new double album, *First Rays of the New Rising Sun*. The Electric Lady Studio had opened on 25 August 1970, so they were able to use the facilities that Jimi had designed to lay down some tracks. Little did they know that this was an album which would never actually be completed.

The Final Weeks

On 30 August 1970, Jimi Hendrix and the Band of Gypsies headlined at the Isle of Wight Festival. This was the festival that proved that the 'Summer of Love' was definitely over. Jimi's drug habit was obviously shared by the majority of the crowd and as he struggled with technical difficulties during his disappointing set, the rest of us were left to watch the massive crowd erupt into violence.

The innocence of those early days with Jimi had faded away and I wondered if there would ever be a way to retrieve them.

Looking back on it now, the end of the summer of 1970 seems like a black time. My marriage was breaking apart, we were losing the Jimi Hendrix we knew and loved to an escalating drug problem and the happy, hopeful days of the 1960s were behind us.

But there were blacker days to come.

They started, ironically enough, with the Love and Peace Festival in Puttgarden, Germany. Jimi Hendrix and the Band of Gypsies performed through torrential rain on 6 September, after delaying for a day, but the festival was disrupted by gunfire between rival German motorcycle gangs.

So much for Peace and Love!

Billy Cox, the Gypsies' bassist, was feeling the pressure and fell ill with stress and exhaustion. The band was, therefore, forced to cut their European tour short so that Billy could return to the States to recover. Jimi flew back to London with Monika and all the parties that he could find.

On top of this there was discussion about a possible management change. I think that Jimi blamed Mike for Billy's breakdown and the poor performances that the band had produced. It was true that Mike was continuing to work Jimi hard. He needed him to keep touring in order to keep making money, but Jimi wanted to take some time off to develop his music and experiment. Despite the drugs, Jimi hadn't forgotten his first true love: the music.

Mike's contract as Jimi's manager was up in three months and he was panicking. He may have allayed the more dangerous of his debt collectors with a little help from Bob Levine's savings, but there were plenty more where they came from and Jimi Hendrix was his only real source of income.

If he lost Jimi, he could lose everything: the clubs in Spain, the business. Without Jimi, Mike Jeffery's only option would have been bankruptcy.

And bankruptcy would only have seen off the legitimate lenders – most of the men that Mike owed money to took a far more physical approach to dealing with debt collection.

So Mike wanted to keep his kneecaps and that meant keeping hold of Jimi's contract, but there were plenty of other people sniffing around. Alan Douglas was one of the major contenders and I even heard rumours (from those who didn't know the real story behind their break-up) that Chas Chandler would be taking over management again. But, really, who wouldn't have wanted one of the world's most successful musicians on their books? Jimi wanted out and Mike truly had his work cut out if he didn't want to get usurped.

The pressure was on and all of us in the Anim offices were feeling it. Mike's black mood was not something you wanted to run into. We were into the September of 1970; Hendrix was in London catching up with friends and I decided to take some time off to move the last of my belongings out of my Devonshire Close home and drive them up to Whitley Bay.

There wasn't much to collect. I packed the car up with a few personal keepsakes and my two beloved boxer dogs. Margaret had agreed that they would be happier up in Newcastle with my father. One of the terrible things about the end of a marriage is how little you have to show for it. Those dogs should have been the playmates of our children and now here they were watching our tearful farewells, their tongues lolling against the back window, their eyes not nearly as mournful as mine.

It was a sad trip, that drive up to Newcastle with the dogs. Margaret and I had agreed to a divorce and I had left London with the papers in the hands of my lawyer. We had tried the best we could; had every conversation, attempted a thousand solutions, but the time had come to go our separate ways. Margaret was planning to travel through Poland, where she eventually settled and re-married. A fitting conclusion for my Polish princess; I'm only sorry that I was not the man to play her prince in shining armour.

I arrived in Whitley Bay late that night. I was grateful for my father's open sympathy and care. He left me to myself, but was always available to talk if I needed it and I sincerely don't think that I could have got through those days without him.

I waited in my father's house for the finalised divorce papers to arrive. My next engagement in London was on 19 September, when I was to pick up Jimi and take him to the airport. Bob Levine had rung me from New York.

'I'm sorry to bother you with this, Tappy; I know it's bad timing, but Jimi's had a bust-up with Gerry and he's refusing to work with him. He says that Gerry doesn't get his sound or something . . . I don't know. Anyway, I should be able to smooth it over, but I need someone to see Jimi over to New York and look after him until I can sort it all out. What do you say, Tappy, it could do you good to get away?'

'I wanted to spend some time with my dad. I've just dumped two dogs on the poor old fella; I don't want to run out on him.'

'He'll understand. You'd really be helping me out, Tappy, and it'd give you a chance to catch up with Jimi. Maybe you can talk some sense into him?'

'OK, Bob, I'll see what I can do.'

Of course I agreed. To be honest, I thought that Bob was probably right that it would be a good idea to get out of the country for a while and maybe some time back on the road would do me good, too. I was also looking forward to seeing Jimi. Gerry Stickles was a great guy and a brilliant road manager and I was sure that I could use my influence to get Jimi to see sense. I told my dad that I would have to leave Whitley Bay sooner than expected.

'That was Bob on the phone; I've got to go to New York in a couple of days with Jimi Hendrix.'

'Jimi?' my dad said, looking puzzled. 'That a pal of yours is it? You two off on holiday?'

I laughed and hugged my father. The most famous artist in the world and my dad didn't have a clue who he was. To Joseph Wright, Jimi Hendrix was just another of my pals from London. The swinging

Sixties and crazy start of 1970 hadn't even touched my dad in Whitley Bay.

The morning before I was due to leave I got a call from my solicitor's office in Newcastle. The divorce papers had arrived and he needed me to come in and look them over before everything could be finalised. It was late morning on 18 September.

My driver, Willie, picked me up from my dad's house and took me to the solicitor's. When we arrived I asked him to wait and walked into the reception. He must have switched on the radio while he waited, because I'd only just taken my seat in the waiting room when he came cannoning in after me.

'Tappy! He's dead! I can't believe it, he's dead!'

'Jesus, Willie, what's up with you? Who's dead?' I grabbed my driver by the shoulders. 'Who's dead, Willie?'

Willie stared at me, his face full of emotion. 'It's Jimi. It was on the radio, Tappy. Jimi Hendrix died this morning.'

'Jimi Hendrix? Oh, I love him!' the pretty young receptionist exclaimed.

I tightened my grip on Willie's shoulders and steered him back towards the door.

'Stop fucking about, Willie,' I said through gritted teeth. 'Jimi is *not* dead. He can't be dead. You're driving me down to meet him tomorrow, remember?'

'You actually *know* Jimi Hendrix!' the receptionist squealed. Jesus, this was not the moment that I wanted to be fielding autograph requests.

Willie eased my hands free and gave his shoulders a rub. 'I'm not lying, Tappy. Christ, I wish I was. You had better come with me, this can wait until tomorrow.'

I followed Willie outside to where the car was waiting. He'd left the car door open and I could hear the radio still blasting out the news that Jimi had been found dead in a London apartment that morning. It was true. Jimi Hendrix was dead.

I fell down into the passenger seat with my head in my hands and started to weep uncontrollably. Willie laid a hand across my shoulders.

'I'll take you home, Tappy.'

Once the initial shock was over and Willie had got me back to my dad's house and pressed a cup of strong, sweet tea into my hands, the questions started to throb through my brain. How had this happened? Why Jimi? Why did that sweet 27-year-old boy with the world at his feet have to die? It was all so pointless. All such a senseless waste. My dad and Willie fussed around me, not knowing what to say.

'I have to phone Bob,' I said suddenly, startling them both. But, as soon as I got Bob Levine on the phone, my tears started afresh. 'He's dead, Bob,' I sobbed. 'I can't believe he's dead.'

'I know, Tappy,' Bob replied, his voice little more than a whisper. 'We're all in shock over here, but I think you should come over as planned. Well . . . not quite as planned.'

There was a pause while Bob recovered himself. 'We're like a family; we need one another at a time like this.'

'I'll be there in a couple of days, Bob. I don't think I could face it right away. I'll spend some time with my dad and then I'll fly out. I'll see you soon, Bob.'

I could hear Bob begin to sob as I laid the phone down.

CHAPTER 11

Gone But Not Forgotten: Resurrecting Jimi Hendrix

Pulling Together

It was only afterwards that I discovered how Jimi Hendrix had spent his final days. He mostly had been seen in the company of Monika, in whose apartment he had been found dead. I ran into Eric Burdon in London. It had suddenly become important to treasure all those old friendships that I'd taken for granted and when Eric and I met, we embraced immediately. He told me about the last time he'd seen Jimi alive.

'I was playing with War at Ronnie Scott's and Jimi was in the audience. He'd been in the night before and tried to jam with us, but the guy was off his head. He couldn't even hold a guitar, let alone play one. He was wobbling all over the stage. It was a shock, you know, to see him like that.

'That girl Monika was with him, they'd both come with my friend Alvina, and in the end Monika took him home. When they came back the next night they both seemed more together. He was all dressed up and he had his Strat with him. He asked me all politely if he could jam and then sat down with Monika, waiting for me to give him the nod. We played some music together.

'Man, the way that he drove out "Tobacco Road"! He was back on form. He was incredible. After the gig, he left with Monika to go to a party. That was the night he died, Tappy. I never saw him again.'

We were all in shock and compelled to share our stories of Jimi's life in order to try and make sense of his death. It made me sad that I no longer had my wife to talk things over with. I flew over to New

York soon after seeing Eric; I was taking the flight that I should have taken with Jimi, but I was alone.

Bob met me at the airport and, as I had with Eric, we unashamedly clung to one another.

'How are you doing?' Bob asked. 'Flight OK?'

'Yeah, I think that the flight crew knew who I was. They were really sweet and looked after me.' I shook my head. 'I can't believe it, Bob. I still can't believe he's gone.'

On 1 October 1970 we buried Jimi Hendrix in Seattle, where his father had organised a family plot. There had been talk about Jimi expressing a wish to be buried in England, but the ceremony in his home town was an emotional experience. It was a bright afternoon and everyone who had known and loved Jimi was there. We all gathered to weep together in that hilltop cemetery for the young boy who had died too soon. At one point the coffin was left open so that we could file past and pay our respects. Jimi looked waxy and small, but peaceful. As I wiped my eyes I realised that Mike Jeffrey hadn't been able to face the open coffin; he was still sitting in the back of his limo, staring straight ahead. I couldn't even catch his eye.

After the funeral Bob, Gerry and I flew back to New York. Bob drove me to the Electric Lady Studio in the Village after we landed and Gerry went back to his apartment. This was Jimi's place, the studio that he had designed and which he would never use again.

As we walked through the studio and got ourselves a coffee, an eerie silence hung over the building, broken only by the members of staff that we saw openly weeping. Bob and I spoke in whispers, not wanting to intrude on the atmosphere. Electric Lady was so much Jimi Hendrix's baby that it felt as if he could walk into the room at any moment. Although it had opened earlier in the year, Electric Lady Studios were still under construction, a process that Mike would now have to fund alone. It was just another part of the tragedy that Jimi would never be able to see his dream studios fully completed.

'Where can we all go from here, Bob?' I asked, looking around me.

'On, Tappy. It's all that the living can do.'

We left Electric Lady to its mourners and Bob drove me to over to the New York apartment that I would be sharing with Gerry Stickles. Bob had warned me that Gerry was in a mess over Hendrix's death. I understood just how close you got to the artists that you worked with

The locksmith's receipt for opening Jimi's apartment door after his death.

as a road manager and Gerry and Jimi had just had a row, days before Jimi's death. I truly felt for the poor guy; it's awful when you are unable to make your peace before somebody dies.

Bob and I let ourselves into the apartment spotting Gerry coming out of the sitting room.

'Hey, Tappy! Good to see ya.'

Gerry had been drinking on the plane from Seattle to New York and had started again when he'd arrived back to the apartment. He was not looking too great after all the drinking to drown his sorrows, as Gerry had flown back with Jimi's body from London for the funeral in Seattle.

I opened a window, stumbling over some half-empty cans. 'Let's get some fresh air in here. What's going on, Gerry? The place is a mess.' I started to stack up some of the cans, balancing an ashtray in each hand.

'Leave it, Tappy. You need to relax, man. Have a drink with me.' He dug a hand behind him and pulled out yet another beer can. He toasted me and took a long swig.

'I think you've had enough,' I said, easing the can out of his grip. 'Let's get you into the bath and I'll clear this place up. It'll all seem better when we're clean, son. Then we can sit down and have a chat, eh?'

I ran Gerry a bath and, after some cajoling, I managed to get him into it. I quickly set to work on the apartment and had a hot cup of black coffee waiting for him when he emerged.

'How you feeling?' I asked, sitting down next to him on the couch.

'Better, I guess,' Gerry said, sipping at his coffee. 'I'm sobering up, now. Sorry about all that, Tappy.' He gestured at the now clear living room.

'Don't worry about it.'

'Oh.' Gerry stared at the floor and put his cup down on the coffee table. The mention of Jimi's name seemed to have been enough to pull him back down into the darkness I had found him in.

'Look Gerry . . .' I stopped as Gerry broke down.

'I'm sorry, Tappy,' he said, wiping his eyes. 'I just can't believe that he's dead. We had a row and I said awful things, things I didn't even mean. He knew that I didn't like his music, but I loved the guy, you know?

'I'd never had the nerve to stand my ground with him before and I thought that I'd let him sweat it out for a couple of days. Let him come and apologise to me for a change. I knew that you were coming out to New York, Tappy. I knew that you'd be able to talk him around; Jimi always listened to you. I thought that it would all be fine. And now he's dead and I'll never be able to make it up with him. After we arrived this morning and I got back from the airport, I've just kept drinking and hoping that when I came to he'd be here. That it would all be some kind of sick joke and Jimi would be alive.'

I sat and listened to Gerry pour his heart out. Everyone in New York had been so busy dealing with their own grief that they'd forgotten about Gerry. He needed to be heard and it was good to feel useful at last.

'Life goes on,' I said, quoting Bob Levine's words of comfort, when Gerry finally seemed to have exhausted his story. 'Jimi's probably sitting up on some cloud now laughing at the state of us all without him.'

'Yeah, I suppose he is,' Gerry said, trying for a smile.

'And he's probably driving them all mad with some new musical arrangement!'

Gerry laughed.

'Thing is, Tappy. I really did fucking hate his music.'

Where There's a Debt
There's a Scam

It wasn't until the following year that I found out exactly how Mike Jeffery was to commemorate his most famous artist. And, to be honest, I think that I found out the same time that Mike did.

Bob Levine, Gerry Stickles and I were back at Electric Lady Studios; Mike buzzed down to ask me to join him in his office. Since Jimi's death, Mike had become rather reclusive. He'd always been a bit of an elusive character; with his homes all over the world, you never really knew when he was going to show up, but he'd taken to locking himself away. Maybe the stress of Jimi's early death had affected him more than we realised?

I walked into the office. Electric Lady Studios may have been built under Jimi Hendrix's designs, but Mike's office was his own empire. He'd had it decorated in a Japanese theme and its carefully orchestrated look was guaranteed to stop people in their tracks. Mike was sitting behind his grand ebony desk, his hands moving over the engraved ivory inserts as he shifted paperwork.

'Hi there, Tappy,' he said, glancing up and nodding towards a chair. 'Take a seat. I've just got to finish up here and then we can talk.'

I sat down and watched Mike work. It seemed that all Mike was doing was working these days. I'd heard rumours that there were still money worries at Electric Lady (there was still obvious work that needed to be done on construction). Despite the expensive silk shirts and the classy office, I thought that I could see the strain showing on Mike's face.

Finally, he pushed the last of the papers aside and faced me. 'Tappy, we're off to Woodstock. I'd like you to join me at my house there for the weekend. I'm working on some ideas and I need some peace and quiet to finish them off. I'm thinking of doing something for Jimi, I just can't grasp what it is yet. I could do with your help, Tappy. Is that OK with you?'

'Sure. I'm not busy at the moment; I'd be glad to help if I can.'

'Great. Oh, and we need to make a stop at RCA Records on the way. I've got an appointment.'

Half-an-hour later we were in Mike's Mercedes on our way to RCA. I saw an Electric Lady Studio tape tucked in the side pocket of the passenger door and pulled it free to inspect it. There were no details written on the side.

'Is this what you're taking to RCA, Mike?' I asked, holding up the tape. 'Who is the band?'

'Ah yes, *the band*,' Mike said mysteriously. 'I think the less that you ask about that the better. Don't worry . . . I'll tell all after my meeting.' He grinned and we pulled up outside the RCA building. 'Here, Tappy, you take the car. I'll be about an hour here, so why don't you drive over to your apartment and pack a bag for the weekend? Then we can set off straight away for Woodstock.'

I did as I was told and then hurried back to meet Mike. I wanted to hear more about the mystery band that he was pitching to RCA. Mike was waiting for me, a huge grin on his face. 'Woodstock here we come,' he laughed, jumping into the passenger seat beside me.

'Successful meeting, was it?' I asked. I wasn't going to let him get away that easily.

'Oh yeah, it was fantastic,' he adjusted his dark glasses, his smile still in place. 'I know I promised you an explanation, Tappy, but I'm not sure I can even explain it to myself.'

'Do I really want to know this, Mike?'

'Sure you do! You know that we've been having problems at Electric Lady?'

'I've heard a few things.'

'I bet you have. Jesus, Tappy, that place is costing me a fortune and it's still not finished. I thought when the money came through from Hendrix . . .'

'What money?' I interrupted, puzzled. 'You mean record sales?'

'Well . . . yes and there was some more – but that is something you *don't* need to know. I thought that I'd have enough to cover it, but there never seemed to be enough.'

'Until that band on the tape?' I offered.

'Ah yes, the band on the tape,' Mike was laughing now. 'RCA just loved my new band. They've bought them outright, $100,000 cash, in advance! Can you believe it? $100,000!'

'Congratulations, Mike, that's some deal. But I haven't heard anything about them. Who are they?'

'That's the best part!' Mike laughed. 'I haven't got one. That tape you picked up was just a recording of a jam session. Some of the guys were testing the equipment and they recorded it to test the quality. I think Jimi might even be on there somewhere.'

I twisted in my seat; Mike was crying with laughter. 'You're kidding me? You've just got $100,000 from RCA for a band that doesn't even exist?'

'I'm the fucking best, Tappy Wright,' Mike replied, settling back in his seat. 'Hadn't you heard?'

The Big Idea

We drove all the way to Woodstock with Mike singing any song that he could think of at the top of his voice. I hadn't seen him this happy for years, the business's money worries must have really been playing on his mind. He ignored the looks that we were getting from passing motorists and just carried on singing. It was great to see him like this.

We were just pulling into the grounds of Mike's Woodstock house, when he suddenly stopped and frowned. 'That's it!' he yelled. 'Stop the car, Tappy!'

'What? We're almost at the house.'

'Just stop it.' We pulled up on the gravel drive and I turned to face Mike. 'Tappy, what do you know about cine projectors?'

'Cine projectors? Jesus, where did that come from? I don't know anything about them.'

'Well, you had better go and buy a book and learn. I've got a great idea, Tappy. A brilliant idea. Let's get to the house; I need to start work.'

Mike shared his home in Woodstock with his gorgeous Canadian girlfriend, Lynn Bailey. It was a useful weekend retreat from his New York apartment. It was a private place for Mike and his loved ones, and I was honoured to be asked to stay. It wasn't like Mike to mix business with pleasure, but I'd known him for so many years that I think we were already guilty of that – old friends and trusted colleagues.

I enjoyed my time in the grand white mansion, which Mike had jokingly titled his own Graceland. I made myself at home and lounged by the swimming pool. Mike had excused himself after dinner on our first night and locked himself away in his study; I'd barely seen him. Not that I minded that much; he hadn't forgotten about my study of cine projectors and had thrown a book at me early on Saturday morning with the barked instruction to 'read and learn'. I kept busy with my book by the pool and filled the rest of my time with swimming and chatting to Lynn.

I didn't see how I was really helping with the development of the mysterious master plan and I was intrigued to find out what Mike was working on. I knew that he'd placed a couple of calls through to the Chrysalis Agency, but aside from that and my enforced study of cine projectors, I was none the wiser. Mike wasn't giving anything away. He said that he'd tell me when it was all complete and, eventually, on the Sunday night, my patience was rewarded.

'Come in, Tappy,' Mike said, ushering me into his study. He looked excited and I quickly took a seat, eager to finally discover what his long weekend's work had all been in aid of. 'I've got it all sorted at last. It's the perfect tribute to Jimi's memory and it will make me a fair profit along the way. We haven't got Jimi to tour for us any more, but I have got a film of him performing in Berkeley. I've managed to get hold of a couple of unknown acts to go on tour through the UK and Europe as support.'

'But what would they be supporting?' I asked.

'It was that deal I made with RCA that gave me the idea – they wouldn't be supporting anyone. That is nobody in person – we'd play the film of a Jimi Hendrix concert as the headline act. Imagine it, Tappy, all those people that never got to see Jimi perform and we could give them the next best thing. All we need is a cine projector. It'll be the easiest tour we've ever had.'

I was wondering when the cine projector would come into it. To be honest the whole idea sounded bogus to me. Who in their right mind would pay to go watch a film of a concert? And I wasn't that happy about that 'we' that kept cropping up. I was quite sure who Mike had in mind for running this tour and working the projector, and I wasn't convinced that I wanted to lend my name to a plan that sounded doomed from the start.

'So, that's why you bought me that book is it? Mike, this is never going to work.'

'Tappy, you're wrong: I guarantee it will be a success. I've been checking it out and the feedback I've had so far has been terrific. It's the break I've been waiting for.'

'Yeah, but you're not going to be the stupid bugger standing there introducing a movie as the main act!'

'Trust me, Tappy, I'm the best in the business. This is a winner.'

Well, what can you say to that? At the end of the day, Mike Jeffery was my boss and I had to trust that he knew what he was doing. The supporting acts were brought in: Cat Mother and the All Night Newsboys, a band from California, whose first album Jimi Hendrix had helped to produce at Electric Lady Studios, and Jimmy and Vella, a brother and sister act. I convinced my UK driver, Willie Nicholson, to act as projectionist and passed on all the knowledge I'd gained during my study weekend in Woodstock to help him in his new post.

We started the tour in Bristol and, despite all my misgivings, it was a success. I really hadn't seen how it would work, but on that first night I realised that it was just a display of how the power and originality of Jimi Hendrix's musical performance was enough to transcend even death. The nostalgia welled up in all of us as we watched that film reel every night. Jimi may not have been able to be there in person, but in this, his final tour, his spirit was right there in celluloid. Listening to the crowd's reaction every time that film was played, I knew that we may have lost Jimi far too soon, but his music would live for ever.

It was an emotional time, that tour, and I was thankful to Mike for making me a part of it. Thank God the man knew when to ignore my complaints and thank God that I knew when to trust him. It really was a fitting tribute to Jimi Hendrix's memory and it gave me the chance to say a proper goodbye and to take up the job that I'd rejected all those years ago. Finally, I was able to be Jimi Hendrix's road manager.

Duty Calls

After the 1971/72 British and European tour of the Jimi Hendrix Live at Berkley film was over, I returned to New York. With my marriage finished, I was based mainly in the States these days. Mike Jeffery and

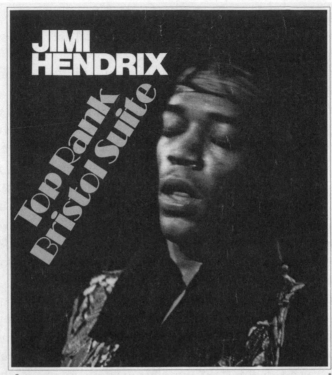

The poster advertising the first night of the Berkley film tour in Bristol in 1972.

Bob Levine had not been idle in my absence. Bob had put together a new American band with Mike's guidance, and this time a real one: Group Therapy. Bob was getting ready to start recording them at RCA studios. As I arrived back in New York, I was immediately dispatched to help Bob with taking care of the band.

It was the night before their first recording session when Bob and I met the boys in their hotel bar. They were obviously excited about the pace at which their musical career was progressing and were ready for a night of partying to celebrate. After a couple of drinks, Bob had enough of the party spirit and left me and the boys to it.

'You guys get acquainted; I'm off to get some sleep. And you, Tappy,' he said, pointing at me, 'make sure that this lot don't go too over the top. They've got a big day tomorrow and I don't want anything ruining it. You hear me, guys?' He gestured round at the group and left with the shouts of reassurance echoing after him.

But after a few more hours laughing and drinking in the bar, all our promises to Bob had been forgotten. Michael, one of the members of Group Therapy, took one look at my bleary face and laughed. 'I thought that you were meant to be looking after us, Tappy? Listen, you shouldn't go trying to get back home in this state; use my room.' He nodded towards a pretty blonde who was propping up the bar and winked at me. 'I don't reckon that I'll need it tonight.'

I grunted my thanks to Michael and staggered over to the elevator. The hotel porter helped me through the doors. I waved goodbye to Group Therapy and headed upstairs to sleep it off. I plunged into Michael's bed and fell immediately into that deep unconscious sleep that only comes after serious drinking.

The next thing I knew was a crashing sound. I was still in a drunken stupor, but I pulled my head up from the pillow and listened. It seemed to have stopped. I decided that I must have been dreaming and settled back down to sleep. Then there was an almighty smash that drove me right out of bed and on to my feet. Two men with severe crew-cuts were standing by the hotel room door, which looked as if it had been kicked from its hinges. As I jumped up they raised their pistols so that they were pointing directly at me. I raised my hands in surrender.

'Don't move a goddamn muscle, do you understand?' I nodded meekly. 'You are going to do exactly what we say. No questions.' I nodded again.

I wasn't about to start questioning this man while he still had that gun in my face. But I did wonder what the hell was going on. Was this a set up for some huge practical joke? Or was I being robbed or kidnapped? I could hear noises coming from one of the neighbouring rooms. It sounded like someone else was getting the same treatment as me.

'You're under arrest,' the man told me. 'I want you to keep your hands up and move over to the door. We're going to be behind you all the way, so don't go thinking that now's the time to do something stupid.' His partner grinned and tightened his grip on his pistol as they snapped a pair of handcuffs to my wrists. At least there was no need for me to change; I'd fallen into bed the night before, fully clothed.

I walked ahead of them to the elevator and then they pushed me out of the hotel towards a waiting car. Why wasn't anyone trying to stop them? As we drove away I saw Art, the bass-player with Group Therapy, being bundled into another car. It did cross my mind that Mike Jeffery's newest band may be the subject of some revenge plot from one of Mike's more dodgy connections. But as the car moved along, one of the men read me my rights. The haircuts should have been enough to give it away – the men were FBI agents and I really was being arrested, but it was the charge that surprised me most of all: failure to report to duty for the US Army.

I thought back to the time when I'd been tempted to apply for American residency in order to accept a job offer in Hollywood, but I'd cancelled all that before it began. Where the hell had these charges come from?

'Hey, listen to me,' I tried to explain. 'Do I sound like a Yank? I'm a British citizen. I'm a Geordie, for Christ's sake; I've got nothing to do with the US Army!'

'I don't know what you're trying to pull. All we know is that you and your friend have absconded from duty to start some *rock 'n' roll* band.' The man next to me spat out the words 'rock 'n' roll' with obvious disgust and raised his gun again. 'And FBI agents are not interested in any stories that deserters have to tell. You and your friend can explain yourselves to your Sergeant downtown.'

My 'friend' was bound to be Art and, as I'd only met the Group Therapy guys the night before, I guessed that they thought that I was

Michael. Talk about being in the wrong place at the wrong time! Michael was probably tucked up in the bed of that sweet blonde that he'd been flirting with and, just because I'd bedded down in his room, I was now facing the FBI arrest that was meant for him. That would teach me to listen to Bob Levine when he told me to take it easy on the booze.

With the gun back in my eyeline and some better idea of where we were headed I decided that it was better to keep my mouth shut for the time being. I could explain it all to the Army and I may as well use the time getting there in catching up on some sleep. I tried to forget about the tough FBI agents either side of me, laid my head back and closed my eyes. The US Army would have this all sorted out in minutes; I had nothing to worry about.

I must have drifted off because soon I was experiencing the second rude wake-up call of the day. So much for having nothing to worry about; I was dragged unceremoniously from the car by one of the FBI agents and dumped at the feet of a waiting Sergeant. We had arrived at the Army base and I gazed up, still bleary eyed, at the massive man in front of me.

'The American Army does not take kindly to draft-dodgers!' he bellowed, the stench of his breath hitting me full in the face. The Sergeant grabbed me by the back of the neck and, with an FBI agent flanking either side, I was frogmarched to the Sergeant's office. The FBI men left us at the door. Their job was finished; I was in the hands of the Army now.

I sat down on a chair in the middle of the room and the Sergeant started to march around me. God, I felt terrible. I'd managed to sleep off the last of the booze in the car and now I was just suffering from a horrendous hangover (that and having a huge Sergeant breathing down my neck, accusing me of being a draft-dodger!) Then I remembered Bob. Oh Christ, he'd be collecting Group Therapy for their recording session round about now, only to discover that the bassist and the man he'd trusted to keep the band in order were both missing. I didn't even know what had happened to Art. Bob was going to kill me.

The Sergeant was still ranting at me, but I struggled to my feet, fighting back my pounding headache and the bile that rose in my throat.

'Look here, Sergeant, there has been a mistake . . .'

'SIT DOWN!' he screamed. 'You will only speak when I ask you to speak, soldier! And I did *not* ask you to speak.'

I fell back into my seat. What else could I do? Getting out of this was definitely going to be more complicated than I'd imagined. After pacing the room for a couple more minutes the Sergeant took a seat behind his desk and faced me. 'Do you realise why you have been arrested?' he asked, pulling a sheet of paper out of a drawer and poising his pen over it.

'No, not really,' I replied. Finally my chance to explain had come. 'I didn't realise that things were so desperate in the US Army that they had to start conscripting British citizens.'

'I'm sorry, what did you say?' The Sergeant's bravado seemed to be slipping. I was going to enjoy this.

'My name is James Edward Wright and I am a British citizen working in New York. So, I don't see how I could be a draft-dodger, do you?' I had to stop myself from laughing at the look on the Sergeant's face.

'If you'll excuse me. I just have to check some details with my superior.'

'You do that.'

I sat and waited and after a couple of minutes the Sergeant returned. 'It seems that we owe you an apology, Mr Wright,' he said, not meeting my eye. He gave an embarrassed cough and continued, 'Obviously there have been some mistakes relating to the FBI's information. I assure you this never usually happens . . .'

'Well, it happened this time, didn't it?' I stood up so that I towered over the Sergeant, who was seated in his chair behind the desk. How quickly our roles had been reversed; it served the bastard right for screaming at me like that. 'Always treat visitors to your country like this, do you?'

I gave him a talking to, but didn't tell him the exact circumstances of my arrest and that the FBI's information had actually been right in every detail save that the man who was sleeping in the bed wasn't the one whose name was in the register. I rather liked the idea of those bully boys who had shaken me out of bed this morning getting their own share of the trouble.

After I'd exhausted the apologies of the US Army, I asked to make a phone call. I had to get in contact with Bob Levine. I may have sorted out my own situation, but I could now see that it wasn't going to be easy getting Art back and, now that they had realised their mistake, it would only be a matter of time until the FBI or even the Army tracked down Michael. Group Therapy wouldn't be much of band with two of their members missing.

I'd managed to convince the Sergeant to let me make my call in private. So I got to sit alone and listen to Bob swear at me, as soon as I'd managed to get hold of him.

'You stupid fucking bastard! Where the fuck have you been? I ask you one fucking favour and . . .'

'Good to speak to you, too, Bob,' I cut in. 'I'm at the Army base downtown. It seems that Michael and Art were dodging service. They realised that they made a mistake with me, but they've got Art here somewhere, I'm sure. I need your help, Bob. If we don't do something, you and Mike are going to lose half your band.'

There was silence on the line as Bob took in what I'd just told him. 'Stay put, Tappy. I'm on my way.' He hung up.

Within half-an-hour Bob was standing next to me in the Sergeant's office. I couldn't see what he could have managed to achieve in so short a time, but I was glad to have him there. He didn't look happy with me; didn't even meet my eye as he came through the door and approached the Sergeant.

'These are for you, sir,' Bob said, handing the Sergeant a handful of official-looking documents. I noticed that he was out of breath. 'We had thought that the authorities were aware of our "situation".'

The Sergeant looked at Bob and then at me and frowned. He obviously didn't have a clue what Bob was talking about. As far as he was concerned Bob was just a friend who was coming to pick me up. Then he glanced over the papers.

'Ah, I see. I won't be a moment.'

Within minutes, Art had been released and we were in Bob's car driving back to Group Therapy's hotel. Bob sat at the wheel looking furious, but I couldn't help asking what had been in the papers that had granted Art's speedy release. It was Art who answered.

'Bob's gone and got Michael and me certified as fucking faggots!'

'Prefer army service, would you?' Bob replied.

The car lapsed back into silence. I wondered how Bob had managed to get hold of the doctor's certificates so quickly, but thought that it was better not to ask. It was a brilliant idea, though; then, as now, homosexuality immediately rendered both Art and Michael ineligible for any position in the Services.

'The recording session has been cancelled,' Bob stated.

'I'm sorry, Bob,' I replied. 'But I don't know what you expected me to do about the Army bursting in and arresting us.'

'*That* wasn't what I was worried about, Tappy. You promised me that you would keep an eye on the boys and if you'd done that we could have sorted this all out hours ago. It takes me a long time to forgive someone for breaking a promise.'

We pulled up outside the hotel and Art got out. Michael was there waiting for us and Bob and I watched as Art explained what Bob had done to remove them from the call up list.

'I think that it might take them a long time to forgive you, too,' I said as we drove off. 'Did you see Michael's face when he heard how you'd rescued them?'

'Yeah, I saw it,' Bob replied and then, despite his bad mood, burst out laughing.

Life and Death in New York City

It may have been my British citizenship that saved me becoming a conscript in the US Army, but I was enjoying life in New York. I was still sharing an apartment with Gerry Stickles on West 15th Street and we both loved the pleasures that New York City and the American lifestyle had to offer two single men.

Not that we let ourselves forget our English roots; we always made sure that we had a large Sunday dinner every week. There were some English traditions that were worth holding on to and a plate of roast beef and Yorkshire puddings was something to hold on to. But we were to discover that even the most English of occasions could take on a New York flavour.

It was my turn to cook and Gerry's turn to laze about on the sofa and watch American football. But I didn't mind too much; as I slaved away I gazed out of the kitchen window and thought of the Sunday lunches that I'd cooked at home for my father.

My reverie was broken by the sight of a large man staggering past our window on his way up the fire escape, with another man in a fireman's lift across his shoulder. He struggled on to the flat roof and then tipped the man off his shoulder and over the side of the building. We were on the 30th floor.

I'd been stirring a Yorkshire pudding mix and the bowl slipped from my fingers and smashed at my feet, as my mouth fell open in shock. The man had moved away from the roof edge and was heading back to the fire escape.

He caught sight of my horrified face at the window and smiled and waved as he passed by. Instinctively, I raised a hand to wave back and then stopped myself. Had I really just witnessed a murder? And had the murderer then casually acknowledged me as he walked away from his crime?

I managed to pull myself together enough to call out to Gerry. He appeared in the kitchen doorway, looking dishevelled.

'What you doing waking me up?' he asked with a yawn. 'I was having a great dream there. Is it lunchtime already?' He looked down at the Yorkshire pudding paste that was splattered over the kitchen floor and raised his eyebrows.

I just pointed at the window. 'I think I just saw a man get killed.'

'Killed? In our kitchen?' Gerry looked about him. 'You sure that you haven't been on the cooking sherry, Tappy?'

I managed to choke out my story and Gerry and I made our way out on to the roof. We both lay out flat and tried to see over the edge of the building.

'You sure about this, Tappy?' Gerry asked, just as the scream of a police siren echoed below us.

'I'm sure. But I think that we had better get back inside, I don't think that we want to get caught hanging around up here.'

We got back into the flat. I turned off the oven; witnessing a murder had killed my appetite (if you'll excuse the pun). Gerry told me to forget about it; the last thing we needed was to get mixed up in a murder inquiry. I tried to do as I was told and was on my knees clearing up the mess of Yorkshire pudding when four NYPD burst through the door.

The cops grabbed Gerry and me and, once again, I was held at gunpoint by the US authorities.

'Up against the wall, motherfuckers,' one of them shouted. 'You were spotted looking over the roof ledge, just after one of you threw a guy over. You're both under arrest.'

Gerry started to gibber as I protested our innocence. 'I saw the guy who did it,' I cried. 'I saw him through the window. I was cooking Sunday lunch and . . .'

'Sunday lunch?' said the blond cop who'd arrested us. 'Are you guys English?'

'Yes, we are,' I said, hoping that this wouldn't mean that we were in more trouble.

But the cop's face broke into a grin. 'My wife's English. Have you ever been to Coventry?' I caught Gerry's eye and we both nodded. 'Hey, that's great!' the cop continued. 'It's a great place Coventry. That's where I met the wife; I was serving as a GI.'

He continued to smile at us, then put his gun back into its holster and nodded at the other cops, who followed suit and disappeared. Bizarrely, we ended up sitting in our living room, drinking coffee with our arresting officer, as he regaled us with stories of his time in England. Nice as this was, in the end Gerry risked an interruption. 'Excuse me officer, but what about the murder? Are we still under arrest?'

'Hey, forget it man. Nice pair of English gents like you? I don't think so. There's murder all the time here; that's New York City, isn't it? Now where was I? Oh yeah, Coventry . . .'

Only in the Big Apple . . .

A Helping Hand

But, along with the horrors, there were pleasures to be had in New York City. I awoke one morning to the shrill ringing of my telephone.

'Hello, yes?' I muttered, with my eyes still closed. Who the hell would ring me at this time in the morning?

'Hi, Tappy, this is Tracy.'

'Right. Tracy . . .'

'We met at the Peppermint Lounge last week. I was the girl with the red hair.'

'Tracy! You're the girl that's into porn!' I was awake now, that girl was a stunner and dirty with it.

She laughed. 'That's me! I was wondering if you'd be interested in doing a little work for me?'

'Porn work?' I asked, with my fingers crossed.

'Not quite. I'm putting together a feature for a girlie magazine, *Escort*; we're going to call it "One for the Ladies". I need some photographs and I thought of you. It would mean posing naked, but you'd be paid $700. What do you think, Tappy, would you be up for it?'

'Sure I would. In fact, I'm up just thinking about it!'

Tracy laughed again. 'That's great. I'll pick you up at one o'clock, be ready.'

Talk about your dream job offer! I was going to get to pose for a picture that thousands of women could drool over and get paid for it! I was flattered that Tracy had thought of me to do it for her and a little intrigued. Any time spent naked in that lady's presence couldn't be wasted and, when she turned up to collect me at 1.00 pm sharp, I was ready and waiting.

'So where exactly are we heading?' I asked, as I climbed into her car.

'It's my boss's ranch in New Jersey. I thought that you'd appreciate a picturesque setting for your photo-shoot. She's a great lady; you'll like her. Her ex-husband was meant to be a complete rat, so she packed his bags and slung him out. The ranch is all hers now. I've told her a lot about you, Tappy . . . you better not disappoint.'

I grinned. This was looking better and better and I couldn't wait to see what Tracy's female boss looked like. I didn't have to wait long; soon we pulled up at an impressive ranch, surrounded by acres of land.

'Beautiful place, isn't it?' Tracy said.

'Yeah!'

'Well, you should see the boss! There she is, over there. That's Alison.'

Tracy pointed at a pretty, blonde woman with curves to die for and I whistled my appreciation as Alison spotted us and wandered over.

'You must be, Tappy,' Alison said, shaking my hand, her bright blue eyes sparkling against her tanned skin.

'Very pleased to meet you,' I muttered and, believe me, I meant it.

Alison took me upstairs to her bedroom and handed me a yellow towelling robe. I undressed quickly, whilst Alison looked discreetly away and then she took me back downstairs to meet the photographer.

'Tappy, this is Clive.'

We shook hands and smiled at one another. It suddenly struck me that this was really going to happen. You could hardly accuse me of being shy, but this was different. I wasn't just going to be naked in front of friends or lovers; I was going to be standing there in front of strangers.

'Are you OK, Tappy?' Alison asked, catching my mood.

'Sure,' I answered, trying to sound confident. 'I'm fine.'

Clive caught my arm. 'Don't worry about it, man. Just relax and enjoy.'

I grinned. 'I'll try.'

Clive and Alison discussed my photographs and I looked around. I was obviously not the only one to be called in for a photo-shoot; women were strewn around the house and grounds, pulling their naked bodies into comprising positions under the flash of numerous cameras. I wondered if I'd really be able to compete.

'You know what,' I heard Alison say to Clive, with a glance over in my direction. 'It's always made me real horny to think of a guy wearing nothing but a Stetson and cowboy boots.'

Who were we to argue with the lady? A pair of boots and Stetson hat were brought over and I put them on. Alison eyed me critically and then burst out laughing.

'The boots and the hat look great, but I'm afraid that robe will have to go!'

So, robe-less, I was taken to the location of my shoot: the ranch gate. Clive handed me a guitar, to add to the look that they'd worked out for me. Thinking that if anyone would appreciate my present situation it would be The Animals, I strummed out the chords of 'The House of the Rising Sun'.

'Hold it there a moment, Clive,' Alison instructed. 'There's something not quite right.'

She walked over to me and pulled the rim of my Stetson forward, then let her hand trail down my chest until it closed gently around my cock.

'Sometimes a helping hand makes all the difference,' she whispered huskily into my ear.

My cock immediately began to stir under her fingers, stiffening into an erection as I noticed her nipples hardening under the flimsy material of her blouse.

'That's great, Tappy!' Clive shouted from behind the camera. 'Much better.' Alison winked at me and stepped away as the camera started clicking.

It was all over far too quickly. Clive thanked me and with a smile at Alison I wandered back over to the house to find my clothes. I was on my way there when I bumped into Tracy.

'How did it go?' she asked.

'No problem,' I said and then, thinking of Alison, I grinned. 'In fact, I enjoyed it.'

'I thought you might.' Tracy pulled an envelope from her bag, 'This is your money, as promised. But I wouldn't rush home too soon; I think that Alison has taken a liking to you, Tappy. You should hang around for a while.'

'I might just do that,' I told her.

So, after I'd dressed, I walked back through the grounds of the ranch, until I found Alison. She was supervising the remaining photo-shoots of the day, but I was glad to see that none of the other male subjects were getting the 'helping hand' that she had given to me.

'Hi, Tappy,' she said, looking up with a smile as she saw me approach. 'I thought that you'd left.'

'Well, I was enjoying myself so much I thought I'd stay a while. If that's OK with you, of course?'

'Oh, it's fine with me.' Her smile broadened.

When the last photo-shoot was over, Alison took me up to the house and poured us out a pair of large gin and tonics. We sat down on the veranda and she stretched out on her chair, slipping of her shoes and sighing contentedly.

'A long day,' she stated. 'But a good one. I usually wind down with a soak in the Jacuzzi.'

'Well, that's fine with me, as long as I can join you.'

Alison laughed. 'You're on!'

Carrying our drinks, I followed her around the house to where the large hot-tub stood. Alison switched it on and the water started to bubble and swirl. We quickly shed our clothes and jumped into the water.

There I was, laid out in warm bubbling water, beautiful pasture stretched out around me and a gorgeous naked woman by my side. I took a sip of my drink and took it all in. The crickets chirping could be heard over the rush of water and the sun was just setting, sending its red glow over the sky. It felt like so long since I had been able to relax like this; since I had felt so content.

Alison shifted until she was sitting behind me and began to massage my shoulders. I felt my cock harden as her naked body moved against my back. I put my drink down and twisted around to face her. She smiled and bit my bottom lip, slowly releasing it. This girl was driving me wild. Soon we were thrashing about, the water splashing out of the tub as I pursued her. She kept giving me just enough to bring me to the brink of orgasm and then drawing away.

In the end I couldn't take any more. I grabbed Alison. I just had to fuck her. It was incredible and, after so much build up, we both climaxed quickly. We shuddered and laughed, pulling ourselves to the surface and shaking the water from our hair. We collapsed back into the water, letting the warm bubbles sooth and invigorate us, and in the end things progressed to the bedroom. We spent the whole night together, most of it spent in hours of long, passionate love-making. Alison was an amazing girl and I was smitten.

The next morning she drove me back to my New York apartment. We said our reluctant goodbyes and I headed for the door. Suddenly, I wondered what I was doing. I liked this girl; why was I letting it go?

'Alison?' I said, turning back. 'What are you doing tonight?'

She smiled. 'Nothing planned.'

'How about letting me take you out for dinner?'

'Yeah, OK. I'd like that.'

We went out for dinner that night and we had another great evening. The relationship lasted a couple of months and, though our work schedules eventually meant that it fizzled out, I had a wonderful time with Alison. She signified a shift for me: since my divorce women had come and gone, but Alison was the first one really to have an effect on me. She gave me hope for the future.

My picture did appear in *Escort*. I was the centrefold and I was very pleased with the results. Not only had Alison showed me a great time, but she'd also ensured that the immortalisation of my cock was something to be proud of – thanks to that helping hand of hers.

CHAPTER 12

In Conclusion

Losing Mike

I was back in the UK in early 1973. I loved living in the USA, but I continued to feel disillusioned by the way that I was living my life over there and I thought perhaps living back at home would do me some good.

I've mentioned that Mike Jeffery's behaviour had been increasingly odd, but he had spent most of the last couple of years in Majorca, concentrating most of his attention on his Spanish nightclubs. Dealings that he had with the Anim offices were conducted on the telephone and he rarely returned to his house in King's Road, Chelsea.

Occasionally, though, business demanded that he be present in London. It was on one of those brief visits that Mike was arrested. He had failed to appear in Newcastle Crown Court on a previous drugs charge and the authorities had finally caught up with him. Mike was taken to court at last, but he brought one of the country's best solicitors along with him. There was no one who could outsmart Mike Jeffery and that included the legal system. The charge was processed and Mike applied for bail. This was granted on the condition that he surrendered his passport, but Mike's barrister successfully argued that his client needed to keep his passport in order to attend an important meeting in Majorca the following weekend. Amazingly, the judge agreed and, with his passport safely in his pocket, Mike left the court with a smile on his face.

It was horrible to think of what could have been avoided if the judge had not granted Mike that passport, but it seems that fate had finally caught up with Mike Jeffery.

225

That last success was to be his greatest mistake.

I took Mike to the airport so that he could catch his flight to Palma. He'd called me as I was packing for a trip up North to visit my father. Shifting my base back to London had still not completely alleviated the low mood that had resulted in my move away from New York and I hoped that some time with my father would be just the tonic I needed.

I arrived early in the morning and met Mike at his London home; we went through some paperwork together over morning coffee. Mike was not intending to skip out on the charges that had been brought against him in the UK; he had too much to lose to risk going on the run. Besides, as he explained, his barrister could make anything happen and he didn't think that he'd ever see the inside of a prison cell. He was in high spirits and looking forward to getting back to Majorca, even if it would only be for a couple of days.

'I'll be back before you know it, Tappy,' he told me. 'I'd like you to pick me up from the airport when I arrive; I'll give you a call from Spain and let you know the flight times.'

We finished our work and headed off to the airport. Mike was always nervous before a flight. He said that, as an ex-paratrooper, he never felt safe in a plane unless he had a parachute strapped to his back. As I unloaded his luggage, I saw him looking pale as one of the planes was taking off.

'You should be used to this by now, Mike,' I said. 'You look just like Alan Price before take-off.'

Mike grinned ruefully and took a determined step towards the departure gate. I tried to reassure him as we moved through the airport. 'It's only a couple of hours, Mike. No sooner are you up in the air, than you're back on the ground again. You should think of me: flying back and forth to New York all the time.'

'Yeah, you're right, Tappy. I'll see you in a few days' time. Say hi to your dad for me and make sure that you place that call to Bob Levine . . .' He carried on reminding me of the business decisions that we'd made that morning.

'Don't worry about a thing, Mike. Have a great flight and I'll take care of everything back here.'

'Thanks, Tappy.' Mike shook my hand and, with a nervous smile and a swift wave, he was gone.

I heard a lot from Mike over the next few days; he called me at my father's house from the Sergeant Pepper's office. On the Sunday evening he called to ask me to drive down and collect him from Heathrow Airport. I said goodbye to my father and drove down to London to meet him.

It was Monday mid-morning, 5 March 1973, a date I will never forget. I had arrived in good time at Heathrow and bought myself a newspaper, settling down to wait. After about an hour, though, I still hadn't heard any details of Mike's flight mentioned on the announcements. I walked over to the Iberian Airways desk to find out what was happening and just stared as I realised that the staff behind the desk were all in tears.

'What's happened?' I asked, but I thought that I already knew. This couldn't be happening again. It was like reliving that day hearing that Jimi was dead and when I'd been asked specially by Bob Levine the day before to go to London the next day to collect Hendrix to get him back to New York; the years dissolved and the old horror returned. I willed the woman at the desk to tell me that everything was OK . . . that Mike was OK.

'There's been a plane crash over France,' she sobbed, wiping the tears from her eyes. 'It was a mid-air collision. No one survived. We don't even know how it happened.'

'What flight was it?'

'An Iberian DC-9 . . . it left Palma an hour ago.'

I sank to my knees. 'My friend was on that flight. I'm here to pick him up. I'm . . .' I couldn't continue; the emotion swept over me and there was no containing my tears. The woman came out from behind the desk and gave me a glass of water. She guided me into a private room and tried for words of comfort, but I barely heard her. I'd only spoken to Mike the day before and now he was dead. It was so sudden and so horrible. I just couldn't believe it.

I caught a flight straight from that airport back to Newcastle; I needed to see my father again. No matter what happened my father was always there for me and I knew that he was the only person whose company I could bear just now.

We both sat in shock, trying to absorb the news. My dad had known Mike and I was able to ease some of my numb grief by talking about him. Eventually, at a reasonable hour, I phoned Bob Levine to pass

Passport to Majorca led to his death

POP music businessman, Michael Jeffrey, 39, formerly of Hawthorn Gardens, Whitley Bay, who was killed in the French air disaster, died only three days after successfully applying to a court to retain his passport, so he could fly to Majorca.

Cullercoats man 'saw' crash in a dream

MIKE JEFFREY opened the first big Whitley Bay night club in York Road, and booked many famous "blues" artistes.

His assistant, Tappy Wright, 29, born and still based in Naters Street, Cullercoats, said: "It seems weird but about eight weeks ago I had a dream in which I visualised the crash.

"His death is a tragedy. He was a keep-fit fanatic, a strict vegetarian, and he hated flying. He was an ex-paratrooper and never felt safe without a chute.

"He had a three million dollar empire in America owning the Electric Ladyland Studios, the biggest studios in New York.

"But the truth was that he was in Spain to buy a villa where he could retire."

Surrounded by souvenirs of Jimmi Hendrix and the Animals, including four £800 guitars, stage clothes, and eight gold albums, Mr Wright added: "He had no relatives here but a lot of friends. I started with Mike 13 years ago after appearing in a group at the Hotspur Hall. He was a good businessman but never greedy with his money."

It was during a civil action in the High Court last week that Mr Jeffrey, once a Newcastle club-owner, was arrested on a warrant for failing to appear on a drugs charge on which he had been committed on bail for trial.

After his arrest, Mr Robert Johnson, his counsel in the civil case, applied to Mr Justice Reeve in chambers for bail, and this was granted.

Last Friday, Mr Jeffrey appeared at Inner London Crown Court, when Mr Douglas Skene, junior counsel, represented him and asked for an extension of bail.

Pop group

The judge said this was no problem if Mr Jeffrey surrendered his passport, but Mr Skene successfully argued that he needed it for the weekend.

Mr Jeffrey, of Kings Road, Chelsea, was manager of the late Jimi Hendrix and once represented the North-East pop group The Animals.

A civil case, involving a dispute over recording contracts, continued on Tuesday. After hearing of Mr Jeffrey's death, the judge appointed Mr David Landsman, solicitor for Mr Jeffrey, to represent his estate for the hearing of the action.

Mr Jeffrey had a fear of flying, a dislike shared by Alan Price, who later left the Animals partly because of this problem.

He had lived in New York, where he had recording studio interests. He also had business interests in Majorca.

Mike Jeffrey's fear of flying finally caught up with him.

on the news. It was a horrific call to make. It seemed like only yesterday that we were sharing the trauma of Jimi's death and now here I was again in my father's house, mourning the loss of another young friend.

Mike Jeffery's funeral was a quiet affair held in Kent. Mike had known so many people, but the funeral was limited to close friends and family. It was an intimate and moving day. He was only 39 years old when he died and both his parents were there to watch their son's remains lowered into the ground. I watched Mike's mother, a small lonely figure at the graveside.

Mike's father moved over to wrap a protective arm around his wife's shoulders. There is no greater cruelty than a parent who has to bury their child. I passed on my sympathies and left for the airport. I was heading back to New York. As we had done after the untimely death of Jimi Hendrix, all Mike's friends and colleagues felt the need to gather together, to try to make sense of another sudden loss.

That Historic Night

I know that I promised you truths; I know that I gave you that scene, right at the beginning of this book: the one with me and that old friend of mine sitting down together over paperwork. That day when he revealed to me that he had been involved in the death of Jimi Hendrix . . . that he had 'no choice' but to do what he did to save himself.

I promised to expand on all this, but I couldn't tell you until I'd told the rest; until Mike Jeffery had plunged from the sky and died in the air over France; until my promise to him could finally be broken and I could tell the truth without fear of repercussion.

Let's first recap on what is now known as proven facts: Jimi spent most of his last day alive in the company of Monika Dannemann. (She took her own life on Friday, 5 April 1996.) She was supposedly the only person there when Jimi died.

Her story of events on the 18 September 1970 changed from day one. Every time she spoke of that fateful night, there were constant inconsistencies in her version of events. To highlight just a few:

1. She claims that she and Jimi went to bed and slept at 7.00am.

2. She called for the ambulance at 11.18am which arrived at 11.27am, claiming Jimi was still alive, but very sick.

3. She travelled in the ambulance with Jimi to St Mary Abbot's hospital where, on arrival, she was told that Jimi would be fine, later to be told that he had died.

4. Post inquest, all known officials, both ambulance men and the attending police officer who went to the Hotel Samarkand have stated that Jimi was alone and fully clothed in the apartment, Monika was not there and Jimi was clearly already dead.

5. Monika never travelled to the hospital with the body.

6. Although there was only a small amount of alcohol in his bloodstream, all who witnessed what has been described as 'a horrific scene' state that:

a) Jimi was covered in red-wine vomit and

b) copious amounts of wine was extracted from his lungs when admitted to hospital.

7. On arrival at the hospital it was estimated that Jimi had been dead for several hours and the time of death could have been as early as 3.00–4.00am.

8. Mitch Mitchell, Gerry Stickells and others all received phone calls as early as 8.00–9.00am informing them that 'there was a problem with Jimi'.

9. None of the officials involved in this sorry tale knew, at the time of death, that they were attending to the world's greatest guitar player.

From the day Jimi died no author, journalist, interviewer or friend ever managed to obtain continuity in Monika's accounts of what happened in the early hours of that tragic day.

Was she there? What did she really know? Unfortunately, she took those secrets to the grave with her.

The conversation took place in early February 1973, when I sat with Mike in his London apartment in the King's Road, Chelsea, working out the preparations to extend the 'Jimi Plays Berkeley' Movie Tour.

It had been a long evening; the ashtrays were full and our glasses were empty. We were talking about Jimi; I was still in shock about his death and organising the tour had thrown up memories. I was keen to reminisce, but I noticed that Mike was getting more and more agitated as I talked over the details of Jimi's last days.

That was when it happened; his face pale, hand clutching at his glass in sudden rage, 'I had to do it, Tappy. You understand don't you? I had to do it.'

'What are you talking about?'

'You know damn well what I'm talking about. That son-of-a-bitch was going to leave me.'

I think I knew then; maybe I'd always known. That was what ate me up inside, that I'd pushed the conversation in order to confirm my suspicions. Now I was going to hear what happened. The truth. I'd been crossing the room to fetch a fresh bottle of bourbon; I grabbed hold of it and brought it back over to the coffee table, sitting down to face Mike.

He had his face in his hands, but it seemed that now he'd started, he had to tell me it all.

'My management contract with Jimi was going to expire in December. I knew that I only had three months of safety left, not that Jimi cared about that. I also knew that Jimi called his lawyer, Henry Steingarten, in New York asking him to draw up papers cutting all strings with me and to finalise the transition for Alan Douglas to be his new producer and manager . . . How crazy, Tappy? Henry Steingarten was also *my* lawyer.'

Mike lent forward and broke the seal on the bourbon, pouring himself out a generous measure. He took a sip and continued, still not meeting my eyes. 'I knew that it wasn't all him, Tappy. They all wanted a piece of the action, but I was scared; there was a queue of men forming, all wanting to take my place and I couldn't do anything to fight it. I had to keep Jimi working; he was the only financial security I had and, if I lost him, I'd lose everything.'

Mike turned and looked at me with his cold, steely eyes and said in a voice heavy with menace, 'Tappy, I don't need to convince you what will happen if you grass on me or tell anyone what I'm telling you!'

Those words are still ringing in my ears today.

I was scared. I knew only too well what Mike was capable of.

Mike saw I was scared and carried on. 'However, I know I can trust you, Tappy. If I didn't know that I wouldn't be telling you this, but you know I was in debt – serious debt – and the people I owed money to didn't take kindly to late repayments. Then there was all that stuff with the IRS . . . I had to pay them $30,000 every month back-taxes or they threatened to take the studio from me. The building of the Electric Lady Studios was draining every last dime, that's why I sent you and Bob to New Jersey to collect some more money I'd borrowed from the Boys, otherwise I would have lost everything.

'That bastard Alan Douglas was about to take my place. And that little bitch Devon Wilson had put Jimi on to him. Jesus, Tappy, I would have been finished! I hated Jimi, I hated him so much. After all I did for him. He knew what leaving me would do to me and that bastard didn't even care! I'd hated him from the time I found him sleeping with the love of my life Lynn, just like he did to Chas.'

I felt the colour drain from my face. Devon Wilson was a girlfriend of Jimi's and had been good friends with Alan Douglas' wife, Stella. But the thing that made my blood run cold was the fact that Devon had recently died herself in mysterious circumstances. She had apparently fallen from a window of the multi-storey Chelsea Hotel in New York and friends of hers were claiming that she had been pushed. Was Mike admitting to two murders here? I knew Mike was capable of murder as I remember sitting listening to Mike's stories about his days in the British Secret Service and how many people he had killed.

Mike continued, 'Tappy, I was in London the night of Jimi's death and together with some of our old friends from up North we went round to Monika's hotel room, got a handful of pills and stuffed them into his mouth . . . then we poured a few bottles of red wine deep into his windpipe.'

I couldn't move. Although I knew Mike was physically capable of murder, could he actually have killed the world's greatest rock star? Was I really hearing the confession of a cold-hearted killer?

As I was falling apart, Mike seemed to be pulling himself together. He drained the last of the bourbon from his glass, got to his feet and stood over me. 'I had to do it, Tappy,' he stated calmly, 'You understand, don't you? I had no choice; I had to do it. Jimi was worth much more to me dead than alive.'

It was then that I remembered Bob Levine telling me how Mike gave a pile of contracts to Jimi to sign, which he did as it was normal practice, but in the middle of the contracts was an insurance policy for $2 million, naming Mike as the beneficiary.

The conversation was over. Mike knew he had said too much, and I needed to talk to someone about the things I had just heard. As soon as I got home, I called Bob Levine in New York, but Bob didn't seem that surprised by what I had to tell him. Between us we pieced together the story of what must have happened. There had been so many unexplained events and questions surrounding Jimi's death over the last few years, but Mike's confession suddenly made it all so clear.

We talked about the stories that Mike had shared with us both, concerning his days in the Secret Service and his callous talk of the murders that he had been instructed to commit in the line of duty. We reassessed Mike's strange behaviour after Jimi's death and at his funeral – he could not even look at Jimi's coffin, instead kept a safe distance, remaining in the back of his limo.

After Jimi's death, Mike was able to raise a quarter of a million dollars to pay Leo Branton, The Jimi Hendrix Estates Lawyer, to buy out Jimi's interest in Electric Lady Studios. It was becoming clearer that the $2 million insurance policy on Jimi's life that Mike had arranged was being used to save himself from his debts. These were debts which, as we had both witnessed when Bob had supplied his life savings to get Mike out of trouble, were owed to the most dangerous of people.

Noel Redding, Jimi's bass player, had always said that the timing of Jimi's death was very kind to Mike Jeffery.

We both knew that Mike Jeffery could be ruthless, but I didn't think that either of us really wanted to accept that a murder plot could have gone on under our noses. Monika Danneman would have had to have been involved, but her confused and contradictory accounts of how Jimi met his end only supported the idea that she had something to hide.

Poor Jimi's cause of death had been listed as barbiturate intoxication and inhalation of vomit, but the tablets he had taken were German painkillers, Vesparax, belonging to Monika, which were supposedly eight times more powerful than the regular brands.

He would have been paralysed, unable to move as he choked on his own vomit. A horrible way to die, but there were more questions here, too – Jimi had vomited red wine; it was found locked in his lungs and all over his clothes, but an autopsy revealed that there were no traces of red wine in his stomach contents.

Could it really be that Mike had used his contacts to arrange an assassination? Had Monika allowed Jimi to drug himself and then let in the heavies, so that they could force the red wine down Jimi's throat and watch him drown, helplessly encased in his own drugged body?

It made too much sense to be ignored and we knew that we held the truth of Jimi Hendrix's murder, but we agreed then to keep it to ourselves. An agreement I have adhered to until now. Despite my fear of Mike, it has taken me over 30 years to realise that some truths are better told. I have kept Mike's secret for too long; I owed it to Jimi's memory and to my own conscience to reveal all that I know and what I listened to on that historic night.

Epilogue

Now that I have opened up my soul to you the readers, I need to confess that over all these pages of my life I have no regrets and, if given the opportunity of youth again, would do all the same over and over.

My only regret would be that some of my closest buddies are no longer here to share the precious moments of my memories. Without the close relationships that I forged over the years in this business, I doubt that the experiences I enjoyed have made me any less of a person but, in fact, enriched every cell of my body.

All those departed souls were not only my heroes but my best friends. The void in my life that their demise has created has still left me a legacy of highlights that few others in the world would have ever known or enjoyed, as confessed in this book. And for which I say 'thank you' to them all.

Each and every one of them, I dearly know, would be happy in the knowledge that I have revealed the secrets of the past and finally lay to rest all the untold mysteries of their lives. I know that all those friends that I have written about in this book would be happy it was me, Tappy Wright, writing it and not some pretender.

In December 1982, when my now best friend, mentor and collaborator in this book, Rod Weinberg, called me at my Whitley Bay hotel to invite me to join The Animals in their 1983 Reunion World Tour as 'special' Roadie, much to Eric Burdon's delight, my legs turned to jelly. The thought of being back on the road again, after more than 20 odd years since the start of an episode in rock 'n' roll history was like being reborn.

However during the tour, the funny thing was, that after all those years nothing had changed with the bands' personalities except that we were all that much older and you would have thought that much wiser. But no, we were all still crazy but, by then, had the maturity to realise that deep down we really enjoyed the fights, the arguments and the brotherhood that went with it. But that's another story!

To all my departed friends, may God keep you in the palm of his hand and may your dear souls rest in peace. I love you all and dearly miss you all. To all my living friends, and non-living, I thank you all for helping me to colour in this book. Amen.

Tappy